D0402067

BELARMINO AND APOLONIO

Belarmino and Apolonio

Ramón Pérez de Ayala

Translated from the Spanish
and with an Introduction by
Murray Baumgarten
and
Gabriel Berns

University of California Press
Berkeley Los Angeles London

University of California Press
Berkeley and Los Angeles, California
University of California Press, Ltd.
London, England

BELARMINO Y APOLONIO copyright © 1921, by
Ramón Pérez de Ayala
Jiménez E. Molina, Impresores
Madrid, Spain

Editorial Losada, S. A.
Buenos Aires, Argentina
1944, 1948, 1956, 1967

First English translation copyright © 1971, by
The Regents of the University of California
with permission of the heirs of Ramón Pérez de Ayala

Library of Congress Catalog Card Number: 79-126795
First Paperback Printing 1983
ISBN 0-520-04958-6

Designed by Ikuko Workman
Printed in the United States of America

1 2 3 4 5 6 7 8 9

Acknowledgments

The translators would like to take this opportunity to thank Grant Barnes of the University of California Press for the help and personal encouragement he so generously and warmly extended to us throughout our efforts; to thank Ray Ford for his alert and expert editorial advice; to express our gratitude for the secretarial assistance afforded us by the staff of the University of California, Santa Cruz, especially the members of the Cowell and Stevenson College steno pools, as well as for the aid of Gaye Cook and Harriet Spiegel in transcribing the manuscript; to thank our colleagues on the Board of Studies in Literature at Santa Cruz who by their interest and encouragement kept us enthusiastically at work; to our families for their patience and the pleasure they afforded by joining us in speaking Belarmino's language and enacting Apolonio's drama; and to the University of California, Santa Cruz, whose unique structure encouraged us in our collaborative endeavor.

Foreword to the Paperback Edition

Reading this novel, a drama of contrasts unfolds before us. We encounter a divided world defined by the clash of opposites, bitter hatreds, and the unmitigated conflict of absolutes. Spain.

For everything here, there are opposing interpretations and contradictory views. Belarmino, one of the two characters who give the book its title, defines this state in his dictionary.

Belligerence, n: opposition, resistance, adversity, misfortune.

The meanings of this world constantly shuttle back and forth between their opposites. Like Lirio and Lario, the characters who fight over Ruera Street in chapter two, should we praise the ancient buildings of Pilares for their eccentric beauty or condemn them for their irrationality?

Belarmino provides us with the power to believe simultaneously in the truth of opposites. He is "ecumenical," which he defines as "conciliation, synthesis." Unlike other Spaniards he refuses to be caught in

System, n: stubbornness, obstinacy; refers to those who go around proclaiming one idea, if it could be called that.

He will teach us how to be

Illiterate, adj.: disinterested, impartial, without intellectual prejudices,

so that we will be able to have

weight, n: deep feeling,

and be in a position to

Imprison, vb: to understand, to take possession of an idea,

rather than being possessed by one side in the conflict.

Like a commentary on a history that Spain tried for centuries to deny, in the world of this novel each character is implicated in the others, whom he or she mirrors and refracts. Crisp and clear, they pursue their obsessions to the point where their absurdities double back upon themselves. In their self-parodying existence, we recognize ourselves. The Duchess "was very frank and occasionally . . . how can I put it? . . . well she swore a lot." Since she was a woman, and an unusual one, she "would give the words a slightly feminine form by changing the final *o* to a final *a*. She also smoked like a chimney." Eternally tragic Spain here finds its comic evocation.

In this novel, society is a tangled skein of intertwining, overlapping, knotted and unravelling quests. The comedy is due to our ability to see the entire multicolored skein, while each character can only trace the thread of his or her own life. As we follow their adventures, we come to discover the ways in which lust and love overlap, how hatred and envy eventually give way to friendship and admiration, and the fanatic pursuit of a single-minded goal can become transformed into the ability to contemplate the wholeness of the cosmos. With Belarmino, the philosopher, we come in this novel to the discovery of the idea of humanity.

It is a conception which his rival, Apolonio, eagerly puts into practice on the stage. Belarmino, the shoemaker, is a philosopher; Apolonio, the shoemaker, is a playwright. Belarmino has one daughter, and Apolonio one son. Between them these two shoemakers give voice to the contradictory qualities of the Spanish world that would split apart in our century and clash violently in the great civil war. Like Dickens, Pérez de Ayala does not shrink from discussion of the contradictions that characterize his world. Again, like Dickens, whose work he knew and loved, Pérez de Ayala suggests through his fiction that reconciliation is possible. Not only will Belarmino and Apolonio finally speak to each other, their children will be reunited in love.

Like the Hispanic world, this novel is full of secrets that disclose themselves to the eyes only of those who know how to see with the heart. *Belarmino and Apolonio* is an education in feeling. Bumping into businessmen and philanthropists, scholars and scientists, who constantly seek to convince them to live differently, Belarmino, Apolonio, their children, La Pinta and Don Guillén, as well as the Duchess of Somavia and Father Aleson—in fact all the variegated characters of this novel—persist in their quest with such intensity as to endow it with religious overtones. In a society where weights and measures figure so prominently, characters learn how to feel, just as the brave reader discovers the value of all those things that cannot be reduced to numbers and dollar signs.

The seriousness of this novel's exploration of the Spanish character is perhaps disguised by its comic incidents and tone. Nevertheless, it is haunted by the persistent Spanish question of identity. Rooted in the landscape of contradiction and dialectic, these characters are obsessed with discovering their true nature.

Amused by Apolonio's manners, bemused by his ambition to recover the ancient drama of Greece in his own work, Beatriz Valdedulla, alias the Duchess of Somavia, becomes his patron. Apolonio's son, Don Guillén, describes her in the contradictory tones which prevail in the novel: "The beneficence that great lady bestowed on my father and myself is of the kind that cannot be repaid. I think she must have been over forty at the time and she was what you might call a fat, middle-aged woman; frankly speaking, she was ugly. But she had a love of life, an openness, and a sense of humor that made her far more attractive than beauty itself. I assure you that when she let loose with one of her obscenities, which in her case was really a sign of contentment, you would just stand there fascinated and smiling, as if you had been listening to a nightingale's song." And suddenly we gain a comment on the medium, now that we have been hearkening to the message. "Where words are concerned, structure isn't as important as tone and intention. Words are like containers. Although they may have a similar form, some are made of clay whereas others are of pure crystal and contain a delicious essence."

Belarmino has qualities of sensitivity and compassion Apolonio neglects. Both make shoes by hand—wonderful second skins for the feet. Out of craft come forth philosophy and drama. Apolonio used to say, "Each man carries his destiny written on his forehead with invisible letters." And then he would add, "Each type of foot is destined for a particular road." (p. 65) Belarmino invents his own language, which he teaches to his daughter. The book concludes with a glossary of the Belarminian lexicon, as recorded by his only disciple, The Grind.

Hump, *n*: responsibility, because it is bulky, heavy, and annoying.

Irrigate, *vb*: to have a vision of unity, to encompass at a glance; when one looks at objects, they are refreshed and unfold.

Rah-rah, *n*: life; constant restlessness; the palpitation of the passions.

Belarmino and Apolonio are both put out of business by the advent of the mass production of shoes and retire into their true selves, Apolonio to write and stage plays, Belarmino to rediscover the true meanings of words.

Free at last to realize their individuality, they pursue their purposes. Their search invites parody. The students of the university town of Pilares know that Belarmino and Apolonio are both extraordinary beings, and provide them with an audience before whom they can perform. Like students everywhere and at all times, these undergraduates recognize and hearken to the prophets the rest of society ignores. Combining the sublime and the ridiculous, as only they know how, the students stage a mock lecture to which they invite Belarmino and unknown to him play a secret recording they have made in which he explicates the meanings of his private language—that realm where words are reunited with their truest values and take flight. To launch Apolonio's career as a playwright, the students cause a riot on opening night. Since Apolonio knows of similar events that greeted Aeschylus's debut, he is overjoyed. And Belarmino is entranced at his discovery that someone besides his daughter speaks the true language of humanity.

This is a novel of peripatetic activity. Parallelling the characters who cannot afford train fare, we travel from place to place at a leisurely walking pace as part of our education. Arriving at a new place, we settle into a boardinghouse. All over Spain, the boardinghouse provides shelter, a feeling of home, and an education. One character learns Greek from a fellow boarder, graduating to the field of medicine which he "studied freely and capriciously." Like Plato's academy, this one teaches its students while they move about.

Character also gives way to character with a Dickensian swiftness, a Shakespearean vividness. "Scarcely had five minutes passed when the voluminous and ruddy Don René Colignon, chicory and candymaker, burst into the shop. His ruddiness was so flammiferous it projected reflections against the walls. His epidermis was tightly stretched and seemed to have been varnished. He looked like a greased bladder. He had a very carefully constructed little goatee, the color of wheat, and his white chin rose up out of it like an egg in a brass eggcup. He had Gallic, almost Rabelaisian, eyes—blue and sparkling they were and they denounced him as a man who delighted in the pleasure of the table as well as of the bed." Colignon is evoked the way buildings are described in this novel. Behind their facade lie the surprises of humanity.

Some of the funniest exchanges in the novel occur when Belarmino explains to Colignon the ways in which his baker friend is the shoe-maker's opposite and alter ego. Playing with language, Belarmino calls Colignon the yes to his no, or the no to his yes. The resulting encounter becomes a veritable aria of language.

Like the narrator, we too have a Cervantine curiosity. With him we seek to know "other people's lives," not to condemn but to participate in their situations. Thereby we amplify our own experience. In this tangled web, people try to take advantage of each other. Nevertheless, the prostitutes of this novel who sell their bodies for bread have their virtue. They too can redeem. They are the patron saints of lust who, like the Duchess, make it possible to transform a baser instinct into love. As we move from event to event, we discover a tale of sexual discovery and harm. Who is responsible for the fallen woman? Is the young man who loves her at fault? The cruel parent who separates them? Are the social norms in a world of business ethics to blame? Touched by the tale of La Pinta and the young Don Guillén, we encounter the family of humanity. The novel's magic makes it possible for us to voice once more the classic statement: nothing human is alien to us here. These people are not ready-made even though their world is rapidly being mass-produced. They are each unique and one-of-a-kind, like the wonderful shoes of Belarmino and Apolonio.

A very great novel, *Belarmino and Apolonio* presents the translator with the difficulties of all great literature, to which it adds its own dimension. In focusing his fiction on figures, one of whom is a playwright and the other a philosopher, Ramón Pérez de Ayala implicates characters and readers in the formal questions of literature and philosophy. His novel summarizes as it parodies the history of western drama beginning with the Greeks just as it plays with philosophical thought from its beginnings before Socrates to our own time. Not only do Belarmino and Apolonio as characters synthesize and symbolize these powerful and even determining movements in western culture, but the very material of their daily lives is the matter of drama and philosophy.

For the translator the challenge of dealing with this novel is the encounter with the historical forms of literature and of language. To translate this novel, we at times had to turn to the history of English literature and language to find equivalents for the brilliant Spanish original. Our effort has been to recreate it in such a way as to make it clear to the English reader that Pérez de Ayala's novel stands like Joyce's *Ulysses* in the great modern tradition, bringing western culture, literature, and linguistic practices to a supreme moment of synthesis.

Ultimately, the novel returns us to Spain—to a world that for a time married the contradictions of east and west, thereby for a golden moment offering the possibility of harmony to a world riven to its foundations by the clash of opposing religions, cultures, and languages. Apolonio's is the world of the stage. His fierce pride in theatre recalls if only as a parody the greatness of Spain on the stage of world history. Belarmino's way with words reminds us that Spanish was the language bringing European culture to the New World and millions of people. Freeing words, he could ideally make the work of liberation and renewal—ancient Spanish ideals—available to us all. As he evokes the history of Spanish greatness, Pérez de Ayala affectionately parodies Spain's pretensions. He reminds us that the process of the reconciliation of opposites—of being ecumenical we might say, following Belarmino—which is resurgent in that country today and has attracted the world's attention, is a process as old as its history of conflict. Reading this novel, we participate in Spain's dialectical dance of contrasts, knowing that *Belarmino and Apolonio* marks the beginning of a *new* moment of reconciliation.

Introduction

Belarmino Pinto, shoemaker-philosopher and creator of a new language meant to express the essence of all things and all knowledge, has only one disciple. The lean, vegetarian Escobar, alias "the Alligator" and "the Grind," spends his short life defending his teacher while himself struggling to fathom and decipher the master's linguistic discoveries. Confronting the unbelievers in public debate, Escobar has a moment of illumination—"Every man who has a part to play speaks a special language which another man who does not play that same part cannot comprehend, for each is animated by a different spirit." In his vision, the world becomes a confused market where each individual shouts his particular language at his uncomprehending fellow men. Since no one listens to anyone else, nothing ever gets done. Can the mad world be redeemed by a universal language?

In this novel, Pérez de Ayala offers us two self-appointed redeemers who seek to bring sense and order to the chaos—the shoemaker-philosopher, Belarmino, and the shoemaker-playwright, Apolonio. Both are obsessed by words. Belarmino attempts to renew language. For him, "everything is badly named, the labels mechanically applied, and instead of stimulating one to an act of knowledge and creation, they perpetuate routine, ignorance, stupidity, empty chatter and a parrot mentality." He believes that "names exist in the cosmos—that is, the dictionary—like caged birds or like human beings that have been drugged and put away in heavily sealed coffins." Belarmino finds "a kind of mystical pleasure," a way of communicating directly with the absolute and gaining a sense of intimacy with the essence of things whenever he breaks the "sepulchral seals," resurrecting the living dead, or when he opens the cages to let the birds fly out. Apolonio, on the other hand, returns to the Golden Age of language. He does not innovate new meanings but reverts to traditional ones, composing heroic

xiii

verse drama and speaking in rhymed couplets at the most inopportune moments. He has no disciples and his great tragedies turn out to be farces. Yet many of the characters in this novel live by the codes that animate Apolonio's fictional creations. His own son, Guillén Caramanzana, is the victim of Apolonio's misplaced and misguided sense of honor. At one point, Don Guillén says that his father used to imagine everyone as "necessarily a victim of some passion"; of love, hate, envy, anger, or avarice. In his mind, every individual was "made up of just one simple element," making it difficult for men to get along with each other. But this state of affairs gives rise to dramatic conflict—"Only nobles understand other nobles, but even then it might be difficult if love is involved." Apolonio's sense of drama is founded on what might be called his pedestrian theory of tragedy—"Each type of foot is destined for a particular road." Here, playwright and shoemaker meet.

As in *Don Quixote,* which in many ways it resembles and evokes, the pleasures of *Belarmino and Apolonio* do not stem from the plot but from the telling. In Cervantes' classic, the scene of story-telling and listening is often the inn; in Pérez de Ayala's novel, it is the Spanish boardinghouse. There is no better place than the dinner table of such an establishment to partake of the feast of language. Unlike the thin and unappetizing meals generally served in these *pensiones,* the book serves up a banquet of stories and tales within tales, creating the process by which they are made. As the narrator tells us, boardinghouses are stores of "individual dramas neatly packaged," and we participate with him in the action of unwrapping and unfolding. Although this novel was published in 1921, the narrator approaches his tale as observer and investigator somewhat in the manner of a contemporary Argentinian writer, the labyrinthine Jorge Luis Borges. "I came upon this drama purely by chance," the narrator tells us, thereby divesting himself of the role of omniscient author. As a listener, the narrator becomes involved in the different versions he hears of the melodramatic, mock-heroic drama of a thwarted love affair between a seminary student and his childhood sweetheart. Both narrator and reader, however, come to realize that this story of the hapless lovers is merely a preface leading into the more important tragi-comic tale of their parents, Belarmino and Apolonio. Here, the narrator does claim some authorial responsibility— "Let me assure you that I spent years of investigation on it and did some assiduous digging in order to compile all the data. For that reason I consider it to be almost an original story of my own." The Cervantine complexity of this narrative structure constitutes one of its greatest delights. Scholars might also discover this book to be a compendium of traditional classical learning as well as the more recent social and philosophical thought of the last two centuries, reflecting Pérez de Ayala's erudition and skill as an essayist and commentator on his age. But new readers of this Spanish writer will undoubtedly be struck by the irony, humor, and humanity contained in the novel. The work of a fertile imagination, it fuses many layers of event and action into a dazzling display of the pleasures of language and storytelling.

The world of this novel constantly moves from the mundane to the imaginary, blurring in the process any distinction between the two. Its landscape is a corner of Spain—the province of Asturias—but to read the work only as a study of regional manners would be to overlook its subtleties. Pilares is Oviedo; the hills, the mountain villages, the ducal palaces, the inclement weather are all part of a Spanish reality— *tertulias,* political discussions, priests, shoemakers, nuns, loan sharks, pastry cooks, *pensiones,* seminaries, were and are essential ingredients of life in Spain, and yet here they play a part in forming a landscape of the imagination. The novel is peopled by individuals who are carica-tures, and the reader sympathizes with their predicaments rather than with them as persons. This is a book filled with names and nicknames which ironically play against the situations in which the characters find themselves: Felicita Quemada, Novillo, La Pinta, Caramanzana, Don Restituto, Doña Basilisa, Father Aleson, Xuantipa, all bear the names of their obsessions.* Belarmino and Apolonio are the most fully drawn characters, yet they do not escape the humorous and burlesque treat-ment accorded to the others. They do, however, bridge the worlds of everyday life and classical myth. We move from shoemaking to language-making, from cutting leather to dramatic encounters, from disquisitions on the metaphysics or physiology of the foot to ardent lyric poetry, all without benefit or need of transition.

Belarmino and Apolonio exalts the joy of playing with language and the pleasures of make-believe. Such a work defies translation while at

*In Spanish the name Felicita Quemada suggests "burned-out happiness"; Novillo, "small bull"; La Pinta, "stained"; Caramanzana, "apple cheeks, apple face"; Don Restituto, "restitution"; Doña Basilisa, "basilica"; Father Aleson, *eleéson* (Gr.), "merciful"; Xuantipa, Xantippe, Socrates' irascible wife.

the same time demanding it. In this case, the act of translating contributes to the growth of language and thus continues the task undertaken by Apolonio, Belarmino, and Pérez de Ayala. Like the reader, the translators have accepted the author's invitation to join in the process of speaking, naming, and creating language, which is the focal theme of the novel.

Belarmino's experience with the magpie, whom he wished to teach to speak the conventional language understood by most men, was unsuccessful. He fed it bread soaked in wine, but the bird, squatting at the bottom of its barrel, never reached the necessary state of intoxication required for speaking. Belarmino's over-indulgence, his deep drinking at the source of language, made him so drunk that it increased his vocabulary by five hundred words (Escobar's estimate). Paradoxically, his eloquence also made him mute. The Alligator translated one of his master's last lessons into everyday language.

Once upon a time there was a man who, because he felt and thought so much, used to speak very little and very softly. He didn't speak much because he could see so many things in each individual thing that he could never find an adequate way to express himself. Everyone called him a fool. This same man, when he learned to express all the things he discovered in one single word, spoke more than anyone else. Everyone called him a charlatan. But when the man, instead of seeing so many things in one thing, reached the point of seeing one and the same thing in all different things—because he had penetrated the sense and true meaning of everything—he never spoke a word again. And everyone called him mad.

The novel, however, does not end in silence. As their tale concludes, Belarmino and Apolonio speak to each other for the first time.

Contents

Prologue

THE BOARDINGHOUSE
PHILOSOPHER

Don Amaranth de Fraile, whom I met many years ago in a boardinghouse, was an unusual individual not less noted for his distinguished
air and almost aristocratic bearing than for his sagacity, character, and
idiosyncratic manner. Some day I may even collect his doctrines, opinions, aphorisms and paradoxes, and add what can be ascertained of his
life. Perhaps I could make it into a book, and if such a work did not
measure up to the *Memorabilia* in which Xenophon set down the
reverent and filial record of his master, it would only be because I am
not a biographically inclined soldier, although Don Amaranth often
made me think of Socrates—a threepenny Socrates with principles. But
this is much beside the point right now.

When I met this extraordinary man, he was already past seventy. He
had been living for the last twenty of those years in the boardinghouse
where I encountered him, and he had spent the previous twenty-five
in other establishments very much like it. That particular one where
fate temporarily threw us together was repugnant in every way. I remained there two whole months only because the warmth of Don
Amaranth's personality and the charm of his discourses induced me to
extend my stay. His ironic pedantry and picturesque erudition put me
under a spell, but what moved me to admire Don Amaranth most of all
was the fact that he had lived for so many years in such a place without
becoming physically warped or mentally unhinged. Privation, dirt, and
venomous back-biting had not kept him from swearing allegiance to

1

boardinghouses. I was amazed at his capacity to endure their debilitating and near-murderous regimen. Difficult as it may be to understand, the fact remains that he had taken vows as a perpetual novice in the order. He told me this himself one day during dinner.

A distinctive feature of meals at that house was the lack of toothpicks, which was due not to reasons of economy and even less to scruples of hygiene and etiquette, as is common among the English who consider the act of picking one's teeth a bodily necessity of a shameful and clandestine nature, but because there was simply no reason to have them around. The stews were extremely liquid and the meat of such a texture that the use of those chewing tools with which ordinary human beings are endowed was completely unnecessary. No residue ever remained between the teeth, making toothpicks superfluous. You might understand now why I make a point of noting that this conversation was able to occur during rather than after dinner.

"In Attica," Don Amaranth said to me, didactically wielding his fork as if it were a pointer, "those in search of wisdom used to go to the market place or the arch of Jupiter the Liberator, where Socrates wittily and smilingly served as midwife of ideas; they frequented the shady groves of the Academy where Plato, with his broad shoulders and mellifluous lips, hatched those winged desires in young souls that would allow them to fly from the realm of the sensory to that of the absolute; or they would go to the Lyceum where the dry Stagirite dismantled piece by piece the mechanism of the world, demonstrating interrelationships, the engagement of its gears, and its general mode of operation. In the Middle Ages, the storehouse of knowledge—all that was still left over from antiquity—was the monastery. Later, science found a home in the universities.

"Nowadays," he continued, "all of these—the multiversity, the true convent, the best lyceum, the most fertile groves of academe, and the genuine modern version of the arch of Jupiter the Liberator, as well as the classical market place—all this, my dear friend, can be found in the Spanish boardinghouse, particularly the Madrid model. Of course, nature is a book, but it is hermetically sealed. In the boardinghouse, the pages have already been cut and the book lies open. You *do* have to know how to read, but that's a simple enough requirement.

"Now, to dwell in a boardinghouse on this earth is like taking vows in a religious order. You've got to have that strange inclination, although God knows it's common enough among Spaniards—an ascetic vocation. The boardinghouse is no place to encourage, let alone satisfy, voluptuousness or carnal desire. Luckily, a Spaniard has such thick skin, such dried out insides, and such dulled senses, that he is an ascetic by birth and predestination; nothing abrasive mortifies him and there is scarcely any sensual pleasure that appeals to him, unless it be the generative one, and that in its simplest and broadest form. Although the average Iberian may call it love, and even the great Lope de Vega wrote that there is no other love than that which by will of nature is satiated through the coupling of those who crave each other, pleasure of this kind is nothing but a matter of slavish instinct, common to men and beasts alike, and merely allows us to tend to the propagation of the species. In his generic pleasures, however, man chooses with discernment and not simply by instinct that object or goal which he is seeking. Through education he perfects both the means of reaching it and the art of enjoyment.

"Although it is at the bottom of the pile, one of the greatest human pleasures is eating. Animals take their food raw; man has his cooked. With a little garnish here, a pinch of salt and pepper there, he elicits all its flavor. Asses munch grass now as they did in the Stone Age and they ruminate as they did then without ever discovering or enjoying complex new taste sensations. On the other hand, the culinary arts and sciences are evolutionary and perfectible. At Maxim's in Paris you don't just feed, caveman style.

"Yes, my dear friend, from the womb to the tomb the Spaniard is an ascetic. For that reason there are innumerable convents and boardinghouses in Spain where Stone Age watery soups and stews are perpetuated and where you can even occasionally find raw food. Once I decided to carry on a scientific investigation that could come under the rubric of comparative sociology, or even ethnography, choosing as a starting point and theme the boardinghouses of Spain as contrasted with those of other nations. After intense methodological scrutiny and extensive sampling, I arrived at this indisputable conclusion: the boardinghouse is a typically Spanish institution. It's a lot like bullfights, Madrid stew, and the cultivation of hairy moles for aesthetic purposes. To compare the English boardinghouse with the French or Swiss *pension de famille,* the Italian *pensione,* the German *pensionhaus,* and the *casa de huéspedes* in Madrid, is to find as much similarity as there would be in taking the Thames, the Seine, or the Tiber and comparing them all to the sickly Manzanares. Paradoxically, in such an analogy the Tiber, Seine or Thames would correspond to the *casa de huéspedes*.

"The English boardinghouse is a small wax museum, an issue of *Punch,* a short collection of caricatures; almost without exception, the English respond socially with clammy and comical simplicity, eschewing effusiveness and intimacy. The Swiss *pension* is like a restaurant in a railroad station; everyone is just passing through and totally oblivious to what is happening in the immediate vicinity. The Italian *pensione* is a public gallery whose visitors trade verbal explosions and artistic clichés like Bazaar merchants ('Have you seen Botticelli's *Primavera?* Ah!' exclaims a female Swedish painter of cyclopic proportions as she guzzles her minestrone with feigned elegance. 'Ah!' repeats a Yankee in a baritone voice which he is training in *bel canto* in order to become another Caruso and earn as much money as Caruso did. His chest swells up like a pigeon's whenever he opens his mouth. 'But what about Giotto's frescoes?' 'Oh!' interjects a matronly Russian lady who has a book by Ruskin propped open in front of her against a potbellied bottle of Chianti); it is a den of aesthetic philistines, of false imitators of Apelles and Phidias, of prospective opera stars who drive the quiet, innocent guest into martyrdom with their howlings and musical pauses. The German *pensionhaus* is a miniature pandemonium, a place consecrated to the worship of a folksy Aphrodite with broad hips and overflowing bosom. Then there are the family-style French boardinghouses which justify their name by exploiting all the virtues and demonstrating all the defects of family life. They couldn't exist without the single long refectory table, the one dining room fixture which in Spanish boardinghouses is also absolutely *de rigueur*.

"Now, I don't deny it is possible to learn something in foreign inns and hostels, but it can only be superficial knowledge, fragmented and irrelevant—like the monographs of the experimental sciences. But the Spanish boardinghouse is an encyclopedia . . . a mail order catalogue . . . a *summa* . . . the Bible.

"Not so many years ago, during my novitiate as a student of boardinghouses, I struck up an easy friendship with another inn-mate, a medical student who was the first to arouse my curiosity about the Hippocratic mysteries. I was initiated later when he took me to San Carlos Hospital to witness a birth. An everyday affair, you might say.

4

But in my opinion there are two spectacles a man ought to witness at least once in his life; one is a sunrise, the other is a birth. The first one teaches us to respect the idea of God; the second, to respect woman. In Spanish marriages women do not receive the respect they deserve because it is a common practice among midwives to insist that the father remain outside the room while the painful mystery is being enacted. As a result, the husband doesn't know why maternity is a sacrament, a martyrdom, a beatification. Saint Augustine says that a woman *nisi mater, instrumentum voluptatis*: either we see in her the figure of the mother, or we lower ourselves to possess her merely as a receptacle for our carnal desire. Failing to experience anything but those fugitive epileptic moments that accompany copulation, ignoring the meaning of the act of engendering and conceiving, man learns nothing about the mystery of maternity, and husband debases wife. How in the world is he to respect what he himself degrades?

"Well, to go on, I studied medicine freely and capriciously. Since that time, I have always subscribed to some medical journal or other. The first thing, I always say, is to have some knowledge of the delicate and complicated machinery with which we feel and think. For, after all, ideas—even the purest of them—are biological evaporations, vapors arising out of ethereal flesh. They are like clouds born of the heavens, outside the earth's jurisdiction, even though they do really spring from the earth and go back to it, fertilizing it on their return trip.

"Thanks to other boardinghouse habitués and a few transients I met there, I became interested in and knowledgeable about several areas of learning. On one occasion a German happened to turn up at my boardinghouse; pushy he was, just as those Teutons usually are. He was interested in learning Spanish in its natural habitat. 'Wait a minute,' I thought to myself, 'you'll learn my kind of talk but I'll damn-well learn yours too.' And so I did. To my great surprise, a candidate for a university appointment taught me Greek practically overnight. I met many candidates and I became their devoted disciple. In Spain they form an institution—the profession of university candidate. They are frail, delicate characters, perpetual dark horses who do nothing but wait in the wings for their big chance. For in Spain, academic appointments are made through connections, family ties, or bribery, not on merit; consequently, it stands to reason that you can learn more from the candidates than from the professors themselves. But now I'll stop boring you with the long list of my scholarly attainments. After all, what difference does it make if a man knows a great deal or if he knows nothing? Every science, taken by itself, is basically an abdication of integral knowledge, a gesture of fatigue, a tacit admission of pettiness and ignorance, an attitude of forced humility. Like a hired workhorse, the wise man has let others put blinders on him so that he can only see what is under his nose. While the universe is an ecological system compounded of infinite heterogeneous phenomena, every science is content to collect powdery grains of homogeneous petty events, unwilling to admit that any reality could possibly exist outside of, separate from, beneath, or even above it.

"The scientific age follows the theological one. That is to say, after having been convinced that it had penetrated the sense of life and death, holding the cosmos in its hands as a little child hangs on to a balloon, humanity took another look and discovered in wonder and fear that everything had been a dream; life not only made no sense at all, but even the cosmos was an illusion. Then it was as if an auction had taken place in which the dwelling places and furnishings of the gods had been put on the block. Some people sold all kinds of articles at rock-bottom prices, and although these items were moth-eaten and worn, some of them still could have been put to good use. Other individuals, more prone to hopelessness and ennui, turned their backs on the already empty and unoccupied heavens, lowered their eyes to the ground, and devoted themselves to making compact collections of miniscule facts—just like the idle man who goes about collecting his batch of unusable objects out of a desire to find oblivion. Thus, the individual sciences were spawned.

"I must emphasize that every branch of science is nothing but an incomplete collection of cancelled stamps or rusty cowbells. In the theological age, man had become used to the immanence of the absolute; the world was filled with myths, and the essence of life floated on the surface like the morning mist over rivers. Integral knowledge was right at hand, like raspberries in a thicket. In a laurel tree man saw Daphne, felt the invisible presence of Apollo; and he used the leaves to cook or to make wreaths for fighters and poets. What else did he have to know? But in our scientific age, a single tree is multiplied into as many trees as there are branches of science. Not one of them is the real tree. The botanist gives it a name, the mathematician calculates its

6

dimensions in relation to the circumference of the equator, the architect makes it a supporting beam; the nautical engineer thinks of it as a mast, the telegrapher views it as a telegraph pole, the economist as a valuable stock, the agronomist as a possible product to be cultivated, the doctor as a therapeutic medication, the chemist as a retort in which certain reactions take place, the biologist as something almost like a human being, and so on and so forth *ad nauseam.*

"Once in a French essay, I read what it would be like to have the retina of a fly. Imagine! What a wonderful panorama of creation has been granted to the common fly and denied to those who call themselves the rulers of the earth! . . . The fly has a retina split up into thousands of facets with which he sees the outside world reproduced in myriad images. Well, by penetrating a little into all the sciences, be they pure or applied, an image is immediately broken down into thousands of images like those I sketched in the paradigm of the tree. Familiarity with the sciences and the subsequent myriad vision can only be obtained through faithful attendance in Spanish boardinghouses. 'The true university of our time,' said Carlyle, 'is a library.' Now if that mad Englishman had been a Spaniard, he would have made it a boardinghouse. But once a person is wise in all the sciences and looks at an object from every angle, taking all its possibilities into account, what then does he really know?

"It's like going round and round on a carousel. Opposite me, on the other side of the turntable, a pretty girl is eating. I'm riding a pachyderm on the merry-go-round—this imaginary, scientific merry-go-round—and as I spin with it, I observe that beautiful creature.

"First, I begin to narrow my vision and I see her physiologically. Then I penetrate the hidden alchemy that is functioning in her stomach as she digests her food. I know something about the proteins, fats, and carbohydrates she is delicately placing in her delightful jewel of a mouth; I know how they all become converted into organic tissue . . . but I prefer not to go any deeper into such intestinal observations because that would be depressing. I go a mere quarter of a turn on the spinning pachyderm and now I observe the girl from another perspective—a philological one this time. From certain words and nuances of pronunciation, I know without the slightest doubt that this girl was born in August, is Galician and comes from the town of Mondoñedo. As if by some enchantment, the girl has just said she is from Mondoñedo and was born in August. My pachyderm leaps forward and I am now at another angle of observation, the one that has to do with horoscopes and astrology, which while it is somewhat neglected nowadays, is not for that reason less respectable a science than any other. This girl, because she was born in August (Napoleon Bonaparte was born in August), is passionate, warm, given to gratifying Venus, vivacious, and she should take care of her headaches. (We all know that Napoleon did not win—I was going to say consummate—the Battle of Borodino because that day he was suffering from sinusitis and a local nasal obstruction.)

"If I were young, I wouldn't go on like this. What, after all, is the value of science compared to two simple facts: (1) the girl is pretty, and (2) she has, let us say, certain tendencies. But although I am not senile, I *am* aging and so with a slight effort on my part I overcome the weaknesses of the flesh. Completing the circle, I examine the girl from the four cardinal points. And I end up where I began. What have I learned about her? Nothing. Nothing. Not a blessed thing.

"Now, if her room were only next to mine and if through the thin walls I could hear her sigh, laugh, or cry and in that way know if she was happy or sad, *that* would be real knowledge. One day I might overhear a sentence, on another day a dialogue could emerge, on yet another I would speak to her, subtly encouraging her to confide some small secret, and then, finally, I would put together what she told me about herself and what others have said. Thus, little by little, I would come to know her purely. I would become part of her comedy. After all, are not all lives dramas—some more intense than others?

"And yet every life is nothing but an inconstant and fleeting shadow. Do you remember Plato's allegory of the cave? Well we have to go even further; the chained figures whom Plato places in the cave are not material bodies, but dramatic and tormented shadows. What is projected on the wall are shadows of shadows. You would probably tell me that the same thing happens in hotels, streets, in railroad cars—in fact, wherever people congregate. True enough. The only thing is that in all those places, the shadows and the dramas are silent, isolated, hidden. In the boardinghouses, the forced familiarity that begins at the dinner table solidifies those ephemeral shadows, raising the curtain on each one. How often, looking around the table at my companions, whose private lives will soon be opened to me as though they were acted out

8

on a stage, I feel suddenly elevated above them. Almost against my will, I begin to contemplate them philosophically, *sub specie aeternitatis,* as so many ephemeral and fleeting shadows. I feel a pathetic chill; I almost cry; I am even capable of swallowing the petrified piece of meat which has been set down in front of me.

"In order to reach the concept, the emotion of a forest, either you skirt its entire perimeter to see it all together, or you immerse yourself in its depths. Don't stay on the fringes or only go in a little way, because then you won't see the woods for the trees. In the same way, to grasp the concept or emotion of life, and to enjoy the vantage point of Sirius (as the philosopher does), you have to dive in with all you've got and swim around in the individual dramas. Now that's the real point: drama and philosophy are the only ways to knowledge. Here in these cavernous centers, these boardinghouses, we find the true sources of knowledge. The important thing, after all, is to uncover underground springs.

"The history of Spain in the nineteenth century has passed through its boardinghouses. Yes, I mean just that; nineteenth-century Spanish history is a boardinghouse history. That's the way it is, and we can't change it. Don't think for a minute that the history of other civilized nations of the nineteenth century is superior to ours. Here and there, everywhere, the history of the nineteenth century is nothing but the saga of the rise of the middle class, richer and more educated elsewhere, less comfortable and not quite as tame down here. Its history is that of a period of anarchic freedom—freedom for exploitation; a whirlwind of senseless and incoherent atoms; a brutal and egotistical period that tried to suppress pain by attempting to overlook the fact that it existed. The bourgeois epoch boasted of *appreciating* ideas and beauty because it defiled them and put a price on them in the market place as if they were commodities. A period, all told, in which the businessman defeated and annihilated the philosopher and the poet."

Now you can understand why I haven't forgotten the lectures Don Amaranth delivered on the subject of boardinghouses. After leaving Señor de Fraile, I roamed through many of these heteroclitic inns. Finally, I came to rest under the protection of the household gods of Doña Trina. Due to the abundance (if not delicacy) of the bill of fare, her place was bearable; besides, it was pleasant there, even entertaining, because of the great number of people from all walks of life who sought shelter in it—priests, bullfighters, politicians, crooks, businessmen, petty bureaucrats, military men, students, farmers, inventors, political office-seekers, swindlers—bits and pieces of the social jumble came together there from all corners of the Iberian peninsula.

At the suggestion of my teacher, Don Amaranth, I became accustomed to viewing the different boardinghouses I visited as though they were so many stores where I spent not money, but time; each one had its characteristic supply of individual dramas neatly packaged and tied with twine. All I had to do was untie them and take off the wrappers. If some of the places turned out to be shops that were poorly stocked, Doña Trina's, by contrast, stood out like some huge warehouse full of unusual, unique items. True, you could only pick out the fabric there; then it was up to you to work diligently to turn out a well-made finished garment. One day, the story of Arias Limón and his sisters unfolded before my eyes in that workshop of packaged dramas. I later published it for the amusement of the idle reader in search of distraction.* Many other dramas brushed against me, but they have been lost in the river of shadows, and it is probable they will never reach the shore. But today, I feel like saving from oblivion one that is half-burlesque, half-pathetic. I came upon this drama purely by chance, but let me assure you that I spent years of investigation on it and did some assiduous digging in order to compile all the data. For that reason, I consider it to be almost an original story of my own.

*Prometheus; Sunday Light; The Fall of the Lemons: three lyric novels of Spanish life.

Chapter One

DON GUILLEN
AND LA PINTA

One Holy Tuesday during the noonday meal an unannounced guest, a beneficed priest, appeared. Had I passed him on the street, found myself across from him in a streetcar, or discovered him eating next to me at a lunch counter in a railroad station, I would scarcely have given him a second glance. But we were sitting around the boardinghouse table. The excellent Don Amaranth was right—it was almost out of a sense of moral duty that all those present, myself included, began to stare insolently at our resplendent priest. He was indifferent to the curiosity that filled the room. Bullfighters, comedians, and priests are never disturbed by curiosity and are not the least bit thrown off by a fixed stare, for they are used to being the focus of attention—in the ring, on stage, or in the pulpit.

I called him our resplendent priest and there's no better adjective to describe him. He seemed like a plasterboard saint freshly taken out of the mold and delicately painted. His cassock was made of shiny lamb's wool that looked as if it had been varnished; his collar was a delicate brush stroke of bright purple, almost cardinal red. A bluish violet shadow hovered around his mouth and chin where he had shaved. The rest of his face was a burnished red in which his black eyes were deeply set. He couldn't have been more than forty years old, if that. Once I got over this first impression of an insipid painted saint, I noticed that his physiognomy radiated something personal and suggestive. The red-ness of his cheeks was pathological; he obviously had heart trouble. Since he was surprisingly young and good-looking for the ecclesiastical position and status he displayed, a malicious person would have assumed that he had gotten where he was with the help of those omnipotent skirts. Yet, on the other hand, there was nothing about him that suggested he had been a ladies' man or even a ladies' pet. There was no sign of the aplomb that is common to the conquering priest, and he had none of that hypocritically sweet self-effacement you find in the lapdog type. If the admiration of the ladies had put him where he was, it was probably without his having sought after it with any particular determination. Well, at least those were the thoughts that came to me between the soup and the stew.

As a result of the priest's proximity, Doña Emerenciana was coming apart at the seams. A decrepit widow who, lacking more distinguished suitors, spent her life pursuing Fidel the kitchen boy, she was the first to speak to the priest. "Isn't it true that here in Madrid it's much too hot—particularly when you consider it's still April? You're probably from a much cooler place, Don . . . what is your name?"

"Pedro, Lope, Francisco, Guillén, Euripides, as you wish," he said in a strong but pleasant voice and with an attractively easy smile on his lips. Except for the old woman, who couldn't make out whether the reply had been serious or sarcastic, all of us echoed his smile.

"Oh, how cute!" she exclaimed, deciding that it was a joke.

"No, madam; it's no joke," answered the priest.

"But is Euripides a Christian name? If it is, it's probably from the province of Palencia. That's where they give people those weird names."

"No, madam; it is not a Christian name. But it's a fact that the priest who baptized me wasn't aware of it. If they ever canonize me, there will be a Saint Euripides, the very first one."

"Oh, how cute! But thank God you have many other names already."

"One of my father's whims. He was a playwright and a shoemaker, or a shoemaker and a playwright; whatever your preference. All my names were those of famous playwrights of other periods—Pedro Calderón de la Barca, Lope de Vega, Francisco de Rojas Zorrilla . . ."

"When I was a child I heard people talking about that Zorrilla, the one who wrote *Don Juan Tenorio*," interrupted Doña Emerenciana.

"Guillén de Castro," continued the priest, still smiling, "Euripides . . ."

And since there was a pause, Doña Emerenciana cried out, "Euripides who?"

"Euripides López Rodríguez, the noted tragic playwright," pronounced the priest, slowly and deliberately this time.

"Well, it's quite obvious he was from a poor family," said Doña Emerenciana. "And which one of these names are we to use?"

"Some call me by one, some by another. Choose the name you like best."

"Well, I prefer Don Guillén."

"That's the one the ladies usually like," said Don Guillén sarcastically.

"If you don't mind, I'll call you Euripides; it sounds democratic to me," said Don Celedonio de Obeso, a declared atheist and aggressive Republican. At heart, he was an innocent and a complete blockhead.

At Doña Trina's table you couldn't possibly do without an accredited Republican. This Don Celedonio occupied the seat at the table formerly held by the head of the Republican party from Tarazona, a prattling citizen with a bipartisan beard that looked like a goat's udder.

"As you please," answered Don Guillén, spontaneously.

Before the meal was over, he had managed to gain everyone's confidence and sympathy. They were all so comfortable with him that Don Celedonio dared to fire at him point-blank, "Do you believe in God?"

"Do you believe in the Republic?" Don Guillén came back at him without batting an eye.

"As firmly as I am a Republican."

"As surely as I am a priest, I too believe."

"No one who is intelligent believes in God."

"I've known intelligent people who say, 'No intelligent person can possibly believe in the Republic.' "

"Well the early Christians," said Señor de Obeso, lowering his voice, backing down, "were republicans."

"What's more, they were anarchists. Starting with the idea of God, those Christians came to believe in the republic. You could go the other way around and, starting with the idea of the republic, come to believe in God."

"Well, for that trip I wouldn't need any suitcases," concluded Don Celedonio, as Don Guillén graciously joined in the laughter.

It should be pointed out that during the previous dialogue Don

Guillén hadn't made one bitter or polemical response, nor had he been in any way disdainful. As a result, we felt even more kindly disposed to him. As he was leaving the dining room, Don Celedonio whispered in my ear, "He's a great guy. That's the kind of priest I like."

After the meal I found out that Don Guillén was a canon in the cathedral of Castrofuerte and had come to town to deliver the Holy Week sermons in the chapel of the royal palace. Of his eloquence there could be no doubt.

So many transient pupils and guests patronized Doña Trina's establishment that she couldn't handle them all in the large, spacious apartment on Hortaleza Street. Let us call that the metropolitan hospice. She had rented rooms in nearby alleys and contiguous streets, and in one of these colonies located on Reina Street I had my lodgings. I mention this small detail in order to make it clear that those of us who lived in the colonies enjoyed more freedom, especially at night, than those in the metropolis. For, at night, those streets and alleyways were a bazaar trading in mercenary delights, an assiduous exchange for ugly prostitutes and peripatetic pimps. To get to my room, I had to burrow through a multitudinous professional army of occupation which continuously barraged me with licentious thrusts and lustful invitations. I was not only an inviting target for verbal assaults but for physical attacks as well. In fact, some of the girls often grabbed me by the arm. In order to slip away from these nuisances and recover from my fatigue, I would seek shelter in a small cafe where these ladies used to bivouac. It was my custom to invite the most persistent of the lot to have a drink with me so that when I left them they were tame, well-nourished, and satisfied.

I felt sorry for them, for their life was a source of pain to me, and I tried always to treat them decently. I agree that prostitution is a huge, foul-smelling ulcer, but how can one blame the ulcer for belonging to a corrupt body? It is no more than a frank manifestation and fatal result of the suffering body politic. Where everything is prostituted, feminine prostitution is almost praiseworthy because at least it is a clear symptom.

Often, once these poor, unfortunate creatures had calmed down, I would spend a long time in the cafe chatting with them. I benefited spiritually from these conversations, since the compassion I felt for

14

them purifies the soul. I used to look around at the different types who frequented this dive; almost all of them were pretty odd-looking characters. From the very beginning, my curiosity was aroused by a lovely, graceful and patient woman with a dark complexion that hadn't been plastered with powder and rouge like the others. She was always alone and motionless in one corner of the room with a glass of watered-down coffee in front of her, which she seemed never to raise to her lips. She looked like a rumpled Raphael virgin. Since I was looking at her rather fixedly one night, Madam Old-Legs, the noisiest and most offensive unit in the army of occupation (and known by that nickname because of the way she limped), said to me, "What are you looking at? That goose? Her name is Angustias, alias La Pinta. She belongs to Tirabeque, a bum and gambler who keeps her cooped up here until he comes by to get her at dawn."

"Invite her over here to have something to drink with me," I said to Old-Legs.

"Hey," shouted the cripple, "you, Pinta! This gentleman is inviting you for a drink."

Blushing, La Pinta refused the invitation. Old-Legs insisted in vain.

"And that name Pinta, is it a nickname?" I asked.

"Hell, no; that's her real name—Angustias Pinto. It's crazy to use your real name in this business. She's just an innocent who's not cut out for this kind of work."

Little by little, night after night, I began to get to know La Pinta. She was a sweet-natured woman, rather sad and introverted, or, to borrow Old-Legs's technical description, La Pinta was just "an innocent not cut out for that kind of work." She hardly ever spoke. One night she told me she was a little over thirty; she looked younger than that. On another occasion, she told me she was born in the city of Pilares. I remember how unusually communicative Pinta was the night of that very same Holy Tuesday when the flushed and democratic priest appeared at the boardinghouse.

"My father was a shoemaker as well as what he called a 'bilateral philosopher.' As a girl I heard these strange words so often that I have never forgotten them. Professors from the university used to come to hear him at the hovel where we lived. My mother had an evil temper and used to say that my father was a good-for-nothing bum. She was convinced that those who came by to visit were laughing at him. But my father is a saint."

Involuntarily, I thought about Don Pedro, Guillén, Euripides, the son of a shoemaker and playwright. La Pinta continued, "It was a priest who led me astray." She had her head down and her thoughts were somewhere in the past.

"Bastard," I murmured, in spite of myself.

"No. You've got it wrong," La Pinta corrected, looking up at me with a pained expression. "He wasn't a priest yet; he was still studying at the seminary. He wanted to marry me. We ran off but his father caught up with him. My mother didn't want to let me in the house. She did later, of course. I'm sure he still loves me. You know what the trouble was? His father couldn't stand my family. I wonder whatever became of Perico."

"His name is Perico?"

"Yes, Perico Caramanzana. And the name really suited him. His face was fresh, flushed, and happy, just like an apple."

"Is that why they called him Caramanzana?"

"It's his real name. His father was Apolonio Caramanzana. You've probably heard of him. He was the finest shoemaker in Spain. The best people from Bilbao and Barcelona used to go to him to have their shoes made. Besides, he used to compose tragedies."

That night I was troubled when I left the cafe. It took me a long time to get to sleep. In the next room, I heard a rasping sound followed by a deep sigh. It was Don Guillén. A diabolical scheme occurred to me. "What if I were to bring La Pinta around tomorrow night and have her go into Don Guillén's room?" I fell asleep turning that idea over in my mind.

The following day, a fast day, Don Guillén wasn't at the table.

"What's the matter with Señor Caramanzana," asked the old widow, who had already found out his last name.

"He's not eating today. He has an upset stomach," said Fidel. "Haven't you noticed how flushed he is?"

"He probably has pyrosis," interjected Don Celedonio. "All the clergy and religious orders suffer from pyrosis because they eat too much rich food and drink a lot."

"Now you just shut up, you heretic," warned Doña Emerenciana, angrily threatening him with her fan.

"And by the way," he added unperturbed, "I hope you didn't forget about my errand. You did tell the lady of the house I'm not about to submit myself to that disgusting farce of fasting. I want to eat meat and fish during the holy days. I'm promiscuous or a profligate or whatever it's called," said Don Celedonio.

"God have mercy on us all! You're worse than Judas!" she answered. "It's a good thing Don Guillén didn't come to the table today. He would have been revolted by such an abomination."

Fidel, the waiter, was snickering to himself during all this.

After the meal was over, I left the metropolis and headed for my colony. About twenty steps ahead of me, Fidel was carrying a large tray covered with a napkin. I caught up with him in the hallway near my room.

"Pssst," hissed Fidel gesturing with his head for me to approach him. "Lift up the napkin."

I raised one corner of it and discovered an abundance of succulent dishes, including a juicy piece of roast beef.

"It's Don Guillén's dinner," said the waiter. "Although he isn't a profligate, or promiscuous, or whatever it's called, he does eat meat in any case."

At that moment, Don Guillén's door opened and he himself, in person, stepped out of the dark into the gray light of the doorway, catching me in the shameful and embarrassing act of snooping. He was dressed in ordinary clothes and his disheveled hair soaked up the light that formed a halo around his head. He was wearing red slippers made of morocco leather. These two details screamed out at me like high musical notes reverberating in that moment of silence caused by our mutual surprise—the radiant halo and the bloody feet.

"Come in, come in," he said looking directly at me. I obeyed, not having fully recovered yet from my humiliation. "Sit down," he insisted. I wanted to apologize and leave. The priest continued in a tone I took to be imploring. "Won't you do me the favor, if I insist, of keeping me company for a while?"

This plea, and the tone in which it was made, helped me to recover my usual composure. I sat down next to a table covered with books, papers, pipes, and a pair of reading glasses. Presiding over the accessories and utensils of the intellectual life was a photograph of a woman enclosed in an intricately worked silver frame as if it were a holy relic. I

17

couldn't help but glance at it, trying to do so discreetly. The girl looked like one of the young virgins painted by Raphael during his Umbrian period.

"Put the food here, Fidel. Did you bring wine? Take it away; I've got better wine here." And turning toward me he asked, "What are you looking at? The frame? It's a holy relic from the fifteenth century, a priceless jewel."

"No, I was looking at the photograph."

"It's a sister of mine who disappeared."

"Disappeared?"

"She was lost in the shadows."

"Oh! She died . . ." I tried to sound puzzled, hoping that he would offer some explanation.

"Some years ago." There was a slight pause after which he said, "Will you have a glass of brandy?"

He took out a bottle of aged cognac and another bottle of wine which up until that point had been lying in an elegant pigskin suitcase that would have been more appropriate for a successful businessman than a priest. He sat down to eat. The more I looked at him, the less he looked like a priest and the more he seemed a man of the world.

"By pure chance," he said eating slowly, "you have had an intimate glimpse of me as a man. A few minutes ago when I saw you . . . "

"Snooping!" I interrupted. "But it was only because Fidel asked me to look, without my even knowing what it was all about."

"What difference does it make? If I had closed the door on you then, you would have taken me for a false priest and a hypocrite. I couldn't just leave you without an explanation."

"I was the one who should have . . . "

"You? Why? The most you did was show an excess of curiosity. I, on the other hand, in the opinion of some rather timorous people, am committing a grave sin."

"I'm not timid."

"But I must offer you an explanation. Just as in matters of state there are negligible crimes, so too in the Church there are negligible sins. Actions that don't impair justice or violate dogma (those axes on which state and church respectively revolve) are negligible crimes and sins. All they do is go against, and even disobey, certain disciplinary

18

measures that are temporary or accidental. One of those ephemeral measures is the obligation to fast for four days during Holy Week; perhaps the present Pope, or the one who succeeds him, will decide to modify or even do away with this requirement.

"The state is a material community that maintains itself by mutual agreement and the Church a spiritual community that sustains itself through mutual love. Therefore, the disciplinary spirit of the Church is by nature different from the disciplinary spirit of the state. For the state, discipline comes under the heading of controlling selfish pursuits, since without discipline there can be no mutual agreement. For the Church discipline arises in an atmosphere of generous affection, out of the desire for sacrifice, as it does for lovers who keep testing each other's love in order to make sure it is reciprocal, proving it by promulgating edicts and making capricious demands, for to love is to obey. In the same way, the Church imposes disciplinary obligations on the faithful—just to jab those who are a little bit lukewarm—and gives them an opportunity to show and exercise their capacity for love. For those of us whose faith is well established and who know what we are about, whether we be priests or laymen, such obligations are superfluous; what is important is dogma. The state gracefully tolerates freedom of thought, since ideas can hurt no one, but is intransigent with regard to freedom of action because that would disrupt discipline. The Church is intransigent with regard to free thought but is tolerant when it comes to actions; only thinking is sinful. All sins, no matter how monstrous, can be absolved in the confessional, but the slightest doubt in the mind of the confessor makes it impossible for us to absolve him. Now because all this depends on common sense, it has to be kept a secret from those who don't have common sense, be they clergy or laymen. Do you understand?"

"I understand perfectly," I said. And, actually, I had understood everything he had told me, for it wasn't the least bit complicated; but I couldn't understand *him*. What kind of a man was this one anyhow, seated in front of me, swallowing and rationalizing at the same time, chewing and discussing these matters with such cold scrupulousness and elegance? Dressed as a man of the world, he did nothing to suggest his ecclesiastical position. From time to time as he talked, his eyes settled on the photograph of a woman he himself had pushed into the anonymous depths of prostitution. What kind of a man was he? A hedonist? A non-believer? A hypocrite, sophist, nihilist? A man suffering the torments of Hell? I couldn't have cared less about the explanation he had given me. What did I care if he fasted or didn't fast?

As though he had the uncanny gift of telepathy, which often comes to life in intimate and intense duo-logues, Don Guillén had taken my thoughts for his own. "Of course you couldn't care less if I fast or not. What's more important to you is that by chance, and I've said this before, you've had a glimpse of my innermost self. All of us—monks, priests, bishops—under the cloth we are all men. *Homo sum* I say, to quote the pagan philosopher."

And once again I saw him in my mind's eye, his head encircled by the radiant halo, his feet blood red.

"You've seen me without my cassock. You have had a glimpse of me not as a minister of the Lord but as one of His creatures, as imperfect and burdened with care as all of them. Within a few hours I'll be speaking before the King, or really above the King—from a pulpit not just a few feet over the crowned head but from infinitely higher, because I represent the eternal and everlasting conscience beyond the reach of thrones, sceptres, and sovereigns. But here, in this stuffy room, face to face with you, I can't find the voice of my conscience. I'm really no more than a dark chamber echoing that voice."

That was going a bit too far. Not knowing what to say, I kept my head down and tried to focus my eyes on something, which turned out to be the photograph.

"Do you like the frame?" asked Don Guillén.

"I was looking at the photo. I know that woman," I said dryly.

Don Guillén was not perturbed.

"You're wrong," he said. "You may know someone like her but you can't possibly know the lady. I have already told you that she is my sister and that she doesn't exist." He stressed the words *sister* and *exist*.

After dessert, Don Guillén treated himself to a glass of brandy and changed the tone of the conversation by lacing it with anecdotes and humor, leaving no doubt that he was as witty as he was intelligent. When it was time for me to leave, he said, "I won't be at the round table for the next few days. Wouldn't you like us to eat together here in my room, no matter how jealous it makes Doña Emerenciana?"

20

During those secretive and leisurely meals, my friend Don Guillén told me bits and pieces of his life. I heard the story of Angustias Pinto, about her father and his, that is, about Belarmino and Apolonio. Later, on my own, after careful investigation, I came to realize that the tale of young Caramanzana and La Pinta was merely the preface to a more important story.

Chapter Two

RUERA STREET, SEEN
FROM BOTH SIDES

(If the impatient reader cannot wait to find out what's happening, he should lightly skim this chapter, which is nothing more than the stage setting on which the action will unfold.)

Out of the deep, dark, and dormant regions of memory, the stygian lagoon of our soul where former feelings and images have been buried, there unexpectedly arise from time to time old, familiar voices and faces that appear like bodiless phantoms. As at night when the lugubrious and immobile swamps breathe out a white and ghostlike mist, our internal stygian lagoon also releases its vaporous phantoms during those hours in which the darkness of dreams saturates our spirit. But, on occasions, the incorporeal creatures from the other side of memory rise up in the light of day.

Just now as I was getting ready to describe Ruera Street in the very illustrious and ancient city of Pilares, the home town of Belarmino Pinto—also known by the name of Monsiú Codorniú—shoemaker and bilateral philosopher—the specter of Don Amaranth de Fraile suddenly rose up on the threshold and margin of my conscience. He was waving the pewter fork I had always imagined to be the trident of Charon, that Neptune of the eternal sea. Like Brutus turning to the silhouette of Caesar in the Shakespearean tragedy, I address myself to the incorporeal shade of the excellent Don Amaranth, "Speak! Speak!"

And the shade begins to speak with the same wit and penetration that used to delight me so many years ago.

"Are you going to describe Ruera Street? Are you going to describe it or are you going to paint it?" I notice two innovations. First, that Don Amaranth is speaking to me in the familiar *tú* form. Second, that his voice has become somewhat thin and he sounds like a eunuch. The voice continues.

"The cyclopes saw the world superficially because they had only one eye. Because they saw the world superficially, the cyclopes wanted to assault Olympus; but the gods dashed them down into the deep Gulf of Tartarus." (Don Amaranth and his constant mythological references.) "The novelist is like a small cyclops, that is, like a cyclops that is not a cyclops. The only thing he has in common with the cyclops is superficial vision and the sacreligious desire to occupy the dwelling place of the gods. The novelist aspires to nothing less than the creation of a small universe, which is what a novel attempts to be. Although he's much smaller, man has the advantage over the cyclops because he has two eyes with which he sees into the profound depths of the sensory world. Well, then, to describe is really to see with only one eye, letting it flit over the surface of one plane, because the images succeed each other in time and do not build or superimpose themselves on each other. Neither, therefore, do they have any depth. On the other hand, man's vision, that is, diaphenomenal vision which focuses on the object with both eyes each from different sides, penetrates the object on an angle and receives two lateral images that converge into one central image. This is vision in depth. The novelist, as a man, sees things stereoscopically, in depth; but as an artist, he is without the means to reproduce his vision. He can't paint; he can only describe, enumerate. The mission of seeing in greater depth, with greater delicacy and emotion, and to teach others to see in the same way belongs to the painter. The original sin of the novelist stems from his need to extend himself over an innumerable number of objects. The painter, on the contrary, chooses one single object; or if he selects several of them, he groups them in a reduced area, thus concentrating and humanizing them. As opposed to the novelist, the painter doesn't allow himself to be dominated by the vastness of the object but, instead, dominates it. The object becomes the vertex of the angle of the painter's vision and

23

not the painter the vertex of the angle of contemplation of the panorama, as happens to the novelist. The painter who paints canvases that
are more than six feet square is undeniably a superficial painter. The
question for the painter of large dimensions is that of concept; either
he realizes he must be artificially superficial or he is superficial and
inartistic and doesn't realize it. Knowing this, the famous fresco
painters, ancient as well as modern, painted on large planes with
monotonous tones, and in that way evaded the obvious sensation of
volume and depth. They were deliberately superficial."

I interrupt the loquacious shade with his eunuch voice.

"The noon day Angelus has just sounded in the neighboring church.
In an hour I'll have to stop working. If I were to listen to you, I
wouldn't do anything else but let myself be caught up in the leisurely
current of your discursive delights. Tell me, then, how can I describe
Ruera Street so that you will be satisfied with my description?"

"By not describing it. Seek the diaphenomenal vision. Repress your
novelist's role. Have two other people see the street at the same time
but from different lateral angles. Can't you remember some occasion
when you witnessed how that same object, Ruera Street, produced a
duplicity of images and impressions in two observers with contradictory
dispositions? What you should do is amalgamate those images and
impressions."

"I remember, I remember!" I exclaim. But the shadow of the excellent Don Amaranth with the pewter fork on his shoulder, the emblem
of boardinghouse asceticism, has already disappeared.

"Yes, I remember once that . . ."

Strictly speaking, what difference does it make to describe or to
paint? What's the value of painting a two- or three-dimensional vision?
The important thing is to communicate, to express yourself, to make
yourself understood, even if it's through remote allusions, mute gestures, fleeting words. But just so the magisterial and imperious
silhouette of the admirable Don Amaranth won't bother me again, this
time I'll give in and follow his advice .

I remember that while I was living in the old and venerable city of
Pilares, two friends of mine from Madrid, Juan Lirio the painter and
Pedro Lario, whose profession I don't know, though he said he was a
Spencerian, came to visit. I acted as their guide. On reaching the
acropolis, the highest part of the city, whose oldest and most noted

24

boulevard is Ruera Street, Lirio, gesturing enthusiastically, said, "What a beautiful street!"

"What a horrible street!" corrected Lario, frowning bleakly. He added, "What an absurd street!"

"That's why it's beautiful."

"What's absurd is beautiful? What would an ancient Greek have to say about that opinion? For the Greeks, beauty resulted from the most meticulous and refined logic. The world is beautiful and elegant because it is logical."

"As far as Greek beauty is concerned, I can only answer that I prefer the pug nose and quivering nostrils on the face of that cute number who's walking up the street over there to the marble nose of a statue done by Paros. And as for the logical beauty of the world, I'll tell you I'm more attracted by the works of man than by the works of Nature. I prefer a gondola to a shark and if you really push me to it, I'd have to say that I like a ceramic pot from Talavera more than the Himalayas. I get along better with what's capricious and absurd in Nature, or at least what seems to be that way. A giraffe amuses me more than what the geologists call the tertiary stratum."

"You've contradicted yourself. You prefer that pug-nosed girl to a statue and yet her nose is a work of Nature. You prefer the gondola to the shark because the gondola is made by man."

"Over and above the works of Nature I place those of man, and above those of man I place life itself, preferably the source of all life—woman. But I agree that I contradict myself frequently. And so what? That way I know I'm alive. If I didn't contradict myself and merely obeyed pure logic, I would be a phenomenon of Nature and I wouldn't feel I were alive. The works of man and, even more, works of art, are to be esteemed to the degree one feels them animated by this necessity of contradiction, which is what life is. This street is beautiful and alive because it's contradictory. Let me make a sketch of it; I'm not going until I paint it. The only annoying, really sour note is that new house with its frenchified architecture."

"You've really given yourself away. All you painters, philologists, and scholars are beasts of the same species—and the whole lot irritate me. All of you feed on antiques. You're fascinated by what's worn out, eaten by worms or moths. Given the choice between a bulky mummy and a tasty sociological treatise just out of the oven, the philologist and the scholar would choose the first one. Between an Apollonian youth and a horrible old geezer with a wart on his nose, the painter would choose the second and even argue in good faith that he's more pictorially beautiful. What an aberration! But there's something that exasperates me even more. And it's that the scholar imagines books are not meant to play the social role of perfecting and beautifying the spirit, but exist only so he can take notes on them. And the painter imagines objects and beings lack their own finality and collective utility; for him, they exist only so he can make sketches."

During all this, Lirio was busily sketching Ruera Street. Since nobody stopped him, Lario continued, "Here you have this absurd, hateful street. Why should one even call it a street? Every house is the impulsive product of each inhabitant's willfulness. There are not two of them alike. You can find neither norms nor symmetry. Everything is composed of broken lines, silly dull colors, and filth, or what you perhaps would call patina. Besides, there is a forty-five degree downgrade paved with moss-covered granite stones. Neither carriages nor horses nor people with heart trouble could climb it. A lonely place. Lonely. The sun never penetrates this narrow alley. It looks like an intestine suffering from constipation. And now the bells of the cathedral have started ringing. What a deafening noise! They probably ring them at all hours from that swollen mass up there with its long neck pressing down on these dismal shacks, like a brooding ostrich hatching a nestful of beetle eggs. And that you call a street, a beautiful street? A street is an artery of a city along which life and health ought to circulate. Now, the idea, the very concept of a city appears when man realizes there are certain things more important than the impulsive whim of his personal choice; collective utility and decor, the common desire for prosperity, culture, and pleasure that all the people who live together in the city have the obligation and the right to enjoy. Before coming this far, man was rooted in wild tribal villages or he squatted in nomadic camps. But once the individual applied himself to carrying out the concept of the city, that is to say of a scheme, a structure with ideal goals, of which he is nothing more than a subordinate particle, then the Hellenic city arises, the archetypal urban area, and all kinds of other things appear with it—norms, principles, symmetry, sunny streets in regular and homogeneous patterns, civil dwellings with inviting porticos and inviolate hearths, gardens, the market, the *agora,* the harmonious temple—and not that barbarous, belfryed cathedral."

"You're the barbarian," interrupted Lirio, looking disdainfully at Lario. "So as far as you're concerned, a beautiful city, a civilized city, a logical city, is one that is laid out in a regular and homogeneous way?"

"Of course."

"If man were not able to make more of himself than that, a homogeneous city, then it was just a pure waste for the species to have evolved and ascended to the point where it has yielded the fruit that is mankind. Bees and beavers construct homogeneous cities."

"The city of the bees is the ideal republic. I've already told you the world is lovely, beautiful because it's logical. If I'm not mistaken, that's what the word *world* means, *mundus,* mundane. Everything in the universe is subject to a marvelous ordering. What is inorganic is controlled by serene rather than contingent laws, and until man came along even organic living creatures were governed by instincts that always directed them straight toward their ends without hesitation. By contrast, man's symbol was Buridan's ass, which possessed an inkling, a premonition of discursive intelligence, and for that very reason died of inactivity while standing between two piles of hay wondering which one to choose. Before the species evolved and finally produced the human genus, before the rise of man and consciousness, Nature unfolded itself teleologically in a coordinated design of final causes. Beings and things were united by various and subtle means. That animal you like so much because he's absurd, the giraffe, isn't absurd at all; he has a long neck so he can reach those dates that are way up in the palm trees. The tiger has striped skin so that he can hide among the reeds."

"And the palm trees are high," interrupted Lirio, "because the giraffe has a long neck. The reeds exist for the tiger so that he can acquire a pretty skin as he blends in with his surroundings. That street exists in order for me to paint it, because I consider it to be delightful and because I feel like it."

"I'll continue without paying any attention to your ramblings. The advent of man and his precarious intelligence right smack in the middle of Nature brought disorder, discord, doubt, and confusion to the purposes of life. What else is the normal human intelligence but a temptation toward disorder and torpidity in the symbiosis of Nature. Barely raising his head, man disarranges all the well-concerted ecological interrelationships by which the universe keeps its balance; he stands erect as though he were the center of the universe, the focus of all its teleological systems. The end of all things resides in man; that's what *man* says. But what goals does a man have? This is the beginning of the age of absurdity. In its origin human logic is rudimentary and illogical, for it moves by trial and error and does not proceed directly or surely to its goal. This is due to the fact that at this stage of his existence man seeks absolute ends instead of experimental relationships and relative goals; and this is all because he's afraid of death, a kind of pusillanimity unknown in Nature until the birth of human consciousness. When man finally brushes away the metaphysical mists and frees himself from superstition (the word comes from *superesse* and *superstare,* superexistence, superbeing, superlife, or to continue living forever, and expresses the ironic disdain the ancients felt toward Christians because the latter believed in immortality), when man gives up searching for absolute ends and is satisfied with concrete, natural, biological goals, when he perfects himself and submits to the logic of the cosmos and overcomes absurdity, behaves with rectitude, simplicity, and efficiency like a perfect piece of machinery, he then returns to Nature."

Lirio is about to interrupt. Lario stops him, holding out his hand.

"Hold on. I'll be finished in a minute. What is a city? And within a city, what is a street? Concrete teleology; a place where one can live at ease, pleasurably, comfortably. Once man is emancipated from superstitions and gracefully accepts the biological postulates, he will lay out a spacious boulevard on a plain and there construct comfortable, ventilated, luminous, hygienic dwelling places in accordance with that set pattern that best furnishes the necessities of domestic life. The result will be a logical, decorous, and beautiful street. Now contemplate that incongruous alley, that stack of pigsties, not fit for human beings, this shameful vestige of an earlier period of ignorance and superstition. Those who built such houses never intended to live in them permanently. They only wanted to live there temporarily, like transients, while they sought to reach Heaven. They weren't interested in living, but rather in *superbeing,* surviving in another life. They didn't care about humidity, bad odors, lack of air, light and water, but only about eternal salvation. All those huts were squeezed together and piled one on top of another in order to rub against the cathedral's torso or, at least, to be able to bask in the shadow of its tower. There is only one decent house—that three-story building, white and spotless, with its wrought-iron balconies; that one with the confectionery shop on the ground floor and the large, attractive sign that says, '*L'ambrosie des dieux; le plaisir des dames. Confisserie et patisserie de René Colignon.'* "

"Are you finished?"

"I have finished."

"Well I'm going to answer you, but illogically, because logic gives me a swift pain. I'd destroy that white house and I'd hang René Colignon from the top of the cathedral tower. You said man becomes superhuman when he turns into a perfect piece of machinery; what you really mean is he is superior when he stops being a man. Well I'd rather not be a superman. I don't want to free myself from superstitions. I want to feel I'm alive and the only reason I feel alive is because I know I can die. I love life because I fear death. I love Art because it is the most intimate and complete expression of life. I value Art over Nature, since Nature, not knowing it is constantly dying, is an inexpressive and dead reality. The tree whose leaves turn yellow in autumn is ignorant of its own death; I'm the one who knows *that* when I eternalize its dying moments in a painting. Art vivifies things, releasing them from their concrete interrelatedness and their utilitarian teleology; it makes them absolute, unique, and absurd; it saturates them with that radical contradiction which is life, since life is at the same time a negation and an affirmation of death. Only things that live are beautiful. That street is beautiful because it's alive; it's just the opposite of those inanimate and inexpressive streets you advocate. You yourself said those houses are bunched together, pushing against each other, looking for the protection of the cathedral. Yes, you're right. It seems the houses themselves have been endowed with a sense of volition and movement. Each one has its own personality, soul, physiognomy, expression, biography. One of them meditates; another dreams; another is laughing, and that one yawns. The old house with its hewn granite stones and delicate romantic niches, with its great arched doorway and its coat of arms below the eaves, is a feudal lord who, as he keeps his distance, dares to look the church straight in the eye. That other noble dwelling with its baroque entrance and its recently whitewashed, newly carved coat of arms is a noble upstart apparently fond of the church, because two abundantly endowed Dominicans are just now passing through the door. Then you have the 'bourgeoisie,' the untitled, the plebeians. Look at that yellow ramshackle house with its abysmal entrance like the opening of a toothless mouth, the one that has the gallery of windows that look like so many pairs of spectacles. Notice how its rounded, blackish, and half-stripped roof looks just like a dirty beret; a pawnbroker undoubtedly lives in that house. See that thin and gangling little house whose windows are crammed with flower pots and birds? Who but a faded virgin could possibly live there? It's evident a shoemaker has taken refuge in the basement and has publicized the fact by hanging that pair of deformed riding boots from those brackets. From the sign he has put up, there can be no doubt the man is an imaginative soul—The Bosquous and Equitable Nimrod. Belarmino Pinto's Bilateral Shoe Shop. Need I say more? I've already finished my sketch. What do you think of it, Lario?"

Lario looks at the drawing. He removes his hat, shakes his head, scratches the back of his neck, and then exclaims, "The street couldn't be uglier. The drawing couldn't be more beautiful. Now that you have made Ruera Street eternal, they ought to tear it down."

Chapter Three

BELARMINO AND
HIS DAUGHTER

The Republican Circle and Club of Pilares was situated at the entrance to Carpio Street, adjoining the large house of the Jilguero brothers, Don Blas and Don Fermín Jilguero, rich canons who had raised their imposing structure as at once a boast and a threat, for it was face to face with the episcopal palace itself. The intrusion of the Republican Club into the ecclesiastical quarter of the town had greatly disturbed the bishop, the Jilgueros, the city council, and a group of minor clerics who lived in the neighborhood. Whenever there was a meeting of the Circle, those who attended would emerge shouting inflammatory, even blasphemous, cries. Fortunately, the club didn't hold many people. It consisted of one not very spacious room decorated with only two lithographs and furnished with only six chairs and a table. The local party had rented the place from the widow of a harnessmaker who had been a fanatic Federalist while he was alive.

"What is the Republic? A *maremagnum,* the ecumenicity of belligerents, the Roman fidelity of Sastrea's scale. But I am particularly abundant as far as the ecumenical aspect is concerned. And if not, here we are surrounded by four walls . . ." Belarmino Pinto, the person speaking, hesitated while he chose the proper words into which to decant the overflow of his ideation.

"I request the floor because of allusions," said Carmelo Balmisa, a very well-read tailor.

Belarmino turned around to look at him, surprised and almost frightened. Whenever anyone took him away from his digressions and pulled him out of his oratorical self-exaltation, forcing him to pay attention to the outside world, it was more violently disrupting to him than if he had had his pockets picked and turned inside out. His face was drawn, ecstatic, childishly sweet, narrow in the jaw but quite broad and spacious in the forehead; his dark eyes were tumid and lambent, two tongues of flame floating in oil. He was still a young man.

"I am the one who has been alluded to," insisted Balmisa.

"You've been adulated?" asked Belarmino, making every effort to descend to external reality.

"Not adulated, no. The one alluded to," corrected the tailor.

"It's all the same," answered Belarmino, just at the point of evaporating again and exempting himself from the surrounding circumstances. "To allude is a vulgar expression, made of coarse material. To adulate is a compound form. Allusion is always adulation. You prefer this vulgar expression? So be it. In what way have I alluded to you?"

"You've spoken of Sastrea, which must be something like *sastre*, sartorial, from the Latin for tailor, and I assume this refers in some way to my profession. I demand an interpretation to see if I have been offended. What is a *maremagnum*? What is the ecumenicity of the belligerents? What is the Roman fidelity of Sastrea's scale? I would like to think you were commenting on the existence of some beloved creature who sprang from my ribs; that would be my Ramona, and not your Roman scale."

"Oh vulgar brain!" exclaimed Belarmino, resigned and dejected. "I'll have to express myself in common terms to get through to you. *Maremagnum* is just what it says. It's the *non plus ultra*, the best of the best. Ecumenicity is the same thing as uniting by common consent. The belligerents are those who are opposed. Fidelity amounts to the same thing as accuracy. The Roman scale is for weighing things. Sastrea, as everybody knows, is the lady whose picture is painted in the courthouse."

"I understand now; but it's just that you're so mysterious," slyly suggested Balmisa, maliciously winking his eye at two silent witnesses, one being the editor of a local Republican newspaper to which the tailor contributed articles, and the other the owner of an embroidery shop, both of whom were secretly laughing at Belarmino. "What you wanted to say was that the Republic is a desideratum, the conciliation of opposing forces, and the balancing weight in Astrea's scale."

"No, I didn't just *want* to say it, that's what I said."

"But we didn't understand you."

"Did you understand Salmerón,* when he came to Pilares to give his speech?"

"I would like to think I did."

"You understood everything, everything?"

"Well, if you mean everything . . . "

"Well Salmerón said what all of us were thinking; for that reason we are all Republicans. But he said it in a way only some of us could understand; for that reason he's a philosopher. I also am an apprentice philosopher. You are a vulgar brain."

"I give up. Now explain to us that whole business of the four walls."

"That is ecumenicity. Where are we? In a room. What is this room? A square. And what is a square? A circle—the Republican Circle. It's the square of the circle. That's why the Republic is ecumenical."

"Bravo! Bravo!" shouted the tailor, the newspaperman, and the milliner, choking with laughter.

Belarmino began to get carried away, already forgetting those around him.

"We are subscribed in this square."

"By paying dues of two *pesetas* a month," commented the milliner.

"We are circles that are subscribed in a square."

"Oh! Inscribed," the journalist agreed.

"Each man is the center of an infinite circle, just as Pasqual said."

"Which Pasqual?" asked the tailor.

"Unless he means Pascal," suggested the journalist.

"That beacon of humanity," continued Belarmino, referring to the above-mentioned Pasqual, "who hated the Jesuits, as Salmerón told us in his speech. Death to the Jesuits!" shouted Belarmino, beside himself, now on his feet. "Long live Pasqual! Long live Salmerón!" he exclaimed, pointing to a sepia-colored lithograph that was hanging on the wall. It was a portrait of the person being praised.

---

*Nicolás Salmerón y Alonso (1837–1908), Spanish philosopher and politician, was President of the First Spanish Republic in 1873.

"Long live the Republic!" And he pointed to the other illuminated lithograph, which depicted a stout matron with a tricolored tunic, a torch in her hand, a lion and some broken chains at her feet. "Death to the Roman Curia! Death to the Rota Tribunal!"

"Why don't *you* just drop dead once and for all, idiot, adulterer, baboon, before you kill us all with your stupidities," shrieked a mordant voice that belonged to a young, rather attractive woman whose distended face at this moment made her look like one of the Eumenides. A hurricane bearing desolation, she penetrated that circle, which was a square, and seized Belarmino. It was Xuantipa, the legitimate wife of the witty, eloquent, and impetuous shoemaker. The name Xuantipa was a contraction of Xuana the Tippler, an alias or appendage she had acquired through paternal inheritance. Her progenitor, Xuan the Tippler, a wine merchant from the province of Toro, was the first usufructuary of this appendage or alias, owing it to the fact that whenever he was tipsy, which happened frequently, he would become belligerent and threaten to strangle anyone who claimed to be drunker than he was.

Xuantipa was dressed in attractive, genteel clothes like a typical shopkeeper's wife; she wore a yellow silk scarf around her neck, a Vergara shawl of bright colors crossed at the chest and tied in the back, a skirt of blue cretonne with a white speckled design. Belarmino always dressed in high style. The only indication of his professional activities was a leather apron he wore rolled up under his waistcoat, although he carelessly left a little corner of it sticking out so that it looked like one of those leather vests masons wear. There was a notorious incongruity between Belarmino and his wife.

Xuantipa grabbed Belarmino and dragged him outside by his lapels. Belarmino looked around at his friends and made an exculpatory gesture as if to say, "You must forgive her; she's an inferior woman." Before making her exit, Xuantipa shouted to those who remained, "You scoundrels—turning this baboon into a monkey so you can laugh at him!"

As they went down the stairs, Belarmino mumbled to himself, "And this happens day after day after day . . . "

"That's what *I* say," answered Xuantipa angrily; "day after day after day, and you never learn, baboon that you are."

"I've already told you, woman, that I am resigned to everything except to your calling me a baboon. With that vulgar word you seem to be covering me with filth."

Xuantipa pulled Belarmino along by his lapels through the accustomed streets of affliction. The little children followed them at a wise distance, chanting

> *Xuantipa today*
> *Is in a bad way,*
> *You'll pay the price too,*
> *Monsiú Cordoniú.*

Xuantipa threw stones at them. The urchins scattered, but in a moment they again took up their chant. Belarmino walked along with admirable dignity. Finally, they reached the shoe shop. Inside there was a gentleman who had been waiting for Belarmino. Xuantipa disappeared through the back door. The gentleman and Belarmino were left alone. Pointing with his cane at a pair of boots lying on the counter, the visitor said, "Belarmino, I am returning these boots; they just do not suit me. You make seditious, Republican shoes."

"Pardon me, Don Manolito. In my profession I'm illiterate. I mean that as a shoemaker I have no political preferences. As a citizen, I do. The science of shoemaking doesn't know anything about political clauses; that's why it's illiterate. It's all the same to me whether I make mountain-climbing boots, hiking boots, riding boots or elegant dress shoes. I even make footwear for the clergy. So you see, Don Manolito . . ."

"Those boots do not suit me. I have decided to have my shoes made outside of Pilares."

"Well, if that's the way you want it. But this pair of boots . . . , " murmured Belarmino turning one of them over in his hands, and discovering to his consternation the wear and tear the boot had suffered from use, he added timidly, "They're very worn."

"Just to please you, I did wear them a few times."

"I would say more often than that," Belarmino dared to reply.

"Perhaps a half a dozen times. When I picked them up I tried them on, and I saw they didn't fit me very well but, I thought, 'If I return them to poor old Belarmino, he'll think I have some kind of a mania!' And so I put them on just to see if my feet would get used to them. Impossible. Well, not willing to accept this, and since I didn't like the idea of returning them to you, I tried them for a few more days, but I did not put them on more than six times, until in spite of myself, I was convinced that they simply would not do. And regardless of all this, you don't seem the least bit grateful. I think you're forgetting whom you're dealing with. But, just the same, before I have my shoes made somewhere else I've decided to ask you to make me another pair to see if this time you can do it right. Well, good-bye."

And he left.

Belarmino took out a book from a drawer under the counter. It was a dictionary of the Spanish language and, tucking it under his arm, he sat down on a small chair next to the door.

"Hey, you, Celesto! Are you there?"

From a shadowy corner of the room there emerged a red-headed lad who couldn't have been more than twelve—he was the apprentice. He stood there with his mouth open.

"Do you have anything to do?"

"Not a thing."

"There aren't any orders pending, are there?"

"No, sir."

"Then why don't you take the child out for a walk in Cathedral Square where it's nice and sunny. I'll stay here and take care of things."

The young boy went to the back of the store and returned a moment later with a seven-year-old girl. Belarmino took her in his arms.

"Do you love your daddy?"

"Yes, I love," she answered.

"A lot?"

"Lots, lots."

Belarmino tenderly kissed his daughter and then turned her over to the apprentice, giving him five cents.

"Here. Buy her a caramel lollypop. And be sure it's a red one because that's the kind she likes."

Alone at last, Belarmino opened the dictionary and began to take notes in a small oilcloth-covered notebook he had taken out of his jacket pocket. Scarcely had five minutes passed when the voluminous and ruddy Don René Colignon, chicory and candymaker, burst into the shop. His ruddiness was so flammiferous it projected reflections against the walls. His epidermis was tightly stretched and seemed to have been varnished. He looked like a greased bladder. He had a very carefully

36

constructed little goatee, the color of wheat, and his white chin rose up out of it like an egg in a brass eggcup. He had Gallic, almost Rabelaisian, eyes—blue and sparkling they were and they denounced him as a man who delighted in the pleasures of the table as well as of the bed.

Even before Colignon had entered the room, the red-hot radiance that preceded him had been like a herald announcing his arrival and Belarmino hastened to hide his book and notepad.

"Oh, *monsieur le cordonnier! Mon cher ami le cordonnier!*" said Colignon on entering, and his voice went up and down in modulations that sounded like the gobbling of a turkey; his arms were open and he used them to press to his huge bulk the gentle, sweet, and lean Belarmino. "How I love you, my illustrious and kind *cordonnier.*"

"I love you too, Señor Colignon, and I'm not angry with you because of the nickname you've given me."

"I have not been at fault, dear Belarmino."

Some of the townspeople, not particularly well-versed in French prosody, had converted *Monsieur le cordonnier* into "Monsiú Codorniú."

"And they have even made up songs about me," added Belarmino.

"I know, I know; but I have not been at fault."

"I realize that. I like to talk to you because you are an educated man and you know about far-off lands; particularly since you come from a republic of foringers."

"Foringers . . . ha! ha! Delightful . . . " Colignon burst into laughter that sounded somewhat like the loud "glu-glu" of a turkey. "I wanted to ask you a small thing that has come to me last night. Why do you call your shop The Bosquous and Equitable Nimrod, saying also that it is bilateral?"

"You'll have your answer in the time it takes to pay a bill. It means to speak well and to think on two levels and so, by association, to be a philosopher."

"Are you a philosopher? I thought you were only a Republican and an orator."

"Orator? I deny that utterly! Orators are the most common of portals [portals = mortals]. I despise oratory. Naturally, I speak in public; but I don't wish to be an orator, merely eloquent, just eloquent like my master Salmerón. But I am also a Republican of the mind; and for that reason, I am a philosopher. That's what Salmerón is. I'm not completely a philosopher yet, but each day I become more of one, and as time goes by . . . Well, the crux of philosophy is nothing more than the stretching of words, as if we were to put them on a shoemaker's last. If we could find one single word in which all things would fit, let's say a last that would be valid for all feet, then we would have philosophy, as my intellect sees it. Some day I'll find the knave [knave = *quid*]. While I'm looking, I'll keep calm by making lasts for all kinds of feet and widening words for all kinds of things, the more the better; the two levels are ecoliquated. Now you will be in a better position to understand. Nimrod is a proper name and it cannot be stretched. Bosquous—adulates, or as the vulgar say, alludes to *buskin,* a type of shoe, and also to *bosque,* a small wooded area, because I make boots for walking in the woods and hills. It is also distantly related to the Spanish word for bear, *oso,* because the material is lubricated with bear grease. Equitable because I make riding boots, that is, boots for equitation; they are perfectly and equitably made. The science of shoemaking disregards political considerations and can thus turn out a dancing pump for the Queen of Scotland as well as a reinforced wooden shoe for the butcher, or a buckled slipper for the King of Aragon's Lord of the Bedchamber—all in all, *equis.*"

The ebullition that was created in Colignon's thoracic enclosures was no longer just the "glu-glu" of a single turkey but the hissing of a whole flock of Christmas geese. He couldn't stop hugging Belarmino, and his eyes filled with tears of laughter. "What a great man you are, *monsieur le cordonnier.* What a great man you are!"

The joyous salaams of Colignon didn't annoy Belarmino one bit— as a matter of fact, he was moved and flattered. The shoemaker was very perceptive, very quick to become aware of the machinery and expression of passions or affectionate feelings; but since at the same time his goodness was even greater than his perception, when he suspected that someone felt hostile or was ridiculing him, he refused to show any reaction. Above all, he knew how to differentiate between one kind of laughter and another. In the loud laughter of the abundant and ruddy Colignon, a type of overflowing *ex abundantia cordis,* Belarmino sensed a delightful personal quality or even a racial characteristic—that of joyful admiration. Of what a different lineage was the snickering and malicious laughter of the tailor Balmisa and the other frequenters of the Republican Circle—the ambiguous expression of an arid heart and unilluminated *cerebellum*! Those were the shoemaker's thoughts. But since he was compassionate and loved his fellow club members because they needed his love, he used to attend meetings daily so that he could train them in the technique of double-leveled discourse.

Although Colignon had finished fumigating the atmosphere with that copious spray of optimism, Belarmino remained a moment in suspense, fearful that his interlocutor might ask the meaning of the word bilateral as it referred to his shoe-repairing establishment. A catechumenical philosopher, Belarmino often used terms that he endowed with mystical qualities he would never have been able to elucidate completely. Fortunately, Colignon forgot to extend his inquiry into the bilateralness of the shoe shop. The Frenchman and the Spaniard continued to chatter until Xuantipa made her appearance.

The shoemaker's consort addressed Colignon with unusual courtesy and respect. Such civil affectations were only brought into play by Xuantipa under extraordinary circumstances and only when she had good reason for them. In this case, the reason was that some time ago Colignon had made a loan of a thousand *pesetas* to the Pintos without asking for any receipt or verifying document, and Señora Pinto was thinking of bleeding the sanguinary and ruddy candymaker once again, thus relieving him of a gushing stream of little *pesetas*. Colignon was very rich. He owned the large house where he lived and carried on his business. He had built it with the abundant profits from his candy store, bakery, and chocolate factory, as well as from a chicory plant he had on the outskirts of the city. By contrast, even the alleycats knew that the Pinto household was in a state of decay, was in hock, and on the verge of disappearing, for Belarmino neglected his business, preferring political shenanigans.

"What boots are these?" asked Xuantipa, pointing to the miserable remains Don Manolito had left behind on the pretext that they didn't fit him. "They look like they belong to a beggar."

"They're Don Manolito's—he left them to be fixed."

"Well don't fix them if he doesn't pay in advance; he's as poor as a church mouse and doesn't have enough money for sardines," grumbled

Xuantipa recovering her usual grim expression and looking again like one of the Eumenides. "What does he owe you? How many pairs have you made for him?"

Belarmino couldn't remember exactly. It could have been fifteen or twenty or even twenty-five. But how could he say this to the irascible Xuantipa without causing an ominous scene in the presence of Colignon?

"Oh two or three pairs," said Belarmino finally.

"You don't know if it's two or three?" asked Xuantipa, drawing herself up with a rapid motion and focusing her venomous eyes on the humiliated Belarmino.

"I have it written down somewhere."

"Where? Let's see. Show it to me," demanded Xuantipa, holding out her hand threateningly.

"But, my dear . . . ," pleaded Belarmino.

"Xuantipa, if Belarmino says so . . . after all, he is an honest man," interjected Colignon.

"You call that an honest man? This dolt, this baboon! You call that an honest-to-goodness man? He might have been one before, when he was still a bachelor. Now . . . he's a blithering fool, a clown, a lazy bum. That's what he is. You don't really know him, Señor Colignon."

"What I have wanted to say is that Belarmino is telling the truth. Calm yourself down now, Xuantipa; don't derange yourself."

"Calm down, calm down! . . . Why it's like trying to get the cheese out of a mouse trap. In this house the mouse could walk right off with the trap because there's no man living here. What's to become of me? What will happen to that poor innocent child? God only knows that I'm forgiving, and I act as if I don't know what's going on here. I'm not just sitting in the corner sucking my thumb . . . but what can I expect to get from that baboon!" roared Xuantipa, her voice going hoarse, her squinting, arid eyes ineffectually trying to squeeze out a few tears. "But this is the end, the very end; I'm fed up. I swear to you by this," and here she made an improvised cross with the thumb and index finger of her right hand, holding them up to her thin, dry lips and making a sucking sound with her mouth that was supposed to be a kiss, "starting today, I'm taking charge of everything, and if this creep is not good for anything else, let him make the beds and clean out the bedpans. He can sweep up and cook and sing the Republican national anthem while he's doing the dishes."

"But do you know how to make shoes? Because that's the important thing," said Colignon smiling while trying to lower the dramatic pitch of the scene to a more colloquial and tranquil level.

Belarmino just stood there with his head down, his precocious bald spot showing; a slanting band of light penetrated this hairless area like a sword piercing the head of a martyr.

"Well if I knew how to make shoes," replied Xuantipa, "everything would be well taken care of in no time flat. But, you see how things have turned out . . . when we got married, we had six helpers, male and female, and we couldn't handle all the commissions and orders. Today, just one miserable apprentice is too much for us."

"Well, you must go back to the way things were before, and you *will* go back," affirmed the optimistic and rosy Colignon.

"May God grant it!" prayed Xuantipa, taking on an expression of conventional and hypocritical piety.

"I think you should be involved in the business, Xuantipa—to take care of the bookkeeping, to insist people pay their debts . . . you are very good at this, but I don't think Belarmino is made for that."

"Oh wouldn't I be good at it though? If this one would only tell me the truth about who is paying and who isn't, I promise you that either they would pay or I'd take out their tonsils."

"What do you think of my plan, Belarmino?"

"It would be fine, excellent," answered Belarmino looking up beatifically.

"Oh sure, that no-good would find glory in anything that'd save him the trouble of working."

"He will do what belongs to him," declared Colignon with conviction. "And now, courage and ever onward!"

A new character entered from the street. He was undoubtedly a neighbor because he was wearing a filthy pointed cap one might wear around the house; he had a miniscule and erysipelatous nose, square glasses with a yellowish tint, a round, toothless, black mouth that was as deep as a cave. He wore a little frock coat that was too small for him, threadbare in spots, and chameleonic in color, that is, somewhat iridescent. He had a scarf wrapped around his neck and his tight checkered

41

pants were prominently baggy at the knees. His feet were wrapped in cloth slippers. Over his right ear was a long feather, the color of a grapefruit; the cuff of his left sleeve was covered with a mesh of black lines, which was nothing more than the web of strokes left behind from cleaning the tips of his pens. He emitted a dark and pessimistic effluvium into the atmosphere as though he possessed a zone of ominous influence that enfolded him. Either by enchantment or metamorphosis, he was the human incarnation of that jaundiced shack on Ruera Street where the painter Lirio had calculated that only a pawnbroker could possibly live.

Just as the jovial, diurnal spirits fly off with ruby-colored wings as soon as the nocturnal incubus sprouts in the East, Señor Colignon, anguished, disturbed, and pale on the inside (because on the outside his ruddiness would not let any other emotion show through), said goodbye and headed for the door as Xuantipa shouted after him:

"We count on your help, Señor Colignon, and may God bless you for it."

"A-ha! A-ha! The Frenchman is on your side? That's perfect, my children, just perfect," commented Don Angel Bellido, since this was the pawnbroker's name—one both suitable and inappropriate at the same time.*

"Yes, Señor Bellido. Where have you been—in Limbo? Who around here doesn't know that we and Colignon are like meat and potatoes?"

"My dear lady, I didn't know you were as close as all that . . . the fact that Colignon is the meat, and thank God he's not without an abundant quantity of that, and you're the potatoes . . . fills me with great satisfaction," said Don Angel. "But since I have the pleasure of calling on you every day to refresh your memory and as you never tell me anything or even hint at anything . . . but, now, just between us the problem has taken on a different aspect . . . since . . . well, well . . . you know what I mean." Bellido was unusually fond of suspended clauses. All of his sentences left behind the hissing sound of skyrockets. Anyone who listened to him was always eagerly awaiting the explosion of his Adam's apple. Generally, skyrockets don't have Adam's apples.

*The name literally means "beautiful angel," but Pérez de Ayala is also referring to the figure of Bellido Dolfos, who appears in the early Spanish ballads as a traitor who killed Sancho II of Castile outside the walls of the city of Zamora in the eleventh century.

But when Bellido's sentences did explode, the bomb was like dynamite.

"Because the loan and the accumulated interest is increasing," Bellido continued. Psss . . . the skyrocket was climbing into space. Silence. Anxiety. "It's reached the figure of ten thousand *pesetas*. It's all in a formal document. I could foreclose right this minute and, not to lose out completely, I could keep these four or five pieces of garbage you have here, which aren't worth half of what is due to me." That was the dynamite bomb Don Angel Bellido detonated over Belarmino's head and over the surly forehead of Xuantipa.

Because she was much less sensitive, Xuantipa was completely overcome by fear. Belarmino with his quick intuition where feelings were concerned, understood what he was supposed to answer.

"This would be a very bad time for you to foreclose, since we hardly have any material in inventory and scarcely any shoes at all in stock."

"Oh for goodness sake don't talk that way," was Bellido's immediate reply. "Did I say anything at all about foreclosing? I just said if I wanted to . . . but I would never think of doing anything like that . . . particularly now that Colignon is behind you . . . behind . . ."

"It isn't that he's behind us," declared the honest Belarmino.

"Aeh?" answered Bellido, very alarmed, craning his neck while the pupils of his eyes peered out over his square glasses.

"What do you mean he isn't? Didn't we just speak to him face to face as Christ has taught us?" interjected Xuantipa, almost choking.

"I see what you mean, you rascal," twanged Bellido, withdrawing his little eyes back behind their windows while allowing one of them a kind of good-bye wink, pulling in his neck as well so that it returned to its normal length. "You don't want the news to get around that the Frenchman is your financial partner, eh? Well, as far as I'm concerned . . . and just so that you are convinced that I'm worthy of your confidence, I'm going to give you another piece of news. A shoemaker from another town, a real high class shoemaker, is going to set up shop on this very street. He's a protégé of the Duchess of Somavia, so . . . keep your eyes peeled, because this is pretty serious business. You'll have to get busy to compete. Tell your Frenchman friend he's got to come up with some cash."

At this point, a lady appeared in a nimble and perfumed swishing of springtime breezes. Her arrival and the pawnbroker's departure were as one. It should be said that the shop had space for only one person from the outside. Each new arrival was like a nail that displaced the previous one.

The lady exhaled prudish puffs of air and bounced from place to place with a gentility that was completely adolescent. Seen from the back, she was a short little thing, refined, and graceful. The other side of the medal did not correspond with the rear view; she was completely flat-chested, had a waxen complexion, protruding eyes, and a totally masculine face.

"Ooof, ooof! What a man that is!" she blurted out. "He looks like he's been disinterred. He even smells like a cemetery . . . Belarmino, I don't understand how you even let him in here. He leaves a smell behind . . . I'm going to have one of my nightmares as a result of this meeting. Aye! If I had seen him I wouldn't have come in. But that other one was close on my heels and I came in here hoping you would give me refuge, shelter. He gets more daring every day. He's even capable of coming in here in hot pursuit. What an Anselmo he is, good Lord! . . . but everybody has his own peculiarities; you have to admit he's handsome, charming, very masculine, as elegant as they come. He even sends his shirts to Madrid to be ironed. I'm amazed that he's taken so long to pass by the door. I'm just going to peek for a minute to see where he is. There he is! He's waiting in ambush at the candy store. How tenacious he is! How insistent! And it's been that way for five or six years. I've even lost count. If I were to yield a bit, we'd get married on the spot, but I just don't dare, I don't dare. The idea of the wedding bed scares me to death. Yes, I realize that a young lady should not remain single, all alone. People have tongues like embroidery needles. But the wedding bed horrifies me, it scares me to death. I had to fly through the streets and he is always behind me, always behind. How assiduous he is! How persevering! Ah me! May I just rest here and catch my breath?"

That eloquent and fickle creature, that irresolute androgynous twig was Felicita Quemada who lived on Ruera Street. Her tenacious and persevering pursuer, a senior-citizen type as one might expect from the looks of the lady, was considered in Pilares to be the arbiter of elegance and occupied a most distinguished position in local politics. He had been appointed deputy to the Duke of Somavia, the political boss of the region who spent most of his time in Madrid. This deputyship or representation was not limited to matters of local politics. Novillo's elegance was also delegated to him by proxy from this same aristocrat, a dirty old man a bit on the foppish side. In dress, Novillo constituted a somewhat faded replica of his protector, for the latter used to send him ties, stiff collars, stockings, and sporty vests from Madrid which were like the Duke's own although made of inferior material. Novillo would also receive suits of Catalonian wool, which were copies of those the Duke wore, although his were made of English cashmere. The love affair between Novillo and Quemada, or, as they used to call her in Pilares, "the Consumptive," had come to be a typical feature of daily life on Ruera Street as well as in the entire town. This affair went back at least ten years; it had begun when both of them were well on in years and had not progressed beyond the purest kind of romantic, platonic, and ineffable relationship. The Consumptive never talked about anything else. Novillo never spoke about their alliance; if anyone mentioned it to him, he felt deeply offended. The people on Ruera Street as well as in the rest of the city considered this love affair comical. Because of his age, or his corpulence, or perhaps simply because people are most sarcastic when they are suspicious, they all called Novillo by the nickname of "the Ox." But beneath its ridiculous exterior, the silent and constant love affair between Anselmo and Felicita hid a truly pathetic emotion. How was it possible to explain his unconquerable timidity (he was so daring in matters of municipal and provincial administration and in planning electoral strategies) except by attributing it to fate? To what could it be ascribed but the furious whims of an adverse nemesis? Anselmo and Felicita sought each other out constantly; they lived only for each other. But this capricious nemesis had struck Anselmo dumb, and, in addition to this barrier of silence, had also placed a wide, impassable hedge of thin air between them. Anselmo would not dare to come closer than fifteen feet to the object of his love. It was as if on reaching that point he came face to face with a transparent and invisible obstacle. This distance was constantly maintained. It was as though Felicita were enclosed in a glass tube or had been placed under a great bell jar. Within that prison imperceptible to the eye, Felicita was being slowly consumed; on the outside, Novillo stood arrested and stupefied, scarcely daring to look at the beloved captive. Out of respect for the truth it must be mentioned that this torment created opposing effects in Novillo and Felicita, for Novillo did not lose an ounce of weight over the situation but, on the contrary,

45

gained quite a few. And it should also be stated in conclusion, that Novillo's fidelity was absolute; no one had ever seen him engaged in other
flirtations or even involved in the kind of illicit relationships for which
one pays money. And all of this in a provincial capital where everybody
knows everyone else's business.

Felicita sat, took a deep breath, but didn't settle down. Barely had
she touched the seat, when she jumped to her feet again, impelled by
the dynamic energy that kept her as thin as a rail and, reaching for
some papers she was carrying rolled up under her arm, spread them
on the counter.

"Look at this, Belarmino. This magazine is *The Mirror of Fashion,*
and the other one is *The Mundane Sylph.* Just take a look. This whole
section is dedicated to shoes. There is a pair here I have simply fallen
in love with. Couldn't you make me a pair just like them? I'm very
demanding about shoes. That's my weakness. You can tell a cultured
person by his feet. A foot covered with bunions denotes an uncouth
spirit. Like me, Anselmo is also a slave to good footwear. You've probably already noticed that. Do you see these cute little shoes in *The
Sylph?* They're made of Scandinavian leather. Do you have that kind
of material? They have zigzag back-stitching of white kid. You probably
have that. In any case, we could always cut up an old pair of gloves; I
have an endless number of those. That's another weakness of mine.
Gloves and shoes; the hand and the foot. Well, I think I am spending
more time than I ought to on all this. And, by the way, something just
occurred to me. Do you think Anselmo would object to my visiting your
house this way, Belarmino, since he is a monarchist and you are so
subversive? . . . but, I guess it's all right. If it weren't suitable, he would
have told me. Well, I'm off. I'll take these fashion magazines with me
and we can speak more calmly about those Scandinavian leather shoes
later."

And in a swishing of perfumed skirts, without ever having left one
little crack through which Xuantipa or Belarmino could have squeezed
through to utter a peep, out she went. This scene was repeated almost
daily. It was absolutely obligatory for her to come in thinking that she
was being pursued, then to talk vaguely about having a pair of shoes
made, and then, as a sort of *P.S.,* be struck by doubts as to whether or
not Novillo would approve of those visits to the subversive shoemaker.

Shortly after Felicita had left the store, Don Anselmo Novillo passed before the doors of the establishment with the solemnity of the corpulent, mature man who is very much aware of his elegance. He began his stroll with Felicita through the streets; this would go on for three or four hours.

Xuantipa withdrew to prepare dinner. Left to himself, Belarmino rested his forehead in his hands and meditated. He stayed that way, motionless, for a long time until the apprentice and the little girl returned. It was getting dark. Belarmino awakened from his meditation to kiss and hug his daughter. All this was done silently, sincerely, and tenderly, even more so than usual. His eyes filled with tears.

Total darkness reigned in the store.

"Shall I turn on the light?" asked the red-headed apprentice.

Belarmino didn't answer right away; his voice had deserted him.

"It's not necessary. We'll save electricity. Go to the kitchen with the girl and see if you're needed in there. You can light the way with this match. Be careful."

Engulfed in darkness, Belarmino withdrew into himself again in order to meditate. This time Belarmino did not dissolve into those philosophical speculations, or what he considered to be such, which lately, for the last two or three years, had totally monopolized his thinking processes and his spiritual desires without leaving room for any other pursuit or sentiment except the love he felt for his little daughter. No; Belarmino was not now delving into the problem of knowledge but rather into the problem of conduct—he was not worried about what he ought to think but about what he ought to do. His external life, the currents and movements of his social life, were like a geared wheel that was enmeshed with others. Every day this wheel mechanically made a complete turn, meshing with the teeth of the other wheels, always the same ones and always in the same shape and position so that there was no way to be sure if his wheel was making the others turn or if the others were making his turn, or if all of them were just regularly turning, impelled by some unknown and enormous mechanism. This day had been identical to innumerable other days in the daily revolutions of Belarmino's life. And yet it seemed a significant and critical one, a day in which a deep intuition of the future had been awakened in him, or, as Belarmino would say to himself in such moments, using the esoteric technical vocabulary he had invented, it was a *Pharaoh's Chronicle*.

Men are divided into two classes according to the way they sleep. Some sleep very little because they fall asleep immediately; others sleep a lot or at least spend many hours in bed because they fall asleep little by little. The head, or dream tank, is like a receptacle with a small drain. In the case of some people, the receptacle is filled to the brim in a flash and they fall into an inert and dreamless sleep. Then the receptacle begins to drain gradually and in the early morning hours their heads are empty, clean, cloudless, and their bodies cry out for exercise. Such people get up from bed completely awake. For other people, the receptacle fills very slowly because less sleep penetrates through one end than is dissipated or emptied through the other, and as a result they suffer from a rather difficult and rarefied slumber filled with incoherent images; the contents of the receptacle reach their maximum volume at the very moment when it's time to get out of bed. Such individuals get up when they are most asleep and walk around like somnambulists during the whole wasted morning until, a few hours later, they have been able to shake off this soporific saturation. The first type is muscular and robust. Those of the second group are lymphatic and nervous. Members of the first group are endowed with the necessary resources for practical success—for war, politics, business. Those in the second category are cut out for intellectual and aesthetic success. Belarmino belonged to the second group. Xuantipa used to get him up by hitting him with a broom the way hunters flush out rabbits that are hiding in the underbrush. For the rest of the morning he was totally useless. He felt as though his forehead were filled with a dense smoke that moved downward over his eyes and made them cloud up and smart. By the end of lunch, after he had drunk his bottle of cider and smoked the two cigarettes he always kept stuck in the waistband of his trousers, he was a different man. His talent, which he always imagined to be a substantive, independent, and even corporeal being, a mysterious guest inhabiting his interior regions, began to bubble, to become restless, and started rapping gently with its knuckles against the inner walls of his skull. It would say to him, "Hey, Belarmino, I'm here! Let's begin to discuss things never heard before." Belarmino used to call this recondite being, this intimate demon, by the name of *Intelet*.

By the time dessert was served, his *Intelet* would make him impatient, and no sooner had Xuantipa gotten up to wash the dishes than Belarmino would furtively head for the Republican Circle. Later, the usual things happened—Xuantipa's violent eruption, Belarmino's afflicted return, some client or other in the shop, all of them morose, the optimistic Colignon, the pessimistic Bellido, and the impossible Felicita. The graph of Belarmino's life was traced on paper that had the guide lines already sketched in. At the top of the page there was a sacred inscription, "the daughter of his entrails." From time to time a brief parenthetical statement would appear on the page referring to some public meeting at the Republican Circle when Belarmino delivered one of his great speeches.

As is the case with all gentle and timid souls, Belarmino had tucked away a supply of anger and violence in a savings account that paid compound interest. When the rare occasion arose for spending these reserves, Belarmino became so wrought up that he actually seemed possessed. Balmisa the tailor, the owner and editors of *Dawn,* and other coreligionaries of the lower intellectual middle class didn't take Belarmino very seriously and even had him pegged as a nut. The clergy and more pious families considered him mad and, although they thought him basically inoffensive, felt that on occasions he could be extremely dangerous, and thus had to be watched more carefully than all the other Republicanites. But the lower echelons of the Party, the humble workers and artisans, showed a superstitious faith in Belarmino and became fired up whenever they heard him speak. Of course they didn't understand him, but Saint Bernard was also able to inflame the Crusaders, sweeping up huge numbers of people who never did understand the language he was using to persuade them. Whenever Belarmino gave a speech it became necessary for the audience to rush out into Bishop's Square and launch a series of inflammatory and blasphemous cries. As a result, there were some devout people who were seriously considering a plan to convert Belarmino.

There sat Belarmino saturated in darkness, his soul languishing as he passed through a terrible *Pharaoh's Chronicle* and contemplated what he ought to do next. Daily incidents that are repeated mechanically end up by taking on a different appearance and can even acquire a precise significance. Depending on the consistency or structure of a rock, the abrasion and aggression of watery currents can make the rock smooth, round, and slick; in other instances it can bring out sharp angles, edges, and barbs until one day, very suddenly, the stone cuts like a knife and plunges in like a dagger. Belarmino had accepted Xuantipa's chafing as a form of discipline that would lead to perfection. From the very beginning Xuantipa had scratched, cut, and jabbed; but as a result of such rubbing, scratching, cutting, and jabbing, the friction seemed progressively less abrasive to Belarmino and he felt that his soul had become rounded, smooth, and almost lubricated through contact with his coarse spouse. He was becoming more and more indifferent to the friction he had previously suffered from his clientele as well as to the agitated and turbulent contact he had with Felicita. Rubbing against the Frenchman was becoming progressively more pleasant. What was horrifying and had brought about the terrifying *Pharaoh's Chronicle* was his contact with Bellido, a contact always bothersome and distressing, but which on that day had suddenly wounded him and caused a rent in the most intimate part of his being. "I am ruined. I'll be out in the street tomorrow, or the day after tomorrow, or in a month. This situation has no *equa*" [this meant there was no hope]. Such were Belarmino's thoughts at that moment. He would have been able to continue just scraping by indefinitely, as he had in the past, but the arrival of the competitor whom Bellido had mentioned would accelerate the onslaught of the catastrophe. Besides, he was right in assuming that Martínez, a former employee of his, was planning to install a shop on the same street and sell machine-made shoes. "Machine-made footwear?" thought Belarmino, making a mental detour. "How could anyone even conceive of shoes that weren't made to order. As if a machine could make decent footwear! Idiots! It's a miracle they haven't thought of inventing a talking machine or a writing machine or some other asinine thing." He immediately returned to the straight and narrow road of his mental meanderings. The problem was that the whole business had no *equa*. One really couldn't count on Colignon. For the moment, it wasn't likely the Frenchman would advance all the money needed to pay Bellido as well as to set his friend up in a high class shoeshop. But even if Colignon had offered, Belarmino would not have accepted, because he knew in advance it would be money down the drain. He admitted to himself in all sincerity that he had not been cut out to run a business. He had been born for nobler and less profitable things; his interior demon, the *Intelet,* clearly told him this. "Belarmino, let's talk about things never heard before." His duty was to give up everything, to live on charity, to suffer hardship, to sleep in the open air, to feed on herbs, all of this so he could follow the voice of his *Intelet* and discover those things never heard before and which his inner genie promised him. But, what about the little daughter of his entrails? When Belarmino said to himself, "daughter of my entrails," the expression took on an almost literal meaning. Whenever he embraced and kissed his daughter, or looked at her adoringly, or thought about her, he felt himself to be more her mother than her father. Actually, Angustias was not Belarmino's daughter but the child of one of his sisters who died in childbirth a short time after her own husband had died. Belarmino took custody of the child practically at birth, and he himself nursed her with a bottle. This had all happened a year before he married Xuantipa. Before their marriage, Belarmino had told Xuantipa the true story and she had accepted it at face value. But after they were married, and because she couldn't have children of her own, she began to hate her husband and to speculate that the child was really Belarmino's illegitimate daughter. The infant was not spared this obsessed woman's hate. In all Xuantipa's shouting and insults, and no matter how she may have tried to disguise it, there always pulsated venomous allusions to this situation. The reader has undoubtedly already noticed this.

Belarmino continued with his thoughts. If he were ruined financially, his obligation would be to get a job as a helper in the new shoe store and to work so that his daughter would have everything she needed. To work . . . they would keep him at it from morning until night and even through the night, just as he had done with his own employees during periods of economic prosperity. That was way in the past, before the demanding little sprite he carried around in his head (that is, the *Intelet)* had made his presence felt and had distracted him from business matters. To have to work for hours and hours on end . . . to have to say good-bye forever to the peaceful and fleeting hours that he had dedicated to contemplative leisure and to the secret conversations with his inner tenant . . . Impossible! This was the horrifying *Pharaoh's Chronicle* that was getting Belarmino down.

"Good afternoon, God willing. Is anyone home?" asked a voice from on high, a thin, penetrating voice that sounded like a piccolo.

Belarmino thought he was dreaming. Was it the voice of an angel with a cold?

"Is there no Christian or human soul in this sanctuary?" repeated the piccololike voice, sounding as if it were coming from the ceiling. Immediately after this, there was a resounding clapping of hands that sounded like thunder.

"Belarmino, are you there?" roared Xuantipa from the back room.

Belarmino said to himself, "Well, it seems I'm not dreaming." He struck a match and almost fell backward. Standing before him was a massive object that practically touched the ceiling. He immediately recovered from his fright and became aware of reality. It was just Father Aleson, a Dominican Friar who had the dimensions of an antediluvian pachyderm. His religious brothers, as well as the parochial flock of worshipers, called him the Tower of Babel, both because of his stature and because he knew twenty languages, some living, some dead, and others that were putrefying. He was accompanied by an anonymous priest of normal size among men of the cloth, although it would have been considered excessive for a layman. Even standing next to this second friar, Belarmino looked like a candlewick. This was the first time the Dominicans had ever visited Belarmino's establishment.

When the shoemaker had lit an oil lamp, Father Aleson began to speak.

"You must be amazed to see us in your shop, given the ideas you profess . . ."

"Reverend Father," interrupted Belarmino, not completely sure this was the most suitable form of address, "the science of shoemaking is ignorant of political phraseology; therefore, it's illiterate. I have also made shoes for members of the clergy."

"Oh, is that right? When, my dear friend?"

"Some time ago."

"What you mean is that in spite of your anticlerical ideas you have no objection to shoeing religious individuals. But it could be that some among the faithful might object to being shod by you."

"Fanaticism is re-incidental," declared Belarmino sententiously.

"What do you mean by re-incidental?" asked Father Aleson.

"What I mean is that it's very common . . . and it's dangerous; you come across it everywhere."

52

"Oh I get it. You meant to say it's frequent . . ."

"No, sir. I meant to say and I said that it is frequent and common and harmful and that one often bumps into it. Antonomastically speaking, it is re-incidental."

Father Aleson was bewildered. Belarmino was speaking to him in an absolutely unfamiliar language, one that Aleson did not know nor could even imagine, since it was not a living language or a dead language but rather an embryonic language.

"And what about you, aren't you fanatical at all?" asked Father Aleson somewhat disconcerted, showing his emotion in the way his flutelike voice cracked as he stumbled on the last accented syllable of the word *fanatical.* "They have informed me that you are."

After this transposition of the third person plural and an indirect object pronoun, a syntactical combination that, naturally, creates a serious and solemn tone, the Dominican had almost totally regained his composure and aplomb.

"Outside the repair shop and subscribed in a circle of paradox, which is a square because it is ecumenical, I am a fanatic and even a pale theist; but inside the shop, and in ridicule, I am illiterate. This is the *maremagnum* of class and of good digestion."

Father Aleson, in a state of consternation, didn't know what to say. Anyone in his place would have had the same reaction. Translated word for word from the technical language he had invented, Belarmino had actually said, "Outside of the shop, and inscribed in the circle of my orthodoxy, which could be called a circle as well as a square, since orthodoxy is the conciliation of opposites, I am a fanatic; and even more than that, I am a violent incendiary. But outside of my own center and inside the shop, I am indifferent. Such is the ideal of good behavior and good works." This language was not yet spoken in the Tower of Babel. Father Aleson thought, "If I devote myself now to linguistic investigations and hermeneutics, I'll never finish. I'll just get right to the point." And he said in an elevated voice . . . and how elevated it was! "Delighted, my dear friend. You have spoken with unusual eloquence and persuasion. Now I understand why your speeches move and affect audiences."

"I assure you, Reverend Father," interrupted Belarmino, tickled by an itch of empathy toward the cyclopean Dominican, "these audiences don't understand my speeches, but I do awaken some enthusiasm be-

cause of my dazzling weight." This last expression meant fiery sentiment.

"It was precisely for that reason I understand their reaction. And
now I would like to talk directly about my purpose in coming here. We
have agreed you are to make shoes for all the clergy in our residence—
that would be five priests and a layman. Don Restituto Neira, a very
charitable and generous gentleman, together with his saintly wife, Doña
Basilisa, both of whom, as you know, have given us the top floor of
their palace as a residence, also wish you to make shoes for their servants. I hope that in spite of your impious ideas you will accept this
standing order. You will not be sorry, I guarantee. Shoes for us will not
be very difficult for you to make. Our vows of poverty oblige us to dress
and shoe ourselves with great simplicity," he said, and sticking his
foot out from beneath his skirts, a shoe of monstrous proportions appeared; a tomb fit for a Philistine.

With his psychological clairvoyance, Belarmino suddenly guessed
they were trying to bribe him. On any other occasion, drawing on the
reserve of anger and violence he had stored away for extraordinary
events, he would have been insolent with the friars. But at that moment, still bleeding from the wound Bellido had inflicted upon him
and still suffering from a case of *Pharaoh's Chronicle,* far from being
angry he felt instead a sense of relief and hope.

"I accept," he said firmly.

"I am very pleased," exclaimed the Dominican without disguising
his satisfaction. "We are agreed, then, my dear friend, that tomorrow
afternoon you will come to our residence and take our measurements."

"What? I must go there?" asked Belarmino, rather disturbed. "What
will my coreligionaries say?"

"What could they say? You are going as a shoemaker. Besides, that
is the fastest and most expeditious way of doing it." Belarmino liked
the word expeditious and he stored it away in his memory so he could
place it on the last, widen it, and give it a spacious, new, and suitable
meaning.

"Do you give your word?" asked Father Aleson.

"Yes, Reverend Father. And may God's will be done."

"Oh how I love to hear that devout expression on your lips, 'May
God's will be done.' God will want what is best. Until tomorrow, my
dear friend."

As soon as the priests had left, Belarmino regretted his promise. He spent the whole night wide awake, in a state of feverish soul-searching. He kept knocking on his head, asking for help and counsel from his inner inhabitant; but the *Intelet* was either distracted or not at home. At any rate, it did not acknowledge his knock.

The following morning, with his head one moment feeling as heavy as a ball of granite and a minute later seeming to want to float off his shoulders like a puff of smoke, Belarmino went to the door of the shop to clear his brain. On the ground floor of a building situated on the other side of the street and a little farther down from where he was, a crew of carpenters, masons, and painters were working diligently and energetically. They were being directed by and receiving orders from a very bristly and strawlike man who from time to time would show the workers some blue papers that must have been architectural drawings. With his stiff mustache, his hat cocked over one ear, a flower stuck in the buttonhole of his elegant morning coat, the man made a disagreeable impression on Belarmino. He struck him as being somewhat effeminate, a cross between a pimp and a peacock. "What novelty is this?" Belarmino said to himself, without clearly understanding the reality of the situation. His surprise was animal-like, as a chicken might feel finding one morning that its corral had been invaded by odd and insolent intruder birds. People were not long in coming to tell Belarmino that all the activity down the street was for the purpose of constructing a new shoe store. The bristly individual was the new shoemaker in person. Belarmino thought, "No doubt about it; I'll move to the Dominican residence this afternoon."

In the gossip and talk of the street, the coming of the projected shoeshop was discussed continually, and everyone contributed what he could to the general knowledge—a supposition, circumstantial evidence, a fact. The new shoemaker's name was Apolonio Caramanzana; previously he had had a shop in Santiago de Compostela; he was the protégé of the Duchess of Somavia. The shoemaker was accompanied by a goodlooking young boy of twelve—his son; father and son were to take up temporary lodgings in the duchess's mansion; the duchess was often seen at the construction site; the new shoemaker was already working for certain well-placed people, etc., etc. And thus bubbled the effervescent curiosity of Ruera Street and the whole town of Pilares. There was only one person who contemplated the trivial and anxious expectation with perfect indifference and disguised irony—Belarmino. Xuantipa's bitterness, harshness, and aggressiveness had risen a few degrees since the coming of Apolonio. She was exasperated and had even reached the point of hitting her husband. Belarmino received the blows and insults with a smile. Bellido, in spite of his cold blood, was vibrating convulsively and would throw several dynamite bombs daily against Belarmino's skull. Belarmino listened to all of this with an angelic smile on his face. Felicita stopped calling at Belarmino's establishment; that was a relief. Colignon admonished him, encouraged him, stimulated him, and insisted upon injecting some commercial aggressiveness and a bit of the mercantile spirit into him; he warned him about imminent risks and tried to describe first a dark future and then a rosy one; and Belarmino, without replying, looked at him with that same affectionate and peaceful smile on his lips.

One day Colignon said to him, "You're very calm and sure of your resources. Have the Neiras and the Dominican fathers promised you a nice slice, that is to say, of money?"

"They have promised me nothing."

"Then, what do you intend to do?"

"Live."

"Live. But how?"

"Better than ever."

"Wonderful, wonderful. But how?"

Belarmino moved closer to Colignon and whispered in his ear, "Do you remember that once I told you how one day I would hit the bull's eye? Well I've done it, I've done it. Belligerence is the doting mother of Greece. *Pharaoh's Chronicle* is extremely puerperal. I have found the recreated solarium." Translated into everyday language: adversity is the mother of wisdom. A serious crisis is always fruitful—and as for the last sentence, Belarmino himself translated it into common speech at the request of Colignon who asked, "The recreated solarium?"

"I will interpret this for you in ordinary terms. *Solarium* is a word that comes from *sol,* meaning sun, and it expresses the idea of a most vivid illumination and the source of light itself. *Recreated* is what no one has made but, rather, has made itself and produces pleasure, recreation or, in other words, uncreated light."

This time, Colignon's hidden and gurgling turkeys remained silent. The Frenchman leaned his left forearm horizontally over the depression or upper plateau of his abdomen, placed the elbow of his right arm in his left hand and then with his remaining unoccupied hand, he covered up his egg and the brass egg cup (that is to say his chin and goatee), in a gesture that was Napoleonic and pensive.

"I understand, I understand, *mon pauvre ami;* the priests have converted you."

It was Belarmino's turn to laugh, and he laughed gleefully.

"Convert me? What a projectile!" Belarmino bunched the tips of the fingers of his right hand together, brought them all up to his forehead, and confidently and clearly syllabized, "The *In-te-let!*" Then, changing the tone of his voice, he added, "I was helped in this by a book belonging to the Dominican fathers . . ."

"Did they lend it to you?"

"No; I borrowed it because I saw it on top of a table."

"And what is the title?"

"Well you wouldn't understand, because it's in Latin."

"But you, you, do you understand Latin?"

"I'll some day have an intuition of it. For the time being it's merely salutary for me."

Colignon left the room thinking, "There is no hope for the poor man."

The opening of the new shoe store caused an unforgettable sensation, extraordinary astonishment. The sign said, "Apolonio Caramanzana, Master Artist." There was a wide show window of limpid plate glass. In the window several pairs of exquisite shoes and boots were placed in a row on green felt. They rested obliquely against chrome supports— one for each shoe. Each pair had its own little label underneath: "Shoes of Swedish leather, commissioned by her Serene Excellency, the Duchess of Somavia"; "Calfskin boot for Anselmo Novillo"; and other commissions granted by various distinguished and elegant personalities. Toward the back of the shop window was an urn in which the authentic skeleton of a human foot had been placed. On the face of the urn, a sign: "Osteology of the foot." A wire came out of each little bone and tags were attached to the ends of these wires. The tags said, "tibia, fibula, interior malleolus, external malleolus, astragal, calcaneus, scaphoid, cuboid, the three cuneiforms, metatarsis, phalanx, second phalanx, third phalanx." On the wall above the urn hung a watercolor that represented a boot in profile sending out rays of light; on the top part of the boot was a sign, "The ideal podotheque," and at the bottom, four lines of verse.

> Although so fine and shiny,
> And with such great appeal,
> No one would dare, if this you wore,
> To cut your Achilles' heel.

And even farther down, the statement, "Tell me what boots you wear and I'll tell you who you are."

On both sides of the central portrait hung two other paintings. One represented a bare foot with high arch and curved instep; this one carried the inscription, "Aryan Foot: Noble." The other portrayed a foot that was stretched out flat with the sole against the ground. The inscription read, "Flat Foot, Plantigrade or Semitic: Plebeian." There were glass shelves on the side partitions of the shop window and these contained plaster molds of feet, some of them quite twisted and deformed. A sign placed against the shelves said, "repertory of extremities, life-size." From the highest point in the plate glass window hung a wide ribbon like some heraldic emblem which announced in gilt Germanic lettering, "A sovereign beauty inspires Caramanzana."

Everyone who saw the window thought about poor Belarmino. The opinion was unanimous—competition would be out of the question. Even Belarmino went to see the famous window. He examined it attentively and calmly. Since his heart was free of vulgar passions, his face did not register any ugly expression of displeasure; on the contrary, he smiled. He smiled with an innocent and delicately ironic expression. Apolonio, who already knew of Belarmino, was spying on him from within the store and felt strangely humiliated. Gorged and inebriated with success, what did he care about the hypocritical and malignant expression on the face of his already ruined rival? And yet he felt humiliated, guessing that the real rivalry between them had nothing to do with shoes. Apolonio sensed that there was something intimate and personal in all this and he had the uncomfortable feeling that in this budding and inevitable rivalry, Belarmino might very well emerge the victor.

Chapter Four

APOLONIO AND
HIS SON

It was the evening of Holy Thursday. We had dined in Don Guillén's room. The canon was smoking a long and expensive cigar; I was enjoying the dark, silky, and full-bodied tobacco of a Havana, so energizing, such a subtle and essential inciter of ideas and images that at times it is an excellent substitute for human relations, less bothersome and uncomfortable than dealing with one's fellow man. In praise of tobacco, a master physician of Salamanca by the name of Cristóbal Hayo expressed this idea many centuries ago: "Smoking, one never feels alone." Don Guillén had offered this particular cigar to me knowing it to be the shape and size I most liked—a delicate and thoughtful gift for which I thanked him. My host had also supplied a fine aged brandy.

Perhaps these details are impertinent, but I mention them to show that Don Guillén was a man who attended to detail and believed in the moderate gratification of the senses. From this it can be deduced that external reality existed for him, that he accepted it for all it was worth, only making sure that any opposition to such a reality was quick and well oiled.

He was laughing to himself as if he were seeing a vision that was comic and touching at the same time. He began to speak.

"I can't think about my father without laughing—in an affectionate way, you understand. My mother died when I was only three years old. I don't remember her. My father was, or to be more exact, *is,* for he is still alive; that is, he lives as a mere shadow of his former self . . . My father is the son of a servant who was employed by the house of Valde-dulla, an ancient Galician lineage that goes back to the Swabians or some such group. From father to son for two or three centuries now, all the men in my family on the paternal side have lived in the shadow of the house of Valdedulla, serving not only in the capacity of domestics, but also as *confidants* to the members of that household. The firstborn always remained in the service of the family, while the count dedicated the other male children to the Church or sent them out into the world to earn a living. In my family there have been quite a few abbots; nor would I be surprised to discover I have a rich uncle in America without my knowing about it. My grandfather was almost the chief adminis-trator of the house of Valdedulla. When I was born, this powerful dynasty had been reduced to just two descendants, the count, Don Deus-dedit, and Doña Beatriz, who had married the old Duke of Somavia and lived in Pilares. The count was a bachelor who suffered from many ailments, and his face was covered with livid boils and pimples. There was no hope he would ever get married, not so much because he was ugly and rickety, for women can accept anything if the suitor has wealth or pedigree, but rather because the count was a misogynist and a misanthrope. He used to say, 'Thank God the line of the Valdedullas ends with me, since from the days of Mauregato they have been a pack of asses.' Nothing interested him. He never left the ancestral home. The only thing that amused him the least bit was my father. The count didn't want my father to inherit my grandfather's position when the time came, 'Because,' he said, 'this is ending with me; the name will be lost, thank God, and the house will be transmitted to Beatriz's son who is a Somavia; let him do with it whatever his little heart desires.' The count wanted to arrange it so that my father could get along on his own and have a profession, a job, or even a career. It seems that my father, from a very tender age, used to compose verses and was very fond of reading novels and poems. Even then he was in the good graces of the count, who was some fifteen years older than my father. In re-sponse to the count's wishes, my grandfather proposed an ecclesiastical career in which, given my father's natural wit, he would probably have attained the rank of cardinal; but he felt no fondness toward the clergy and, more important, the count, who boasted of being an ardent fol-lower of Voltaire, said he would hear of no such thing. They sent my

60

father to the Institute where he studied for two years and was consecutively awarded two series of failing grades in the same courses. One of the professors wrote to the count that my father's excessive imagination made it impossible for him to concentrate or study with discipline and profit. My father has not forgotten that failure; now, however, he is able to explain it in his own way and is perfectly satisfied. He always says, 'I, who have had an academic education . . .' My father wanted to pursue the career of a dramatist, but when they convinced him that there wasn't any such profession, he responded, 'Well if I can't be a dramatist, I will be a shoemaker.' What a strange dilemma! I can hardly keep from laughing . . . these strange ideas and surprising inferences were exactly what amused the count. I'm probably boring you."

"Not at all," I answered.

"I'll be brief. Until I was twelve, I lived on the Valdedulla estate. My grandfather had died there three years earlier. From that time on the count himself took charge of the accounts and the administration. My father had a shoe shop in Santiago de Compostela. Business was going badly because my father spent most of his time talking in cafes and getting drunk with his student friends. Thanks to the benevolence and generosity of the count, he was able to manage. From time to time he would come back to visit the estate. You should have seen how pompous and dandyish he had become, wearing a flower in his buttonhole, his hat tilted to one side, and his cutaway coat, which for some reason or another that I never understood, the count called paradisiac. 'My boy,' the count would exclaim, 'I'm flabbergasted by your elegance and your airs.' And then, doubled up with laughter, the count listened to him recite fragments from a drama that my father was writing, *The Siege of Orduña and the Lord of Oña*. My father explained the plot to him, especially emphasizing the thesis, or, as he used to say, the idea, to all of which the count thoughtfully replied, 'Well, imagine; that's quite enigmatic.' 'Enigmatic!' replied my father, with innocent petulance. 'You'll see how enigmatic it really is when the drama has its first performance on stage.' "

"It was probably more rational than those plays written by his countryman, Linares Rivas,* " I interrupted. As the reader will notice I was

*Manuel Linares Rivas (1867–1938) was a Spanish playwright, author of ideological dramas dealing primarily with the theme of justice.

at that indiscreet youthful age when, on closely examining the world, men, and things, one tends to drop names.

"I cannot tell you, because I don't go to the theater, nor do I ever read frivolous literature. But let me continue. During the three years after the death of my grandfather, the count did not rest for one minute; he visited his lands, checked property lines, counted his cattle, and went through the whole house packing away the china and silverware. He spent hours in his study writing down all kinds of things. One morning, three years later, he was found dead, whether from fatigue or boredom I don't know. Among his papers was a letter for my father which said, 'You are a good man; but you are something of an ass, and I don't think you will be able to get along alone in the world. I am leaving a small legacy for you in my will, but if you administer it, it'll go up in smoke. Therefore, after I am dead take your son and go to Pilares. My sister, the Duchess of Somavia, has instructions from me and she will tell you how I wish you to make use of the legacy. She will see to it that you have everything you need.' I read this letter many years later when I was a young man. My father had turned it over to the duchess and she showed it to me. But I remember that when my father read it for the first time, he was standing near the count's laid-out corpse in the ancestral home of the Valdedullas. I saw my father frown and turn pale; it was undoubtedly when he came to that part about the ass. Then he unwrinkled his brow, his cheek began to twitch, tears came to his eyes, and he dropped the letter without even finishing it, crossed his arms and remained silently looking at the dead man for a long time. Finally he sobbed

'For you, soul so generous,
'Tis not noble nor decorous
To suffer an earthy inhumation.
I offer you a burial glorious
Here in my heart and eternal adoration.'

He then knelt, took the count's hand in his own and held it to his lips.

"I witnessed everything from beginning to end. Children are the best observers, and the intense observations of childhood are never forgotten. You probably have the idea that my father was a great fraud, that all this was just false and theatrical and the kind of thing that would make people laugh in spite of the presence of the deceased. Perhaps it was funny, I won't deny it, but it was also enough to make you cry. My father has always been sensitive to an excessive degree. Anything at all disturbs him. He is moved to tears by the most trivial events. He takes everything to heart. Spontaneously, he can become exuberant or emphatic. He was also very fond of singing, and whenever he sang I had the impression he was going to melt into the atmosphere like a cube of sugar in water. As for improvising verses, this was also very natural for him. You'll soon be convinced of the fact that my father, undoubtedly because he was in constant training, composed verses out of habit. But, in order not to interrupt the narrative, I will continue chronologically.

"My father did not separate himself from the cadaver until the grave-diggers had finished their ignoble and not very decorous earthy inhumation. We returned to the house. My father held me by the hand; he was whining like a child. We entered the room that had served as the Chapel Ardent where the body of the count had lain in state. The posthumous letter was lying on the floor. My father picked it up so that he could finish reading it. I saw that he frowned again, screwing up the corner of his mouth and puffing up his cheek, which he then proceeded to scratch. All this indicated vexation on his part. Before, he had dropped the letter when he reached the section on the inheritance. Now, the whole idea of going to Pilares and settling down among people he didn't know and under the immediate tutelage of the duchess disturbed him tremendously. But what could he do? My father pulled up the roots that had bound him to the beautiful Galician soil, and we headed for another no less beautiful region. My first trip by train, how I loved it! In León we changed direction and transferred to a train that went directly to Pilares. It was at the end of April and after several stormy days, people were wondering if the mountain pass near the Busdongo station between León and Pilares would be closed to traffic because of the snow. Just the idea of going through snow-covered mountains excited me. My father and I walked along the station platform, and I don't know which one of us felt more impatient as we waited for the convoy to be formed. And here you have proof that my father used to compose verses without even realizing it. He was muttering between his teeth, 'Where is the train? This gives me a pain.' 'It has just struck two. What's the matter? What to do?' And more doggerel and more verses. During our stroll back and forth we passed in front of a booth that attracted my attention because there was a sign on top of it that, for me at least, was quite enigmatic: Signalman. During one of our strolls in front of this place, a man with a lantern came out of the shed. My father addressed him, 'Signalman, a word with you; it looks like the train won't go. As there's no sign in view, will we get beyond Busdongo?' And turning toward me he said, 'Tell me, Pedrito, isn't this a sure indication that I am a poet? Without even trying, I have composed a sonorous quatrain. I always seem to express my contentment or displeasure in poetry. Valeiro was right when he told me I was the modern Ovid!'

"I don't want to bore you. Suffice it to say that when my father became even a little agitated, he used to breathe in verse. This peculiarity, or if you prefer, this mania, has perhaps been the cause of his misfortunes, but certainly thanks to it, he has also been able to overcome disaster with amazing resignation and indifference. Let us say, for example, that a tile from a building hits my father on the back of his head. Naturally, poetry couldn't be blamed for this accident. But my father, without losing his temper, would explain that this unfortunate thing happened to him because he was chosen by the gods—my father always speaks of God in the plural as the pagans did—and he would add that all tragic characters are semidivine—this is the result of his education in Santiago de Compostela. He would then give the explanation in verse so as to mitigate the pain from the blow on his head. Another of my father's peculiarities is the instantaneous way his love-passion becomes inflamed. As soon as he sees a woman, he's floating somewhere in the clouds; or, at least he raises her to a height above the clouds, then lo and behold! . . . she is an Elvira, Laura, or Beatrice. He will die sighing for love, evaporating in honor of the woman who happens to be beside him at the critical moment, be she a young nun with whom it is admissible to flirt, or a bleary-eyed cleaning woman. My father, the dramatist, used to imagine that everyone is necessarily a victim of some passion; if not love, then hate; if not hate, then envy; if none of these, then anger or avarice.

"He conceived of men as mechanical puppets all of a piece, activated by a single spring, and he divided them into nobles, phlegmatics, and villains, according to their dominant passion. Since in his mind each individual is made up of just one simple element, one man can rarely get along with other men; that's what gives rise to dramatic conflict. Only nobles understand other nobles and even then it might be

difficult if love is involved. Those who are phlegmatic pay no attention to each other; and villains hate each other and everyone else. My
father classified everyone he came across by physiological characteristics
and especially, curious as it may seem, in terms of their feet. He would
state, 'That one is noble,' broad forehead and Aryan foot; 'That one is
vile,' narrow temples, prognathous jaw, flat, Semitic foot. He would then
immediately devote himself to imagining the biography of the stranger
and the dramatic conflicts which he had experienced or was about to
experience. My father, following the wisdom of Buddha, used to say,
'Each man carries his destiny written on his forehead with invisible
letters.' And then he would add, 'Each type of foot is destined for a
particular road.'

"Well, I am falling behind, just like the train at León, which finally
left when night had fallen and passed, while I slept, through the snow-
covered mountains. Pilares—the first city I had ever seen. Since *illo
tempore* there were no taxicabs, we had to walk asking for directions to
Ruera Street, the boulevard on which the Somavia palace was situated.
Once we had found the street, we were taken right to the door of the
palace by a red-headed waif about my age who was with a young girl.
How delicate the girl was, so sweet and beautiful! . . . The name of the
boy was Celesto; the girl was Angustias. We were friends from that very
moment. I'll tell you about it later. We entered the palace, asked for
the duchess, and were led into a dark room. After waiting for an hour,
which seemed to be more like a century, the duchess appeared, dressed
in a colorful bathrobe. In light of the recent death in her family, I was
scandalized by her outfit. Both of us were dressed in black, and my father
had even had a black shirt made for the occasion, although, of course,
the coal dust from the train wouldn't show on it either. The duchess
opened the shutters and stood looking at us. 'Well, well,' she said, when
she had finally satisfied her curiosity. 'So this is the great Apolonio
Caramanzana; and this other little fellow is the pippin,' " and from that
time on she always called me Pippin.

"The duchess was very frank and occasionally . . . how can I put it?—
well, she swore a lot, although, being a woman, she would give the words
a slightly feminine form by changing the final *o* to a final *a*. She also
smoked like a chimney. All the Valdedulla family were eccentrics. As
for the duchess's heart—I'll use one of my father's phrases to describe it
—it was made of Hyblan honey and was larger than Mount Olympus.

The beneficence that great lady bestowed on my father and myself is of the kind that cannot be repaid. I think she must have been over forty at the time and she was what you might call a fat, middle-aged woman; frankly speaking, she was ugly. But she had a love of life, an openness, and a sense of humor that made her far more attractive than beauty itself. I assure you that when she let loose with one of her obscenities, which in her case was really a sign of contentment, you would just stand there fascinated and smiling, as if you had been listening to a nightingale's song. Where words are concerned, structure isn't as important as tone and intention. Words are like containers. Although they may have a similar form, some are made of clay whereas others are of pure crystal and contain a delicious essence.

"And now the image of Belarmino takes shape in my memory. He was a shoemaker-philosopher, quite a fabulous character, who, naturally, also lived in Ruera Street. As a matter of fact, the previous theory on words belonged to him. 'A table,' he used to say, 'is called a table because we feel like calling it by that name; it could just as well be called a chair. We use the same word for both of them when we say they are pieces of furniture; but we could also call them houses. Just because we feel like it, we use the same word for furniture and houses when we say they are both things. The problem of philosophy lies in searching for one word that will express everything we feel like expressing.' I don't know if he was a mad wiseman or a wise madman. I've gotten off the track. I was going to say that even though the lady was not the most suitable object for his affections, my father nevertheless immediately became inflamed with love for her. Since my father had always lived removed from reality, he consistently behaved in a strange way that both frightened and amazed those who witnessed it. And so, after a very brief conversation with the duchess, finding himself in a state of agitation, my father began to assail her with amatory verses which at that point were still somewhat ambiguous, more the result of artifice than timidity. He declared it was not by coincidence the lady's name was Beatriz and that he, like Dante, had come up from the inferno of Compostela to reach the paradise of her presence and protection. You are probably amazed by my father's knowledge, but that's easily explained. He had an extraordinary power of assimilation. His somewhat absurd and picturesque erudition had been acquired orally, the way the Greeks acquired it. He picked it up under the porticos of Compostela, among the students, an idle and picaresque group who (and I declare this blushingly), in order to have fun at his expense and feed his madness, filled his head with historical and literary events or wild stories, some true and others pure invention. My father absorbed everything all mixed together, and later he made use of this information in his own way, sometimes wisely and sometimes foolishly, going with the grain at times, at other times against it—but always with unabashed familiarity. If he mentioned Ovid or Sophocles, it was as though they had all eaten Galician stew together. The first time my father got carried away by his amorous poetic delirium in the presence of the duchess, I, overcome with terror, lowered my head and thought to myself, 'The lady is going to set the dogs on us and we'll have to make a dash for it.' But my father's ingenuous daring pleased her. She uttered a delightful obscenity, and encouraged him to improvise new elegiac verses. The duchess had known my father as a boy and had also learned of him from the references her brother made in his letters to her, so she was not particularly surprised by this scene. What a great lady! She put us up in her palace while the finishing touches were being made on my father's shoe shop. This establishment was going to be something special, because the deceased count had given instructions in his will that part of the legacy be used for this purpose. The duchess was to preside over all matters involving the investment of the money, look for a stable clientele, and be sure that my father did not get out of hand. At the time she said nothing about the other clauses of the legacy.

"Although the lady was very frank, she was also firm in her hierarchical beliefs. Her affability and benevolence always came down from above as a kind of patronage. Spontaneously, and seemingly without any deliberate reason, she used to place everybody, but everybody, in their respective places, that is to say beneath her—some higher, some lower, and some even in a humiliating position. Of course, she put us in an intermediate category—half servants, half friends. Strictly speaking, she didn't have what you might call real friends. She treated the people closest to her as though they were emancipated vassals, one step higher than we, for we had not yet been completely liberated. This persistence of caste pride, although covered over by relaxed behavior, was the only rigid side of her character, but on this score she occasionally behaved with extreme harshness and insensitivity; all of this was done unconsciously, and therefore without remorse. As for us, we had no reason to complain but, rather, had much to be grateful for.

"She lived alone most of the year. The old duke and their only son, a twenty-one-year-old adolescent, spent their winters in Madrid, a city which she hated mainly because of its bright sunshine. She liked open skies and filtered light. She used to say that the light in Madrid stirred up her blood, forcing her to commit all kinds of barbaric acts. 'With the husband God gave me,' and this I myself heard her say years later, 'the least I would have done had I lived in Madrid would be to commit adultery. Here I can overcome my boredom by gossiping and picking on people. In Madrid, with my temperament, I would not have been happy unless I were able literally to tear other people apart. All my ancestors were slightly wild despite the fact that they always lived in temperate and rainy climates. If they had lived under the barbaric southern sun, they would have turned out to be total savages, worse than the Riffians of Morocco.' I was saying, then, that she put us up in her house as though we were guests, but we didn't eat at her table, nor on the other hand did we dine with her many servants; we were served our meals separately. However, about a week after we had arrived she invited us to join her at meals. She used to get bored by herself, and my father could distract and amuse her. And, in effect, she had worked out a malignant and shrewd plan for her diversion. Whenever my father was near her, he would become extremely excited, poetically speaking, and everything would come out in verse. She prohibited him from saying anything in rhyme. 'Poetry is a sauce that inhibits digestion. So, be on your guard; if you feel a verse on the tip of your tongue, just close your mouth.' My father would endure mortal anguish. I used to see him perspire. His Adam's apple would pop out in a frightening way as if the consonants, all constrained and tied in a knot, were making a lump inside his throat that threatened to strangle him. 'Speak up, man, speak up; but in prose,' ordered the duchess. My father began to speak, carefully weighing everything, and when he least expected it, wham!—a poem. 'Apolonio, be careful of what you say or you will be punished by not getting dessert,' threatened the duchess. She didn't hide the fact she was enjoying herself—I was having a pretty good time myself (children are basically cruel). My father and I had never really lived together

68

till then and for me he was a strange character in every sense of the word. When I think about all that now, I'm ashamed of myself.

"The only thing that made me uncomfortable at the time was not knowing how to eat with elegant table manners and to use a knife and fork correctly. Affectionately solicitous, the duchess would instruct me, careful not to make me feel even more embarrassed. At the end of the meal, the duchess reaffirmed her decree in perpetuity. 'It is understood, Apolonio, that you will never ever speak to me in verse. Your poetry would end up irritating me. We never highly esteem what is squandered on us. And you, of course, would not want your verses to disturb or anger me. Be more miserly with them. Besides, love poetry is not to be shouted aloud before witnesses, some of whom are even servants. Don't you have any scruples about my reputation as an honorable lady? Amatory verses are to be composed in solitude and read with deep concentration. Compose as many poems as you like, but do it in writing; then you can give them to me and I will read them secretly. Now, since you possess that invaluable and rare gift of improvising poetry as easily as other people yawn, it wouldn't be right, dammit! if on certain important occasions you didn't make this public and have the chance to astound your audience. But I will be the one to decide when and where. Let us mutually agree that you will not speak in verse except when I expressly order you to do so, and even then it would be proper for you to let yourself be coaxed a little before you actually perform.' My father respectfully bowed from the waist in obedience. Anyone less innocent and simple than he would have seen through the irony and archness of the duchess. My father, on the contrary, became all puffed up as if he had inhaled a great mass of flattery and vanity.

"Every night after dinner, the duchess received a few friends for discussion and conversation. Actually, it was more like a type of homage paid by the vassals to their liege lord. One afternoon the duchess said to my father, 'I would like you to attend my salon this evening. My friends already know you by reputation, and I have also spoken to them about you.' I overheard this and naturally guessed that my father had been invited so that he could make a spectacle of himself when the duchess ordered him to speak in verse. The fact that some stuffy aristocrats whom we didn't know might laugh in his face, made me feel sorry for him and angry. But my curiosity got the better of me and I wanted to know *de visu* the members of this salon group. And so, after dinner, I clung to my father's coattails with the intention of squeezing myself into the room behind him. My father was so confused and nervous he didn't even realize I was following him. Standing guard at the door of the chamber and dressed in livery was Patón, a lackey with thick lips and bristling eyes who looked upon my father and myself with ill-disguised dislike and envy. When I was about to sneak into the room, this animal grabbed me by the scruff of the neck and without saying a word threw me thirty feet down the hallway. I sat down in a chair, hiding my face and sobbing. At that moment the duchess came by. 'What's the matter with you, Pippin?' 'Patón won't let me in.' 'Well we'll see about that, my son.' She had called me her son; I felt as if my heart would melt; every time I remember the scene, I feel the same sensation. The duchess grabbed me by the hand and as we walked by Patón, who had tensed himself even more, sticking out his muzzle and blinking rapidly, she said, 'Are you the one who chooses my guests?'

Hunched up in a corner under a palm tree, I dug myself in and, to use the vernacular, didn't miss a trick. All the guests had arrived. The only female present was the duchess and she presided over the gathering from her place on a high-backed chair that looked like a throne. The rest of the group formed a semicircle on both sides of her as they smoked and drank coffee and liqueur which had been placed on little tables scattered throughout the room. The duchess was also smoking, not puffing at a cigarette this time but at a good-sized cigar. The only person not smoking was a priest who sat there in a fetal position, his milky skin, overhanging nose, and tearful eyes all comfortably tucked in. This priest, Don Cebrián Chapaprieta, was the one who said mass for the duchess and her servants.

"My father was magnificent. If a stranger had suddenly come into the room he would have said right off—here is a great lord and a great lady. The great lord would have been my father, naturally. His hands were resting on his thighs with his elbows pointed forward, his torso held stiffly, his neck stretched out and his head turned slightly with a vague gesture of melancholy and disdain, a forgotten cigar dangling from the corner of his mouth. He was at least two heads taller than the other guests. Present also at the gathering, since he was a fixture at all these reunions, was a certain Señor Novillo, the duke's political representative and aide-de-camp to the duchess.

"Señor Novillo tried hard to look like a member of the nobility, but he gave me the impression of a servant dressed in his Sunday best. Everyone was speaking except my father and they were all under the baton of the duchess as they spoke of local happenings and the latest gossip. When they had finished drinking their coffee and liqueur, and when the smoke of all the cigars had swirled together, almost forming an awning suspended from the ceiling, the duchess said, 'Don Hermenegildo, it's been a long time since you have honored us with the trout's leap.' Don Hermenegildo stood up. He was a magistrate from the provincial port; already old, bald, diminutive, and very thin, his ears were fringed with little strands of hair that had been curled with a curling iron; his highly waxed horizontal mustache stuck out so far on both sides of his face that it looked like the balancing pole of a tightrope walker. He wore an ascot, a cutaway coat that halfway covered his buttocks, and black and white checked pants that were extremely wide at the bottom to hide his enormous feet imprisoned in shoes that had silk ribbons hanging from them as wide as the ascot itself. Before my astonished eyes, Don Hermenegildo got down on all fours. Then Pedro Barquín, one of the duchess's tenant farmers, who looked rude and coarse, stood behind the old magistrate. Putting his foot between the old man's legs, he lifted him up in the air and tossed him quite a distance. This shameful operation was repeated several times to the great joy and noisy excitement of the onlookers, including the priest Chapaprieta. My father was the only one who remained impassive, because he despised low comedy. I confess that I also laughed like an idiot. Now I feel ashamed both for myself and for the duchess. I can't understand how that lady could find any pleasure in vilifying an old man who, in addition, wore the respectable garments of a magistrate. That was the hard insensitive edge of her character. One shouldn't forget to mention, by way of exoneration, that Don Hermenegildo owed everything to the Somavias and had made his career by vile and underhanded dealings. The acrobatic number concluded, Pedro Barquín, who was a specialist in telling jokes, recounted a few that were not at all hygienic or innocent. After a few of these jokes, in a moment of rest and silence, Chapaprieta secretly mumbled into his surplice, 'It seems confirmed that His Holiness is granting a pontifical title to the Neiras.' The Neiras were a childless married couple, extremely rich and very much involved in Church affairs. The husband prided himself on having noble blood.

71

They lived across the way from the Somavia residence in a palace they had acquired from one Pepona, an old courtesan who, in turn, had gotten it as a gracious donation from her lover, the Marquis of Quintana. The Marquis had disappeared from the world of the living many years ago. Señor Neira had commissioned fantastic coats of arms, which were sculpted close to the eaves of the palace so they could be seen from very far away but not from nearby. This was done intentionally because anyone could tell from up close that they were pure fantasy. He was in the process of trying to obtain a title of nobility from the King. But just in case something went wrong and it wasn't granted, he didn't want to waste any time. He was also trying to get one from the Vatican. The latter possibility was more likely. Naturally, the Neiras wanted to be the equals of the Somavias.

"When the duchess heard Chapaprieta's statement, she commented, 'The Pope can't make nobles.' 'Certainly not,' said Barquín, 'the Pope can only make saints. A king makes nobles.' The duchess replied, 'Barquín, you're a fool; the Pope cannot make saints any more than a king can make nobles. Saints and nobles make themselves. What the King and the Pope can do is recognize them as saints and as nobles. The Pope could no more make me a saint than the King could make you a noble, even if they canonized me and gave you a crowned title. Nobility and saintliness are two opposite things and this is the way it should be. The nobles were the most courageous; the saints, the most timid. Nobility and saintliness are different in that nobility can be transmitted by inheritance and saintliness cannot.

" 'Now there is no longer any nobility that doesn't spring from other nobility. Nor is there any aristocracy other than that of blood ties, since we no longer live in a time when new nobles or new saints can be made. New nobles would be impossible, because in our society there is no longer any opportunity in which to accredit personal bravery; there can be no more new saints because we are all so well protected by laws that not even the most timid have the chance to show their timidity in saintly ways. These days it isn't possible to perform either noble acts or saintly acts, but only profitable acts. I mean the kind that brings in money. Today men can become rich.' It was the voice of Valdedulla. She had heard these same ideas many times from her father, Don Teodosio, and from her brother, Don Deusdedit.

"Barquín answered, 'So, we have to admit that modern aristocracy is a moneyed aristocracy.' The duchess said, 'I shit on that aristocracy.' That's what she said, and then she continued, 'That entire aristocracy of wealth is made up of black slavers, loan sharks, purveyors to the military, in a word, thieves. I'm not scandalized by all this. You know me and you also know that nothing surprises me. I recognize that at the origin of noble dynasties, just as when great fortunes are started, there are always a few thieves. But those crooks performed their activities in the open, not under cover. They were courageous and generous or, to put it another way, they were noble. These latter-day thieves are cowards, traitors, cheats, wretches, rascals, rogues, given to ambush and surprise attacks.'

"Since the duchess had gotten rather overheated, no one dared to utter a word when she finally stopped talking. But my father began to speak slowly, not only so that it wouldn't come out in verse, but in order to give his words a pedantic and aphoristic tonality. 'My lady the duchess is right. Those who hoard gold are villains. What did Iago advise? Fill thy purse. Those who conquer gold and distribute it are noble men. What did Hernán Cortés do? Burn his ships behind him. Those who lack gold are phlegmatic and indifferent men.' I didn't understand the allusion to the ships of Hernán Cortés nor do I think my father understood it. Nevertheless, his words produced an amazing effect. The duchess smiled with pleasure and the rest of the guests mumbled their approval. The reunion came to an end without the duchess even having displayed my father's poetic gift. I didn't attend another one of those gatherings again until many years later.

"Finally, my father opened his shoe shop with great success, and we went to live in the same building where the store was, but in back. An old maid came every day to clean our rooms. Knowing how quick my father was to fall in love, the duchess did not allow him to have a live-in maid; she didn't want him to lose control of himself or cause me to lose my innocence.

"The duchess watched over me as though she were my mother. She often invited me to dine with her and gave me books to read. She also taught me some French. At that time I lived a life of beautiful freedom. My best friends were Celesto and Angustias, Belarmino's daughter. We spent two or three hours together every day, under the arches of the town square if it rained. When the weather was good we strolled in the park or took trips to the outskirts of the city to pick flowers, look for birds' nests, hunt crickets, and catch frogs. I have already spoken to you about Belarmino. Shortly after my father opened his establishment, Belarmino's shop went under. A pawnbroker by the name of Bellido repossessed everything, putting Belarmino, his wife, and his daughter into the streets. Some Dominican friars who lived in the palace of the Neiras—now the Marquis and Marchioness of San Madrigal—took him in and installed him in the conciergerie. It was really just a hole in the wall, but there Belarmino worked as a shoemaker.

"This Belarmino had been a frenetic Republican and a demagogical orator, but after his financial ruin, he became completely pacified. Whenever I visited him in his cell, he was always wearing a seraphic expression, as though he were dreaming. Not even his shrew of a wife could shake him from this blessed tranquility. It was said in the city that the Dominican fathers had tricked and converted him. Tricked, perhaps; converted, never. I can guarantee that neither then nor much later did he ever fulfill his religious obligations. If he wasn't exactly a nonbeliever, he was certainly lukewarm.

"My father, who never truly disliked anyone, nonetheless had a capricious grudge against Belarmino. There was a reason for it. Ever since his days in Compostela, my father had always been used to circulating in a rather illustrious atmosphere—that was how he put it—what he meant was he was always with students. In Pilares there would have been a possibility for such an atmosphere or relationship, but Belarmino was the one who was immersed in it. This strange individual spoke with unusual fluency an indecipherable language which he himself had invented. He was a phenomenon. In order to hear him, a large number of students and even professors used to call on him, at first just to poke fun but later in earnest as they became intent on finding the key to his language. My father could not patiently bear his inferior position. He was consumed by a desire to attract the friendship of these students and to prove to them that intellectually he was far superior to that madman. One day when I told him about my walks with Angustias and Celesto, he forbade me to continue cultivating the friendship of that small company; but since my father never knew what was happening around him, I paid no attention to this order. Needless to say, he had classified Belarmino and all those connected with him as belonging to the category of villains. Things stayed much the same way for about two years.

"In September, after the duchess had returned from her village, she invited me to dinner. I was extremely surprised and perplexed to notice that there was another guest, no less than His Excellency the bishop of the diocese. His name was Facundo Rodríguez Prado. In his youth this very solemn gentleman had been hired by the Duke of Somavia to take care of the duke's cows. The duchess continued to treat him as a servant. Through their influence, the Somavias had made him a bishop. He had originally been a member of the Dominican order, spending some years in the Philippines. While there, he had gained the reputation of being a rather well-informed entomologist and was attributed with the discovery of several families of insects—the Musca magallanica, a fly just like the one found here except it resides in the Magellanic Archipelago; the *Draconian furibundus,* a sort of buzzing mosquito; the *Formic cruenta,* a kind of stinging ant; and other small domestic monsters. The newspapers always referred to him as 'Our prelate, the learned, world-famous naturalist, who has uncovered so many insects.' And the Republican journal invariably included the clarification, 'If our prelate, instead of discovering so many insects, had discovered a good insecticide, he would have had the gratitude of humanity and science and he would have been more worthy of fame.' He was a bossy type, his skull was as round as a ball, he had a somber look and political aspirations. During the meal, the duchess let loose with several spicy phrases and an occasional juicy obscenity.

"After dinner, His Excellency departed, apparently furious, and I was left face to face with the duchess. Very seriously she told me, 'In his will, my brother left some cash, not very much, for me to use as I saw fit in trying to make you into a man. After thinking about it for some time, I have decided that you are to be a priest. These days, my son, the priests in Spain are the ones you can count on as having the rosiest future, particularly if they have connections. Any boob in skirts, even if he comes from the humblest family, will be admitted to the best circles. Although he doesn't have a cent to his name, the wealthiest members of society will not look down their noses at him. Even if he is an ass, politicians and academics will listen to him; he can be as ugly as the devil and still the most beautiful women will gaze upon him, entranced. It all depends on his knowing how to handle himself. If my husband and I can't make you a bishop, we don't know our business. You have already seen that fool Facundo, who is as much a bishop as

St. Augustine. And we haven't made Chapaprieta into a bishop because he is so melancholy, so insipid and mellifluous that nothing can be done with him unless it were to turn him into a mother superior. You, on the other hand, are clever and not the least bit priggish. When you don the cassock it won't look as though you're wearing a hoop skirt underneath. You'll learn how to roll up your skirts whenever you have to. Besides, you're honest, truthful, and have a good heart, all the requisites for a charitable and worthy priest. I'm confident you'll never call me names, not even mentally, for having given you a shove along this road.' I never have blamed her, not even mentally. She did what she in conscience thought to be the most suitable thing, and perhaps it *was* the most suitable thing. I entered the seminary at the age of fifteen. Look, it's already two in the morning. We can continue tomorrow if you're not bored by all this."

"I only regret that it isn't already ten tomorrow night." We shook hands and said good-bye.

Chapter Five

THE PHILOSOPHER
AND THE PLAYWRIGHT

The Neiras—Don Restituto and Doña Basilisa, Marquis and Marchioness of San Madrigal—made a fine pair. Well matched, their marriage was childless. His face displayed a swollen nose, red and complicated, like those the Flemish painters loved to analyze with detailed affection. Her face bore a perpetually satisfied expression, a faintly benign look that people with totally undistinguished features often have when their stomachs are full and functioning well. She was plump and rather delectable, much younger than her husband and still ripe enough to appeal to those who go in for rich dishes and voluptuous Venuses. Both of them were always dressed in black. They lived surrounded by male servants similarly arrayed. All the domestics shared the ravenous looks of seminary students or those young boys who run errands for nuns. Humble, even obsequious, their yellowed faces and hungry movements were infused with the conviction that here God's will was being done. Even the cook looked like the rest of them, and yet everyone in that household ate extremely well.

Don Restituto and Doña Basilisa—or "the Empress," as the multilingual Father Aleson referred to her—were what you might call two simple souls, incapable of consciously doing harm to anyone. But they were equally incapable of doing them any good. Where other people were concerned, they didn't know exactly what good or evil was. The greatest good to which they aspired was the salvation of their souls. Given the chance, they wouldn't have had any objections to helping

77

others along the road to paradise, as long as it didn't interfere with their own trip. Naturally, they wouldn't have wanted everyone to have an equal opportunity for salvation, since in heaven just as in this vale of tears there exist social classes—the Angel Choir, Archangels, Powers, Cherubim, etc. In short, categories. Restituto availed himself of a comparison: heaven is like a theater. Blessed is the public for they shall be saved. God has the leading role. There are other figures on stage as well—supporting actors, the orchestra, the choir—didn't the Church itself promise there would be choirs?

It would be absurd to have all the people in the theater sit in boxes or orchestra seats. Those seats were for the select few; the upper reaches of the theater were for the common man. By way of proof, there was the fact that in mundane theatrical language, the terms *paradise* and *gallery* are used interchangeably to refer to seats in the top balcony. Purgatory, then, was the lobby of this heavenly astrodome, the place where people have to wait with a certain natural impatience.

Since he had paid as much as anyone for his ticket, and probably a bit more, Don Restituto just couldn't accept the idea that he and his Basilisa would be seated in the general admission section, having to strain to see the apotheosis of eternity. They were so simple and deluded they would have believed God guilty of a cruel sin if, when their time came, He didn't order Saint Peter, the chief usher, to show them to a box near the stage where they would see well and be seen by all.

For the time being, this pious and optimistic couple was already enjoying a preview of the future place reserved for them in the empyrean. It was almost guaranteed. Priests, members of mendicant orders, even the bishop himself, came to call, to flatter and adulate, doing everything to make them feel like heirs apparent to the blessed aristocracy. If Restituto seemed to be grasping for worldly goods and titles, it wasn't out of vanity, but really as an expression of class solidarity. You might call it a kind of "noblesse oblige," since he felt that as one of the subscription box holders, it was, in fact, his duty to pursue these goals so as not to disillusion the public up there in the top balcony.

He came from a lower-class family who had lived up in the mountains. On this accident of birth Don Restituto based his patent of nobility, for he believed that all the people up there in the hills had traces of blue blood. As a child he had gone to Cuba, and thirty years of complete seclusion and hard labor had made it possible for him to amass a small fortune. And yet, our Don Restituto was the living proof of the fallaciousness of the Duchess of Somavia's statement that every rich man was a thief. He had never stolen anything—or if he had, it was done unconsciously and that, after all, would be the same as not having stolen at all. In Cuba he led the celibate, sober life of a monk, untainted by the general corruption of that voluptuous lush green island. Or, in his own words, defining the extent of his austerity, he innocently proclaimed, "I never even knew one of those *mulatas,* not to mention the real black ones!" Of the white ladies, he never spoke.

And so he vegetated under the spreading shade of Doña Basilisa, both of them always together, sending out lukewarm waves of mutual marital affection, thinking about the salvation of their souls and not shirking the responsibility of saving their neighbors'.

"Father Aleson," said Don Restituto one afternoon, "Belarmino worries me . . . or rather us. He is a matter of some concern to my wife and myself. Isn't that true, Basilisa? He doesn't hear mass, and yet he actually could attend without ever leaving the house. Could he be a hypocrite? Is he as much of a heathen as he always was? What about the salvation of his soul?"

"Madam Empress, my dear Don Restituto," answered Father Aleson, "dare I trust in your willingness to accept my humble judgment? I may? Here you have it, succinctly. Belarmino is in trouble—he lacks a rational soul."

"Do you mean he's no better than an animal? Is he, that is to say, dangerous?" asked the alarmed Restituto.

"A child, rather. Apparently, he has a rational soul just like any human being, but it's an irrational rational soul. Have I made myself clear? His soul is still in the anal, or, if you prefer, the idiotic stage. It doesn't reason, nor does it cogitate in any but the most primitive way. Still, because he has been baptized, he will undoubtedly be saved when he dies. If he were not baptized, he would be sent to Limbo, to a kind of kindergarten postmortem.

"Here is my judgment, arrived at after much thought and supported by the opinions of authorized theologians—Belarmino is a born idiot and therefore incapable of sin.

"When he was free to come and go as he pleased, he was dangerous. Fits of insanity assailed him, and you know how contagious insanity can be, particularly the impious kind he suffered from. Belarmino's madness, as you know, was uncontrollable. It spread like wildfire, it was extremely hard on people with weak hearts, and it even led some to look askance at holy things, threatening to provoke major incidents. Now, thanks to you both, he doesn't have those seizures anymore. Could you wish for anything more? The old Belarmino is dead, and the one we have now is sweet, idiotic, and crazy. There is no need to worry about his not going to mass. Since when do children have to go to church?"

"Aren't you afraid, Father, that his fits might recur?"

"He says he's a philosopher. So be it. As long as no one takes him seriously, a philosopher is always harmless. You have to bind and gag philosophers with sausages. If you feed them most of the time, you can keep them happy. As long as Belarmino stays in the asylum, as long as he has whatever his heart desires, as long as no one stops him from reading what he doesn't understand and from speaking to a few people—just to prevent a type of intellectual constipation that could be dangerous—as long as everything just stays the way it is, there's nothing to worry about."

"You're a genius, Father Aleson. Listening to you is like watching the sun peep out from behind the clouds! You know, I couldn't help noticing how Belarmino is always reading dusty books and filling sheet after sheet with incomprehensible scratches. To tell you the truth, I was worried his brain would dry up and leave him crazier than ever. Of course, I was comparing him to myself, since I never read anything but the missal, and every time I do that, I get a migraine headache and the oddest burning sensation in my eyes. God forgive me, but the harder I try, the worse it gets. But, of course, your explanation is perfect; no harm is done in Belarmino's case because he doesn't understand what he's reading. Who would have thought it! I mean, most people would have said that just the opposite would be the case. You're absolutely right, now that I come to think of it, because whenever I read the prayers in Latin (and I don't understand a word of that language), I feel no pain at all."

That was Doña Basilisa speaking, and she added, "But what about his wife, Juana? She's . . . she's . . . well, a bit of a shrew."

"A vixen," agreed the Dominican, "but fully tamed. Her domesticity, coupled with her absence, are no small contributions, as far as I'm concerned, to the fact that Belarmino is now living in Augustan calm. We have given orders that Juana is not to be allowed so much as to squeeze her nose through the front door. She's living in the room you donated, and when she's not there, she's strolling around town or offering up novenas in some church or other. As you have probably noticed, Angustias, his daughter, does visit her father quite often. By the way . . . I think this is as good a time as any to let you in on a secret. Belarmino is not that girl's real father."

"What's that?" sang out both Don Restituto and Doña Basilisa together, startled by the news. Restituto continued on his own, "A spurious child, then? Whose . . . his or hers? So, they've been handing us a line all this time!"

"Easy does it, my friends, it's not as literary as all that, though you could say it has the makings of a novel. The girl is the legitimate daughter of Belarmino's sister, a poor woman who was widowed right after her marriage and then died during childbirth, leaving the child behind as a living souvenir. Belarmino took charge and nursed her with a bottle. Therefore, on those few occasions when he speaks a language that's almost intelligible, he says he loves her more than a father would. His feelings are those of father and mother both. I can vouch for it; he loves her to the point of madness."

"Even though he's an idiot?" asked Basilisa.

"Yes, my lady. And this proves that God made men naturally good. Willful transgressions and ugly acts are instigated by man's rebellious intelligence and arrogant reason. That's why Christian doctrine instructs us that the poor in spirit will see God."

It'll be from the second balcony, then, and without understanding the play at all, thought Restituto.

Father Aleson continued, "Belarmino became a putative father and, so to speak, a mother, a year before he married Juana. Juana didn't say anything then, but once she was married her true nature surfaced. She made it quite plain that she wasn't at all deceived by Belarmino, and that she knew Angustias was his daughter, no matter how hard he tried to cover it up. There was no way to convince her she was mistaken. I say that because I actually investigated this claim and can assure you there are trustworthy witnesses to substantiate Belarmino's version of the story. But Juana is obstinate and not too bright.

"Now, to get to the heart of the matter, what made Juana so furious with Belarmino and made her fly off the handle whenever she was irritable was that child. It's obvious Juana can't stand the sight of the girl. Still, if you two, with your usual generosity, could educate the child, send her to a school, and let Juana see you take an interest in Angustias, it's quite possible the woman, partly for selfish reasons and partly out of false pride, would change her feelings. She might even be rather pleased to have a daughter who would eventually rub elbows with the best people."

"It shall be done," man and wife intoned as one. Don Restituto continued on his own—"You're a saintly figure and an inexhaustible source of wisdom."

"And is Juana still whistling the same tune?" asked Doña Basilisa.

"Not at the moment. She's probably keeping it bottled up inside her; it could turn flat and she might let a few sour notes escape, but in general, she is controlling herself."

"That's undoubtedly because you have catechized her, Father Aleson," said Basilisa, enthusiastically. "You've taught her how to be patient, such a necessary virtue for salvation."

"My dear Empress," answered the huge Dominican, "I can't teach anything to anyone, not even languages, the only thing I know a little bit about. True, patience as well as a handful of other virtues are indeed necessary for salvation, though I wouldn't be able to say which of them is more important. But if Juana has set herself on the road to perfection and is beginning to exercise this and other virtues, it is due primarily to a circumstance that may seem insignificant and, strictly speaking, unimportant, but isn't at all. And you are the ones who have done it, not I.

"For the salvation of souls, the most important thing is always to have the table set at a given hour. We men of the cloth know it to be a fact. That is the whole idea behind religious orders. We take vows of poverty that free us eternally from economic worries and we dedicate our being to contemplation, to preaching, to charity—passive and active—asking for donations or merely giving others a chance to be charitable, as the Franciscans do, or even showing *ourselves* to be charitable in our studies, our teachings, our apostolic mission, and the conversion of gentiles. Consequently, we are devoted to an endless series of hard and time-consuming activities, both egotistical and generous, which occupy us from morning till night. We labor secure in the knowledge that we are

82

guaranteed a bed, even though it be a hard one, a roof over our heads, and a table set, however humbly, at mealtime.

"When I entered the Dominican order, I took vows of poverty, but you never know how things will turn out. From the moment I took up poverty, I discovered I had more wealth than the richest and most powerful men on earth. Wherever I go, and I am not only speaking of the cities of this kingdom, but of other nations, as I have travelled widely, visiting England, Russia, France, Germany, Italy . . . and I am not only referring to the European countries but also those of other continents—Africa, Asia, America, Australia—everywhere I go, I have a house of my own—and what houses they are! Bigger than palaces, with a table set, a bed provided, and plenty of money to keep me going even to the ends of the earth.

"You can't tell me it wasn't a clever idea to institute poverty as a way of life . . . why even a king of France wanted all his subjects to put a chicken in the pot every day! In that way, they would be happy and not tempted to transgress against the state. From my point of view, I would like all men on earth to have substantial meals on the table regularly, for then they would almost completely suppress the temptation to deny God. Oh, how well-off we would be if mankind could finally disengage itself from worrying about its daily bread, and the nations of the world could be organized like huge monasteries, in which there were neither poor nor rich, and no one had too much nor lacked a house and a full table, where obedience would be the gentle unifying thread that would not hinder a man from devoting his heart and soul to whatever God-given talent he had! . . . With what devotion, what fervor, what sincerity would the Lord's Prayer be intoned then! Until that happens, and I doubt it ever will, blessed be the rich—like you two—who administer wealth for the benefit of the poor as though it didn't belong to you at all but only to God!"

Father Aleson uttered a flutelike sigh that was not at all priestly. It would have suited a nun. An octave higher, he continued, "My dear and respected friends, I am not sure if I have shocked you by my frankness or just bored you with this lengthy sermon. Where I come from people call a spade a spade. Despite my soprano voice, as a member of the clergy I am obliged to speak in serious tones. It's settled then that Juana and the girl are getting along very well even though things could go better; as for Belarmino, things could not be better even though he is not attending mass."

The voluminous priest got up from what one might have thought was an easy chair, for he had filled it completely, armrest to armrest; once he stood up, it turned out to be a sofa, and not one of those puny ones.

Things couldn't have gone better for Belarmino. He had a table set at a given hour, a clean bed in a fixed place, and the certainty that neither one nor the other was at the mercy of the giddiness and inconstancy of the market. He was no longer afflicted with the thought of tomorrow. He worked whenever he wanted to and on whatever appealed to him, and this was done more to satisfy the Neiras and the monks than out of a need to earn a living or a desire to save a little money for his own pleasures. His only pleasure was to cater to his daughter's whims, and this matter was handled with great magnanimity by his patrons. When Belarmino changed professions from a self-employed shoemaker with his own shop to shoemaker-in-residence, it was for him as though he had come home after a long sea voyage fraught with anxiety, threatening weather, and agony—as though he were now a retired sailor who had abandoned his large and frightening ship to take up cozy housekeeping in one of those small boats moored on the beach. He was still a shoemaker; his little hole in the wall was still a shoe-repair shop, just as those houseboats, though occupied by retired sea captains, are still seaworthy vessels. What he was now was what he had been before, except now everything was reversed. Safely anchored, he enjoyed a blessed inner peace as he contemplated the angry seas of the world! Now Belarmino could relax. Apolonio was beginning to drown in the dark seas of commerce. True, he was going full speed ahead, yet Belarmino found himself asking sadly as he watched the ship of his fortunate rival cut through the water, "How long will fair weather last? Shut your eyes for a second and the storms'll rage. I can see you dancing, floundering on the waves like a cripple without a crutch. You'll sink, and neither Aryan nor Semitic feet will help you a bit. I pity you then if you're not a philosopher!"

One of the things that contributed considerably to Belarmino's present calmness was the fact that in changing ships, he had been able to jettison some heavy ballast. Xuantipa no longer bothered him all day long, nor did Bellido the pawnbroker, or Felicita the old maid, make their daily visits. Rubicund and jovial, Colignon was still fond of Belarmino, and the shoemaker responded in kind.

For professional equipment, Belarmino had only the most indispensable tools of his trade, and all of them had been most generously donated by Don Restituto—a pair of pliers, a ball of leather strips, a scraper, a brush with metal bristles (made in America), a stippling roller, a hole punch, awls of different sizes, and a cobbler's block with a metal last. The block was a faithful facsimile of a small horse. It resembled Don Quixote's Clavileño, though Belarmino's looked even more like a horse than did that volatile mount of the knight of La Mancha. A stout log set on four legs, the animal's trunk was indeed a trunk, thicker in the rump than in the chest. A thin, broad plank rose like a neck out of its shoulders and chest. A metal foot, with the sole facing up, was connected to this plank by a set of moveable joints, so that seen in profile it became a horse's head. Astride this little horse, Belarmino spent his days.

Right after he had been installed in his new cell, Belarmino made a few pairs of dress boots for the servants and monks, but little by little he abandoned this line of work and devoted himself exclusively to mending. One day he said to himself, "At last I've become a shoemaker-in-residence," and his heart filled with joy as though he had finally obtained the secure position he had always coveted. His habits changed and his work sessions shortened, the intervals between jobs becoming increasingly longer. During these rest periods he used to read, leaning his book against the metal last, taking notes in a small oilcloth-covered schoolbook.

The dictionary was his favorite book. At times, completely cut off from external reality, following the strange forms that took shape in the air and were visible only to him as he meditated, he felt that this particular way of reading was based on an extremely original method. For him, the dictionary was the epitome of the universe, a concise compendium of all things terrestrial and divine—a key by which to decipher unexpected enigmas. The whole idea was to penetrate that secret code, to open up the compendium, and see everything in it at a glance. The dictionary contains all there is, because all words are in it, and it follows that all things are in it because word and thing are one and the same. Objects are born when words are born, because without words there are no things and, if there are, it's as if there weren't. For example, a table doesn't know that it exists, nor does a table exist for a chair, because the chair doesn't know about the existence of the table. An object doesn't exist by itself, nor in relation to other things, but only for the *Intelet* which, on comprehending it, gives it a name and affixes a word to it. To know is to create and to create is to know.

Such was one small fragment of the Belarminian speculation. It just goes to show the kind of thing that can come from being in a sitting position over a long period of time while leisurely exercising one's discursive faculty! Philosophers are squatting types, even the peripatetic ones. Although they do most of their talking on their feet, they erect their philosophical systems once they assume a squatting position. To continue . . . it followed for Belarmino that if the dictionary is all he thought it was, then cosmos and dictionary must be one and the same thing. In order to avoid the confusion that could stem from the newly discovered identity between these two words, he resolved to invert normal usage. When he said *cosmos,* he meant *dictionary,* and when he said *dictionary,* he postulated the universe. When he asked Angustias to pass him the cosmos, the child already knew from experience to hand over that heavy volume—for her, of course, it was just as illogical to call it a cosmos as to call it a dictionary.

Because—thus proceeded the Belarminian speculation—most men live in the dictionary, that is to say in the world, without realizing they are alive, by the same token they look things up in the cosmos, that is to say the dictionary, without the slightest idea of what they are reading. To live is to know, and to know is to create, or to give things a name. When a man calls a tree a tree because he's heard it called that, he doesn't know the tree intimately nor does he know what he is saying. If he really knew the tree, he would have created it himself and given it a new name.

And now we come to the most subtle of all Belarminian hypotheses. The cosmos—that is, the dictionary—contains the names of all objects. Still, everything is badly named, the labels mechanically applied, and instead of stimulating one to an act of knowledge and creation, they perpetuate routine, ignorance, stupidity, empty chatter, and a parrot mentality. Names exist in the cosmos—that is, in the dictionary—like caged birds or, if you prefer, like human beings who have been drugged and put away in heavily sealed coffins. Belarmino found a kind of mystical pleasure, a way of communicating directly with the absolute and gaining a sense of intimacy wtih the essence of things, whenever he broke the sepulchral seals, resurrecting the living dead, or when he opened the cages to let the birds fly out. He used to read the words in the cosmos, scrupulously keeping his eyes from glancing at the definitions that accompanied them. He read one—strictly speaking he didn't read it, he saw it . . . in the flesh, escaping from the dusty pages, walking on the pavement, flying in the air, or becoming diffused in a mist against the ceiling. Sometimes they were creatures, other times they were things, concepts, ideas; but they could equally well be feelings or delicate emotions.

To superficial individuals, the results so produced might seem funny, but basically this was a serious matter. Take the word *camel*, for example, as it appeared in the cosmos—that is to say, the dictionary. Belarmino actually saw this four-legged ruminant, greatly reduced in size, leap from the page and move slowly along the floor. But after a few steps, the beast's profile, by nature rather sinuous and vague, became even more deformed. It evolved and was transformed. The animal stood on two legs, appeared dressed in a type of uniform; still maintaining its original expression, the head took on human traits. The humps became briefcases slung over its chest and back; a large sheaf of papers stuck out of one of them. Belarmino had just been introduced to someone living in the dictionary—that is to say in the perceivable world— and after meeting him, he had created a new word. From this time forth, *camel* would represent the King's ambassador-at-large. As a result of a similar evolutionary process, *dromedary* came to mean a priest or ambassador of the Lord.

It is not to be thought that in the Belarminian lexicon the words *dromedary* and *camel* concealed a contumelious or deprecatory intention. On the contrary, they implied an admiring comprehension. They alluded to the desertlike indifference in which the ambassador and the priest must function, to the sobriety with which they act or ought to act, and to the heavy weight they carry on their shoulders. The hump symbolized the responsibility stuck to their spines, which in the case of the ambassador would be double—to God and man—and for the priest, just single—his duty was to God alone. And so, hump = responsibility— a new act of creation in Belarmino's cosmos, that is to say, in his dictionary.

There were other words that conveyed only physical sensations to him. But the words he most eagerly pursued, those which ecstatically transported him as he comprehended and created them, were the ones he took to be philosophical terms expressing spiritual concepts—*metempsychosis, scholastic, scorbutic,* etc., etc. After a revelation not at all easy to interpret, Belarmino had defined these three terms. *Metempsychosis* meant an unfathomable enigma, the unknowable, Kant's *Das Ding an Sich,* derived from *psychosis* (that is, enigma) and *mete* (introduce into, hide), so it all came out meaning "to complicate simple things and make them enigmatic." A *scholastic* became a person who irrationally follows the opinions of a school like a tail appended to the body of an animal. A synonym for *pessimistic, scorbutic* derived from crow, a somber bird of ill omen. Quite a man, that Belarmino!

The niche where Belarmino philosophized and repaired shoes was substantially below street level. You had to go down a few stone steps to get to it from the main door. The walls were whitewashed but the humidity had whimsically decorated them with greenish arabesques. Light entered through a long, narrow window-grate which on the inside was level with the ceiling and, on the outside, was flush with the sidewalk. A stream of grayish light, like the illumination in paintings that depict miraculous apparitions, spilled into the room and splattered over Belarmino's left side in a kind of baptism. Through the window he could see the legs of the pedestrians from the knees down as they passed by, their shoes clicking rhythmically against the flagstones. Belarmino considered himself to be providentially placed in the bowels of the earth, located at the root and foundation of all things, for he was convinced the best way to know men was to see only their feet, which form the base and substratum of mankind. Half buried in that dim, cavelike room, that laboratory where the enigmatic questions of thought and existence were refined and clarified, continuously astride his mounting block, now both Clavileño and Pegasus, Belarmino freed himself from the pull of gravity and the yoke of matter and flew unencumbered through fantastic regions, soaring through Uranic spheres, looking down at the dictionary—that is, the world—from such distant perspectives he would almost get sick to his stomach and break out in goosepimples.

In spite of Father Aleson's view that he was a little touched, Belarmino was a sensible man who realized the irreparable dangers that threatened him in going so high that one day he might get lost above the clouds, unable to return to the mundane world of his fellow men. Every time he shed a dead word and created a new, living one, it was as though he had tossed some ballast overboard and had taken on a new supply of fuel that would propel him upward. "Perhaps the day might come when I'll no longer be able to speak to my daughter, since I won't understand her nor will she understand me, and she might even think I'm mad . . . "; his heart almost stopped beating. What was he to do? He hit on a solution right away. He had to preserve the ballast while making the effort to continue to increase the supply of energy that impelled him upward. Whatever the price, he had to do everything possible not to let himself forget everyday speech, so he could use it with his child and with anyone else he cared for whenever this might be necessary. Yet because he was always alone, how could he help but forget it? From inside his skull, the *Intelet* whispered something to him, and Belarmino rushed into the street and headed for the neighboring village. At the first farmhouse, he asked the owner to trap a magpie and deliver it to his residence. He had heard somewhere that with patience and good wine it was possible to teach magpies to speak. Naturally, he would have preferred a parrot, but he certainly didn't have the money for it, and he had his doubts that such an item could be found in the local market. The farmer arrived a few days later and presented him with a magpie, black and white, like the garments of the Dominican fathers. "Now to teach it the most vulgar language possible," he said to himself, with no little discomfort and perplexity, since it wasn't easy for him to come up with common words, and he was certainly not tempted to exert his ingenuity by inventing them. Gazing sadly at the magpie and its shiny Dominican plumage, it suddenly occurred to him, through an association of images, that Father Aleson could help him out, and he went to ask him for the loan of a book of poetry as well as a written speech or two. Belarmino considered poetry and oratory to be the most vulgar forms of language. The Dominican loaned him a volume of poems by Selgas and a pamphlet containing the speeches of Alejandro Pidal y Mon.*

Belarmino clipped the bird's guide wings and placed the magpie at the bottom of a dark barrel. There he would feed it bits of bread dipped

*José Selgas y Carrasco (1822–1882), Spanish Romantic poet, was the author of *Flores y espinas* [Flowers and thorns] and a novel entitled *La manzana de oro* [The golden apple]. Alejandro Pidal y Mon (1846–1913) was a politician, orator, statesman, philosopher, poet, historian, and the father of fifteen children.

in strong white wine. Leaning over the barrel, he would then read stanzas of Selgas's poetry and paragraphs of Pidal's prose to the creature, clearly spacing the individual words. On one occasion, when he came across Pidal's phrase, "I pride myself on being a scholastic," Belarmino said to himself, "I knew it all along. Even Bellido would undoubtedly brag that he is scorbutic." The magpie didn't learn how to speak, but Belarmino didn't lose his patience. He stoically resisted that heavy shower of vulgarity, more out of self-interest and so as not to lose his hold on the world, than from a pedagogical concern for the ugly bird. His friend, Colignon, noticed that Belarmino had lately taken to speaking to him more intelligibly, though he didn't know the reason why. He mentioned it to him one afternoon. Taking great pains to express himself plainly, Belarmino ran into more difficulties than Apolonio did whenever the dramatist tried to express himself in prose.

"I'm speaking to you plainly for many intentions [intentions = reasons]. In the first place, I like you. I like you because you like me. In the second place ∴ . . . well, I don't know how to tell you this without being emaciated and causing you unpleasant weight [emaciated = cruel; weight = feelings]." Belarmino hesitated while he searched for the clearest and most friendly expressions.

"You're matter and I'm spirit. You find your happiness in things, and I am happiest when I separate myself from them. You're yes and I'm no. Or, if you prefer, you're no and I'm yes. Does that mean that I consider myself to be better than you? Not at all. Yes is not better than no, nor is no better than yes; but both yes and no are better than 'how do I know?' I am fully aware that you are as much a philosopher as I am, although in a belligerent way [belligerent = contrary, opposite]. On the other hand, most men are neither yes nor no, but rather 'how do I know?' Since they don't know, they don't feel anything, they're not really alive, and they don't count. What do I have in common with them? Why should I even try to speak their language? Now, you're something else again. I would really like you to understand my language. But because you are a belligerent philosopher, and I like you, and besides I learn from you and you're my touchstone, because you're the no to my yes, or the yes to my no, and we complement each other, I want to make the effort to speak so you can understand me."

"*Épatant, épatant,* my dear Belarmino," replied the candymaker in merry amazement. "I get your meaning, I'm an Epicurean and you're a Stoic, right?"

Belarmino stored away these two words in the cupboard of his memory—*Epicurean* and *Stoic*—with the intention of later transforming them by means of his speculative alchemy and thereby uncovering their true meaning.

One day, Froilán Escobar, also known as "the Grind" and "the Alligator," appeared in Belarmino's room. He had a pair of boots to be repaired; they needed a complete set of uppers as well as half-soles. As a matter of fact, they were just barely boots, since to be worthy of such a classification they would have required, in addition to the uppers and half-soles, new liners, leather stripping around the top, and a goodly number of buttons. To tell the truth, the only real affection Belarmino felt toward the pedestrian art of shoe repairing came from restoring old footwear, the older the better; he could think of nothing he enjoyed more than creating a pair of flamboyant boots from a pile of castoffs. He liked doing that just as much as philosophizing. And so he took in those sickly boots belonging to the Grind, or the Alligator, with special respect and affection.

Nicknames can be biographical sketches as well as miniature portraits. Escobar's aliases told his history and rendered his portrait. He was by nature remarkably bright and had the ability to do the course work; nonetheless, he had been a student at the university for twenty years. He used to say, "The man who wants to know life is a student until the day he dies. There is nothing more repugnant than the kind of knowledge sought in order to get a degree for the purpose of earning a living. There is no real science other than science pursued for its own sake, for the love of knowledge, the knowledge that you never know enough to be paid for teaching the little you know." He used to come out with other maxims that had the same ring to them. Since he didn't want to buy knowledge, he never registered for classes, but merely audited courses in different fields. For this reason, he was nicknamed the Grind.

He lived in extreme poverty and dressed in rags. His headpiece was coated with two fingers of grease, and he wore a short, light brown topcoat, which had made its debut when he first came to the university. He always kept the collar up to hide the fact that there was no shirt underneath. His pants were fringed on the bottom and, of course, he wore those wilted boots. In complexion he resembled the dead, illustrating the meaning of the oracle's advice to Zeno the philosopher, which, truly understood, meant that from overlong exposure to books he had taken on their pallor. He had a superhuman talent for remaining absolutely still. In class, for hours on end, he kept the same stiff and attentive posture without moving one muscle or even blinking. His eyes were coated with an opaque screen that was like a lizard's auxiliary eyelid. That's how he got the name Alligator.

Sometimes, he had fits of reptilian convulsions accompanied by sibylline contortions, depending upon the professor's subject matter and style of presentation. At such moments, he would take shorthand notes, causing the desk to vibrate ferociously. The students admired and respected him, even calling on him for advice. He was the familiar spirit of the university, the Pallas Athena of that cloistered seat of knowledge —a masquerading Pallas Athena. The official science offered by the establishment was also too frequently invested in grotesque disguises.

As far as Belarmino was concerned, the Grind couldn't have given him a more favorable letter of recommendation or a more valid identification card than that pair of boots—well, strictly speaking, a fourth or an eighth of a pair of boots. Belarmino held these remains lovingly in his hands, viewing them as the seeds or embryos of a brilliant future. He was looking at the Alligator with warm interest when both of them suddenly noticed that four or five cubic meters of air had been removed from the room, which didn't hold much more than that to begin with— Father Aleson had entered, displacing a mass of air corresponding to the massive goodwill of his flesh and bone.

"Good afternoon, Belarmino," said the Dominican, modulating the tone of the more resplendent and endearing notes that floated out of his laryngeal piccolo. "I was going in and coming out. I was just going into your room and coming out of my residence. I was leaving my distraction and entering my field of memory." Father Aleson used this abstract and involuted style in order to please Belarmino and gain his confidence.

"What I mean in everyday language is that as I was going out, I remembered that Professor Telesforo Rodríguez of the seminary asked me for a book I loaned to you some time ago, *Nicolai Garciae: tractatus de beneficiis*. Have you already read it? Can I take it with me? If you have not finished with it yet, keep it a while longer. You're bound to get more out of it than Telesforo anyhow."

Belarmino dismounted Clavileño and gave Father Aleson a large quarto volume, covered in parchment. "I've already read it. It's been extremely helpful."

"Well, I am pleased. Ah, hello there!" exclaimed the Dominican, turning toward the barrel where the magpie was stirring and pecking away. "Angustias told me all about this . . . so those Selgas poems and the speeches of Pidal you borrowed were for this little talking bird to learn by heart? Well, how is it going? Is he learning anything?"

Belarmino answered that he had acquired the creature in order to teach it to speak in the only way that could be understood by the common man. But since Belarmino, in his reply to the Dominican, did not use the language understood by the common man, Father Aleson begged him to explain what he meant. Belarmino obliged. Father Aleson *thought* he understood.

"Hm, aha . . . " said the Dominican, smiling sarcastically. "Seeking a diogenean cynic in this bird, you've created your own Diogenes—the one who spoke with hateful clarity. And to complete the picture, you've even enclosed him in his barrel. What about *you*? Are you Socratic, Platonic, Peripatetic or a Sophist?"

"Stoic," Belarmino answered with pride and marvellous dignity, the meaning of the word he had heard on the lips of Colignon suddenly having revealed itself to him.

Father Aleson was struck dumb. "Maybe this fellow is not as far gone as I suspected," he thought. He started to leave. "Well Belarmino, against my wishes I have to abandon this distinguished company, but that is my mission in life—to ambulate, to go from one place to another, with a heavy responsibility on my shoulders . . ."

The priest had already turned his back when Belarmino muttered, "Naturally, since you're a dromedary . . ."

Father Aleson turned around with an expression of disapproval on his face. "Now, really," he stuttered, his voice failing him, "that is rather offensive." The Dominican thought Belarmino might be annoyed with him because he had spoken sarcastically to him earlier.

"I only meant you're a priest," answered the shoemaker.

"Well, that is even worse. As long as you called me a dromedary, personally, it was all right. I thought you were referring to my bulk. But now it seems I am a dromedary because I belong to the priesthood ... to tell the truth, Belarmino, that is in very bad taste. It is not like you at all."

Belarmino made a sympathetic, resigned gesture toward the Dominican, as if to say, "I'll have to feed it to him a spoonful at a time." Patiently explaining the allegory of the dromedary and the camel, which we already know, he left the friar gaping. Belarmino concluded in his original jargon, "I caress camels and dromedaries but I don't kiss them. I irrigate the tetrahedron, I even imprison and paraphrase it, but from its perspective I'll continue to be undressed and illiterate. My timetable functions according to the convulsions of recreated intuition."

Perplexed and puzzled, the Dominican left.

Froilán Escobar, the Alligator, had not moved throughout the foregoing scene. He thought he was dreaming. "Is this real? Is it an illusion?" he asked himself. "If it weren't for the irrefutable testimony of these boots, as alien to me and yet as much a part of me as the callouses on my feet, if not for this flagrant fact that keeps me in touch with objective reality, I'd be convinced that what I have just heard and seen was nothing more than the fantasies of my paralyzed and confused reason. And to think this is happening right around the corner from the university ... I've been here twenty years without even an inkling ... Such a baffling, extraordinary individual ... Is he trying to be funny? Can he be an obscure genius in the rough? ... an unmined diamond buried in the bowels of the earth?" The Grind had tied himself up in knots.

"Would it bother you, Don Belarmino," he said as he was leaving, "if I came by in the afternoon from time to time in order to talk with you?"

"It would be my great convulsion," Belarmino answered, without blinking an eye.

Escobar didn't know what to say. What would Belarmino's great convulsion be like? Did that mean he would receive a friendly welcome, or would he be unceremoniously thrown out? He decided to give it a try, and he soon paid him a return visit.

Belarmino received him with obvious pleasure and honored him with a long and incomprehensible lecture on *rah-rah* and *rat-tat-tat*. The Grind hearkened to him without understanding a word. Still, he hoped someday he would come to master the technical vocabulary of that modern philosopher-in-residence, or Stoic, as Belarmino called himself, not

realizing that in Greece, philosopher-in-residence and Stoic were synon-
ymous terms.

Escobar continued to frequent Belarmino's doorway, taking notes
on what he heard. Since the Grind fortunately had started out by
hearing Belarmino distinguish between the words *camel* and *dromedary*,
he was absolutely convinced each word used by the shoemaker enclosed
a fixed symbol. He was certain that these words followed one another
in a logical, grammatical sequence and that, beyond the shadow of a
doubt, this formal structure implied a wealth of original thought. On
Escobar's recommendation, many students came to hear Belarmino's
lectures, the professors hard on their heels. Naturally, there were di-
vergent opinions and judgments concerning the Stoic, and all of this
generated a good deal of excitement. Soon the Belarminians and anti-
Belarminians established their own sects.

Even among the Belarminians there were different opinions. Some
maintained that he was crazy, others that he was in full possession of
all his senses. Those in favor of his sanity differed among themselves
as to whether the Belarminian language was decipherable or not, while
those inclined to believe in the apparent intelligibility of Belarmino's
speeches couldn't agree as to their meaning. Some affirmed that once
translated into Castilian Spanish, his speeches would turn out to be
strange and interesting; others were convinced their content was sheer
nonsense and the only interesting thing about them their literary form.

As a result of this controversy, Belarmino's vestibule was as crowded
with people as any of the philosophical schools of antiquity. After
listening to his recondite teachings, some would be convulsed with
laughter, while others would go out to Ruera Street perplexed and
irritated by an itch to solve the enigmas he propounded, squabbling
among themselves, debating, and almost coming to blows.

From the doorway of his fashionable shop, looking monumentally
bored, feigning indifference and ennui, Apolonio watched that lively
mob with the same envy and nostalgia with which the immortal gods
look down from Olympus and see mortals spurred on by those ideals
and passions that make life enjoyable and worth living. The immortals
get so bored by their paternal serenity, they're so envious of the battles
and conflicts on earth, that at times they are unable to resist the temptation to descend, transformed into fluffy, fluid little clouds, and

struggle among men. At least that's what Homer tells us. Apolonio knew all this ever since those early days in Compostela. Furthermore, Apolonio felt some human disputes were instigated by mysterious and divine intervention. Those were worthy of a dramatic, even tragic, dignity.

Whenever Apolonio came across two individuals swinging at one another or wrestling on the ground, he would look to see if there were clouds of dust around them. He would then think, "At last the tragic moment has arrived. That is not dust but the violent gods diffused in thin air, envious of the active life of men!" How Apolonio would have liked to be diffused into thin air in order to take part in the bitter disputes caused by his lucky rival, just as the gods did in the Trojan War waged over Helen. To make himself invisible and annihilate all the followers of Belarmino! . . . The gods find pleasure in vengeance . . . One might wonder what vengeful feelings poor mortals could hope to inspire in the majestic gods. Well, they can. They inspire the most revengeful sentiment of all—envy.

Belarmino was a shoemaker in residence; Apolonio had a fashionable establishment; he used to charge as much as twenty-five *pesetas* for a pair of boots, an exorbitant price for Pilares in those days. Nevertheless, Apolonio would have changed places with Belarmino. Apolonio had a good clientele, but he wasn't interested in clients. What he wanted was an audience, people who would listen, pay homage to him, and even contradict him. Apolonio traveled in very distinguished circles. From time to time, the Duchess of Somavia used to invite him to her gatherings. Periodically, he would receive visits at the shop from Pedro Barquín, from the priest Chapaprieta, the magistrate Don Hermenegildo Asiniego, and other notables of the city. Señor Novillo used to stop by the shop every day, lingering for several hours, spending most of the time in the doorway from which he threw humble, blushing glances at the flower-decked balcony where Felicita Quemada kept her birds. Apolonio didn't take his meetings with these distinguished persons very seriously. He deeply felt the lack of contact with important figures, his alienation from the academic and artistic world. Only God knew with what tricks and deceits that infamous Belarmino was robbing him of the applause and attention that was, in justice, due to him. Not even a crumb was left for Apolonio. Belarmino was nothing more than an insensitive quack, a traitor to the awl and last, while he, Apolonio, with his natural gifts composed the most beautiful artifacts, that is, shoes as well as poems. "There is no justice, sense, or order in the world," thought Apolonio. "Even in my innocence, I presumed as much when I wrote *The Siege of Orduña,* subtitled *The Lord of Oña.*"

Apolonio would have fallen into the slough of despond if this had not been made difficult on the one hand by the customary company of Novillo, who distracted him from his somber thoughts and also gave him the chance to display the exuberance of his damaged heart, and on the other hand, more significantly, by the love he had for the Duchess of Somavia, a love becoming daily more exalted, pure, impossible, increasingly delicious and very literary. "With these two for waterwings," Apolonio told himself, "I can stay afloat while those spiritual tempests of mine continue to rage."

Novillo used to appear at the shop, looking serious and reserved, his face somber, his venerable stomach protruding like that of an idol; his skin was bronzed, both beard and mustache were brownish in color, gray at the roots. There was a certain physical similarity between Apolonio and Novillo; their swollen bellies brought certain statues of Buddha to mind. Apolonio's head, however, was held high with Olympian self-confidence, while Novillo's weighed heavily on his thick neck, causing a ring of flesh to form underneath it. His eyes oozed an irrational sadness. Novillo hardly ever spoke. From time to time he smiled, showing his irreproachably white teeth, which, surrounded as they were by that hairy outline, resembled a strip of cocoanut peeking out from its brown, long-haired shell. But the top part of his face and eyes continued motionless and sad.

As soon as he arrived, Novillo would seat himself on a long, green-leather sofa under a mirror veiled by a matching green cloth. He let his stomach drop between his legs so it could rest on the sofa. Apolonio, leaving the work table where he made patterns and cut leather with deliberate, ritual gestures, would also let *his* stomach rest on the sofa as he sat down beside Novillo. In the rear of the shop one could hear muffled hammering, female voices singing, and the clickity-clack of the sewing machines. Without turning his head in the direction of his neighbor, Apolonio broke into speech.

"I am dejected, Don Anselmo, exceedingly dejected. What do I lack? I have a shop, equipped with the latest advances of science and industry; three machines; a Wilson and a Wheeler to sew the leather, a Johnson to make eyelets—I'm sure there aren't half a dozen machines like those on the whole peninsula. My clients are from the cream of society and they all pay their bills, cash on the barrelhead. What more could I want?

> Oh, beloved! Oh, pain! Oh tears of mine:
> Wherefore art thou that thou appearest not in torrents?

as the poet sang. An unhappy love? Yes, but I don't want to talk about it. Who is at fault? She? Never, never, never! The blame is mine. I fell in love with a beauty as exalted as that of the virgin Beatrice. Well deserved is my sorrow; I accept it with infinite joy."

Novillo heard this purring with the same lack of interest with which the carved plumwood images in church hear hymns and prayers. Apolonio continued, not deigning to look at Novillo.

"In an allegorical poem of mine I have portrayed the exact state of this senseless, horrible, and delinquent love affair. Delinquent, yes delinquent . . . because . . . Be still, oh frivolous and evil-speaking tongue! The poem is about a monster of the type that are called gargoyles because they vomit up rain with a particular sound—that is where the term gargling comes from—this stone monster, perched on the cornice of a cathedral, has fallen in love with a weather vane in the form of a dove that naturally sits at the highest point of the tower. Such is the cruel destiny of the enamored monster—me. To be petrified, hopelessly separated from the beloved . . . and gargling. This last bit is a touch of humor that brings the composition to a close. What is comical is always vulgar and negligible. Humor, on the other hand, is a poetic mode. You wish to know the name of the lady? I will never reveal it. I would rather be skinned alive."

Novillo, enthralled by his own amorous anxieties, got up without having heard Apolonio and went toward the doorway to glance furtively in the direction of Felicita's house. Declaiming, his arms outstretched, his eyes all aflame, Apolonio followed him.

"I will never reveal it. First they would have to step over my dead body; and if I were to reveal her name after death, let it be known it was not I, but a malignant spirit who spoke with my voice." After having ejaculated this conclusion, Apolonio quite suddenly calmed down, went back to his worktable, and applied himself to cutting out leather soles.

After half an hour of embarrassed viewing, Novillo returned to the sofa. At the same time, Apolonio returned to his friend's side, taking up once again the thread of his chitchat.

"It isn't this unrequited love that makes me feel languid, melancholic and unhappy. No. Love is the essence of my life and I cherish it in my heart as though it were a pearl of the Orient. Why am I so dejected, as equally prone to rage as to depression, ready to sell my soul to the devil? Why? Because I am an artist, and here in this city no one understands and appreciates me. Right now, I am a master shoemaker. My clients praise the flexibility and the firm fit in all the shoes I make; they comment on the softness and durability of the material I use; they are pleased by the comfort and modishness of the style. For all those reasons, and not for any other, I am well paid. But these qualities are of secondary importance. A shoe, a brogue, a pair of spats, are works of art. With very few exceptions, who around here is capable of appreciating footwear as a work of art? Who, in this town, grants to shoes the enormous importance they have? People think a shoe is only meant to cover a foot, to protect it from humidity for fear of rheumatism, and to keep it from hurting itself when it comes into contact with a hard surface; all they ask of a shoe is that it not give them callouses. If this were the only reason for the existence of shoes, it would be better for men to sprout hoofs, something which could be easily managed by scientific methods. And I am not speaking only of this town. What I am saying applies in general terms to all of Spain. A very erudite friend of mine, a student from Compostela by the name of Valeiro, told me of a book written by a Friar Guevara or other who was a bishop of one of those dioceses in Galicia. It relates how in the time of the great Charles V, when this book was written, Spaniards used to walk down the street on stilts because of the mud. How barbaric! But it really shouldn't surprise us too much. Don't people in this peninsula still wear wooden shoes, sandals, and those disgusting canvas things—*alpargatas*—with laces that go up the leg? How badly this speaks for the cultural level of the Spaniards, and how well it reveals their savagery! As far as I'm concerned, the canvas *alpargata* is an insult to the Deity, a blasphemy, because it denies and fails to recognize the most perfect work of God, the human foot. Why is man superior to the monkey and to all other animals? Because he is the only one who has feet, that is, what one could call real feet. If the foot were less human, less noble than the hand, men would have four hands and monkeys would have four feet, not four hands as they do now. To be saved the sight of women in wooden shoes, I would gladly live among the Chinese. At least they grant more importance to a woman's feet than to any other part of her body."

Without having heard one word of Apolonio's ingenious speech, Novillo once more returned to the doorway. Apolonio went back to work behind his table. After another half-hour, Novillo returned to rest his agitated stomach on the sofa, this time aware of a passionate trembling within. His eyes had chanced to meet those of Felicita, and she had sent him an enchanting and ethereal smile. Novillo felt happy and expansive. When Apolonio settled himself at his side, Novillo patted the shoemaker's thigh.

"Don't you have anything to say to me today, dear Apolonio?"

"I was telling you, Don Anselmo," Apolonio answered without giving any signs of having been wounded by the physical and mental absence of his friend, "the Chinese give to the foot the importance it deserves. All Asians have this merit in common. The Garden of Eden was not haphazardly placed in Asia. In ancient Greece, courtesans as well as chaste matrons used to long for shoes from Asia, shoes that apparently were just delightful, adorned with excellent painted designs and figures etched in metal. Since they were closer to the moment of Creation, the ancients more clearly distinguished the hierarchy, utility, and beauty of the limbs. They placed the foot above all other members in dignity; then came the head; next, something I would rather not mention; in fourth place, the left hand—the one that held the shield; and in fifth place, the right hand, which brandished the weapon; and so on. All those peoples, endowed with great native and revealed wisdom, which little by little has disappeared and become forgotten, worshipped the foot and outdid themselves in constructing with appropriate decorum the tabernacle of this member; call it, for convenience sake, the shoe. Among the Hebrews, footwear was held in such reverence that only nobles and levites were permitted to use it, and even they hardly dared to put on shoes unless it was to enter the Temple. They had special servants, something like acolytes, who followed the priests and nobles and carried their footwear on a velvet cushion. The Egyptians used to place little discs of gold and silver on their shoes. The footwear used by the Persian satraps was a precious jewel. The Roman patricians and senators wore boots made of red leather with a silver half-moon attached to them—the patrician moon. Let's move on to periods closer to ours and look at the popes, emperors, and the dukes of Venice. The foot covering of these great dignitaries of the Church and the republics was made with fabrics woven from precious metals and encrusted with the most valuable stones, emeralds, rubies, sapphires, and diamonds—almost always the size of nuts. I understand that the Holy Father still wears such things on those special days when they really ring out the bells."

"Goodness, the things you know, friend Apolonio," exclaimed Novillo, sincerely dazzled.

"Well, now you know as much as I do, Don Anselmo. And if you would like more details, I'll leave you a manuscript entitled *Esthetic Podotechnology or The History of Artistic Footwear,* which my friend Valeiro wrote just for me and from which I've gathered most of my data. In less than thirty minutes you can learn all this stuff by heart. As a Spaniard, it makes me blush with shame—and I cannot say this often enough—that we have not contributed any innovation to the art of shoemaking. There is no such thing as a truly Spanish science of footwear. You have probably never heard any one talk about a Madrid toe, an Isabel II heel, or a Spanish cut; on the other hand, everybody knows the Florentine toe, the Richelieu shoe, a Louis XV heel, or an English cut."

"Now, just hold on," objected Novillo, who was very touchy in matters of patriotism. Because he was the local representative of the absentee political boss and was himself a big chief in the village, he felt that insulting the good name of the country was the same as slyly criticizing its politics. "We shouldn't give a hoot about all those things. You say we don't have a heel or a toe? Well, we've developed more substantial, more beneficial things," he said, placing his open palms over his stomach—"Galician stew, Asturian pork and beans, codfish *a la Vizcaína,* Valencian *paella,* Mallorcan baked sausage, not to mention *chorizo* and the Jesuits. And, of course, we can't leave out the discovery of the New World. Besides, if I'm not mistaken, when I was studying in the institute, our professor of history used to tell us that one Roman emperor adopted Spanish footwear for his soldiers."

"Pure fable," replied Apolonio contemptuously. "The Spaniards have invented only canvas sandals, the *alpargata*, which, as I have already said, is an insult to God—a pedestrian sacrilege. As a master artist, I reject the *alpargata* with sacrosanct indignation."

"Let's change the subject, Apolonio, or else we'll have a fight. As president of the council and, therefore, representative of the legitimate government, I can't allow any one to put our invincible flag up for discussion. I won't say to you, 'Shoemaker, to your shoes,' because I don't want to provoke you."

"But we *are* talking about shoes, my dear Anselmo."

Novillo got up to return to his contemplative operation, and Apolonio again took up his professional duties. After half an hour, which, for Novillo, seemed an eternity of inexpressible anguish, for during that period of time several meteorlike glances had been exchanged, the shoemaker and the politician found themselves once again side by side.

"You were saying . . . ?" began Novillo.

"I was saying that here, in general, no one appreciates the artistic value of shoes. Let me tell you calmly I feel I have been ignored. I have not been treated fairly either as a shoemaker or as a dramatic poet. Why do you think I became a shoemaker? Because I am a dramatic poet. Why do you think I am a dramatic poet? Because I am a shoemaker. Most people think one thing has nothing to do with the other, but both of them are, in fact, inseparable. There are dramatic conflicts among men and not among animals because men assume the erect position, and they assume this position because they walk on their feet. Let men crawl on all fours, or turn them into paralytics like trees, and there would no longer be any drama. Is this clear? So you see, drama is merely a question of shoes, of standing on your two feet and raising your head as high as you can so as to challenge the heavens, up there where the fate of mankind is hidden. Does it make any sense that men would have invented the drama, just like that . . . for no reason at all? How preposterous! Man invented a type of footwear, the buskin, which lifted him a few inches from the earth; when he did this, he invented drama. Now if you were to mention to any of those starving student types that I am a shoemaker-playwright, they would just laugh in your face. And yet it doesn't shock them at all that a shoemaker can be a philosopher. That makes *me* laugh . . . ha! ha! ha! . . . any alley cat can be a philosopher. All philosophers are clowns, sideshow freaks.

What is philosophy good for anyway? To quote the immortal Shakin-spear, 'philosophy cannot even cure a toothache.' "

"Come, come," objected Novillo, "the dramatic arts can't cure a toothache either."

"But toothaches can inspire one to write dramas. All aches and pains are dramatic experiences."

This scene was repeated daily over a long period of time, and Apolonio's supereloquence was applied to a whole repertory of themes. Novillo actually became very eager to hear the drama Apolonio had written, and the playwright read it to him one night with such bombast and pathos that his listener was sincerely overcome with emotion.

"It's true; you are a great artist," murmured Novillo, wiping away his tears—he was exceedingly sentimental. "As president of the Subscribers Committee, I promise you that the first theater company that comes to Pilares will perform your work."

Apolonio could have embraced Novillo but he preferred not to ruffle the majesty of his own bearing. Unfortunately, many months passed and no theater company appeared in town.

Poetry was tightening the bonds of friendship between Novillo and Apolonio. Novillo thought very highly of the love poems Apolonio composed, and he always asked him for a copy of each new one he had written so he could, in his own words, "totally immerse myself in them" by reading them alone.

One morning, Felicita entered Apolonio's establishment—not a particularly unusual event—but on this occasion the old maid had a strange look on her face. It was an expression trying hard to be one of anger, but it nevertheless couldn't hide a trace of dark pleasure. "What could have snapped inside this old vestal virgin?" thought Apolonio.

"Apolonio, can we be overheard?" asked Felicita, leaning over the counter, breathing rapidly, and nervously looking around in every direction.

"If you keep speaking in that whispery tone of voice, no one will hear us."

"Apolonio . . . you're a villain, a traitor, an ingrate. I'm saying this to you in a whisper but with great conviction, because I wish to avoid any kind of frightful complications, including bloodshed."

"But my dear madame . . . I mean, mademoiselle . . ."

"Silence, you brute! I haven't spoken until today because I thought it was all just a passing madness. But your daring has reached such extremes that I've decided to give you warning once and for all." She reached into her bosom and came out with a stack of papers which she disdainfully tossed on the counter. "Here are your anonymous, impertinent, and unbecoming little notes. I belong to one man, only one! All other suitors merely inspire me with disgust and aversion."

Apolonio looked at the papers.

"These are my poems," he muttered.

"I already knew that."

"But these verses were not transcribed by me. They are copies, and this looks like Don Anselmo's handwriting."

"Water!" was all Felicita could manage to articulate as she collapsed on the sofa in a dead faint.

Apolonio would gladly have tried to revive the old vestal virgin with a few hearty slaps because of the way she had appeared on the scene to disturb him and make him feel ridiculous, forcing the majesty of his bearing into disarray. Because of her, he had been obliged to run frantically to close the front door so the passersby would not be aware of what was happening inside, he had had to get a glass of water and pass in front of those giddy girls in the back room who smiled on seeing him in the role of waiter, and, finally, he had been compelled to splatter some water in the lady's face. He had even considered trying to undo her corset. Fortunately, Felicita came to before Apolonio had recourse to such drastic action. She sipped a bit of water, asked for the return of her papers and, kissing them first, restored them to the shelter of her bosom. Then, she addressed herself to Apolonio, "I want you to swear in the name of your dead Mother you will not tell anyone about this. Swear to it!"

Face to face with Felicita's rhetorical personification, Apolonio found himself in his element. With a solemnity and unction worthy of the Pope himself, he took his vow.

"In spite of everything," reflected Apolonio, "what a curious drama, this affair between Novillo and Felicita! It approaches the suffering of Tantalus. Why don't they get married? It couldn't be because they don't want to, or because someone is keeping them from doing so. And yet, they have not taken the step. And to think there are still people who deny the existence of a nemesis that shackles and destroys the plans of men! I would write their drama, but Novillo is a friend of mine, and he might not like the idea."

He could have written that drama and a handful of others taken straight from reality. For Apolonio, at that time, reality did not go beyond Ruera Street. Without lifting up rooftops, like that devilish spirit Cojuelo in Vélez de Guevara's seventeenth-century Spanish novel, Apolonio imagined the drama hidden in each house on this street. Combining all the individual dramas, he would create a great tragedy—the tragedy of Ruera Street—in which he was the hero, or victim, and Belarmino the traitor. Envisaging all kinds of sorrowful episodes, Apolonio's breast overflowed with vehement impulses. He felt a peremptory need to act, to carry out some cruel action. It was necessary for him to shake off those aggressive desires that were daily becoming more intensely vexing; otherwise he was bound to lose his head at some awful moment and commit a horrible deed. He was suddenly struck by a bright idea; he began devoting himself to raising fighting cocks. Since he had cash on hand, he soon acquired a real cockpit. He brought a good number of English fighting cocks from the town of Antequera, for he had discovered this was the place where the strain of finest pedigree could be found. He became quite skilled in the care and training of these cocks for combat. He gave all his animals mythological and legendary names; the straw-colored one was Achilles; the red one, Ulysses; the yellowish one, Hector; the black one, Hercules; the golden one, Roland; the ashen one, Manfred; another black one was Charlemagne, etc., etc., etc. The usual custom among breeders of game cocks was to use names of bullfighters.

Although there was no justice, no plan or sense in the world, Apolonio believed in God, and every Sunday attended eleven o'clock mass. Then he would head for the cockpit, followed by his young apprentice who carried the baskets containing the cocks that were going to fight that day. He used to take part in the preliminary proceedings, in the examination and weighing-in of the contenders, scrutinizing the scale with such scrupulousness, seriousness and pomp, one would think he was deciding the fate of mankind. After that, it was quite a sight to see the pious pomposity and intense taciturn concentration he displayed as he sat close to the arena and began to clean the roosters' spurs with a lemon half, just in case they had been coated with poison. He wiped them off afterwards with his own handkerchief and finally deposited each rooster gently in the ring, as if he were saying, *"Alea jacta est"*; that there was no longer any earthly power that could stay the will of fate.

And the will of fate was unfailingly that Apolonio's roosters would end up either dead or fatally wounded. Lagartijo killed Ulysses; Bocanegra killed Hector; Mazzantini made mush out of Roland; Achilles went blind from the stabbings he had received from Frascuelo; and a half-breed, lowly white cock called Espartero, owned by a cabinet maker, annihilated Charlemagne, Manfred, Hercules, and six other unlucky heroes. What was surprising was that Apolonio witnessed without anger, one might almost say with pride, the defeat of his gamecocks. The essential thing was that the cocks were never chicken. They died because they had to die, for the hero naturally dies in the end and never at the hands of other heroes, but always cut down by a villainous dagger.

Apolonio's cocks always went in swinging. The others used cowardly combat tactics; that is, they feigned flight, running around the ring, and when the hero was most confidently in pursuit, they would unexpectedly wheel about and lunge treacherously at him. His animals, like the characters in a play of Sophocles, knew how to die beautifully and gloriously, which comes to the same thing. Ajax had said, "To live gloriously or die gloriously is the duty of all those who are nobly born," and the Greek word used to designate glory was a term that also meant beauty. How much Apolonio and his fighting cocks resembled one another! He looked like them in profile, in his proud bearing, in that look of determination, and he even seemed to have a cockscomb, if not spurs. This, however, was purely a surface similarity. Deep inside and in spite of the fact that his imagination harbored or even embraced the most destructive passions, Apolonio, in the words of his son, was incapable of killing a fly. And so Apolonio saw in his game cocks the manifestation of something necessary and deficient in his own personality; they incarnated his personal frustrations, for a playwright is really a frustrated man of action. For this reason Apolonio could calmly, proudly, and with a sense of intimate satisfaction, watch the defeat of his animals. The perfect frustration of his deficient personality could be given free play—it was a type of catharsis. Because, in a certain way, the cocks were an extension of his own person, Apolonio thought that if they were to win frequently, this aggressive spirit, the need for executive action, would have fatally contaminated him. As he was basically a coward, just the idea of committing any foolhardy action gave him the chills.

Finally, the cock fights had two diametrically opposed influences on the life and character of Apolonio—one favorable and the other adverse. Favorable, in the sense that he was becoming known and famous as a picturesque individual and as an improvisor of doggerel verse. This reputation spread from the city to the provinces where occasional interurban fights were staged. Adverse, due to the fact that there was always betting connected with the events, and as Apolonio consistently lost, a certain imbalance in his economic situation was beginning to occur. Apolonio paid very little attention to these financial blows as long as his public activity as a breeder of gamecocks continued to increase his fame. He preferred bankruptcy and poverty to obscurity. He was willing to accept anything in order to gratify his innocent vanity, just so people would know and talk about him. He was obsessed by the need to become more famous than Belarmino and to be able to humiliate his rival someday.

Belarmino's popularity increased. The newspapers had already published articles, some mocking him and others taking him quite seriously. They all expressed the thesis that he was definitely a mental phenomenon, a case worthy of study, and it was even suggested to the director of the local mental hospital that scientific experiments be performed on Belarmino. It was actually recommended that when he died, Belarmino should not be buried until his brain had been removed for purposes of postmortem analysis. When Belarmino read this flattering proposal, he almost choked on his own saliva—but he recovered immediately and smiled beatifically. He adopted the proper attitude of philosophical indifference to the opinions of others, just as a philosopher does when faced with physical pain, the important thing being to conserve life and thought.

The debates about Belarmino became more and more complex and increasingly violent—no one had been able to present conclusive proof that he either knew what he was talking about or, on the contrary, was spouting like a parrot, merely repeating empty and disconnected words. The Grind had not given up his plan to systematize the complete Belarminian lexicon and prepare a corresponding glossary. He had taken copious notes, had already glossed quite a few words, and he even understood the meaning of some of the axioms. But these fragmentary findings did not convince everyone.

About that time the town of Pilares received its first phonograph. A hardware dealer by the name of Ortigüela had bought it in Paris on one of his periodic buying trips. This piece of machinery caused a great sensation. Ortigüela gave several demonstrations at private residences, in the casino, and at the university. When he heard it, the Grind thought up an ingenious project, which he lost no time in suggesting to Belarminians and anti-Belarminians alike. It was nothing more and nothing less than a plan to demonstrate unequivocally whether or not Belarmino spoke an intelligible language. The proposed demonstration was accepted by everyone. The project was to be carried out in the following way: Belarmino would be asked to come to someone's house and succinctly explain his philosophical system. The phonograph, cleverly hidden, would be placed next to him and Belarmino's dissertation would be recorded on one or two cylinders. At the right moment, Belarmino would be told that a visiting philosopher was passing through Pilares and that this stranger had been invited to give a lecture in the casino. Since Belarmino was the only philosopher in town, they thought he would like to hear him, and in that case they would place Belarmino in a room near the speaker's platform, behind curtains, where he could listen without being seen. The idea was that Escobar, the Grind, would take charge of all the arrangements, since he was the one Belarmino most admired and trusted. None of them thought Belarmino would recognize his own voice because even though one could make out the words on that still rather primitive apparatus, everybody's voice had the same homogeneous and rasping quality.

When the Grind asked Belarmino to expound his system, the shoemaker answered with gentle irony, "And what is a system? Perhaps what you call a system is not what I call a system. I, thank God, have no system. What you mean is an abscess. However, thank God, I don't have an abscess either."

"That's fine, Belarmino, although I must confess I still don't fully understand you. This is precisely why I never get my fill of listening to you and why I would like you to give us a kind of brief resume or sum-mary of your ideas. Even if I don't understand you, *you* understand *me* because you're bilingual. You know what I am asking. Do you accept?"

"I do understand what you are requesting, and I have no objections about accepting. But I need a week for meditation."

When the week was up, Belarmino appeared at the designated place. Anyone would have said he had spent not a week of meditation, but many months of fasting; his noble and aquiline face was drawn and almost translucent. His little body was so shrunken and bony, it seemed as though not even the law of gravity could keep him from floating away. He entered the room without changing his expression, and he didn't even cast a curious glance around him. He sat down where they told him to, lowered his head, and spoke softly without moving or modulating the tone of his voice. The speech concluded, he left the room, and returned to his little abode with his usual imperturbable serenity and absentmindedness.

Another two weeks went by. As planned, two students who were also members of the casino went to ask Belarmino if he wanted to hear the visiting philosopher's lecture. They told him they had chosen a special place for him to sit where he might hear without being seen.

"Where is this philosopher from?" asked Belarmino.

"From Königsberg," answered one of the brighter students.

"And what's his name?"

"Cleonte de Merode."

"And in what language does he speak?"

"Well, naturally, he speaks in philosophy. All philosophers speak a special language."

Belarmino thought this over for a few minutes. He knew philosophers have a peculiar language all their own, but he wondered if each philosopher spoke his own invented dialect, or if they all spoke the same one. If the second possibility was the correct one, then evidently philosophers were a privileged group who had reached the absolute truth by means of direct revelation.

"Will many people go?" asked Belarmino.

"Certainly. And among them will be the most elegant and beautiful women of Pilares."

"A philosopher for elegant and beautiful women? Some philosopher he must be!" exclaimed Belarmino, somewhat disillusioned.

That same wide-awake student extricated himself from this difficulty without any trouble.

"Oh, you know how women are . . . they got wind a philosopher was coming to town and they said to themselves, 'Let's *do* go and see him— he's undoubtedly some queer duck.' "

"Oh, I see."

"There's a small room next to the ballroom; you can hear perfectly from in there. You won't be alone, because some people who don't like to mix with the public, and for good reasons, will be there too. For example, Escobar, the Alligator. How could *he* sit next to all the elegant ladies in those beggar's rags he always wears? So it's settled, you'll join us."

After he had learned the philosopher would speak before a group of women, Belarmino no longer had any real interest in hearing him. Nonetheless, he went along with resigned indifference.

The whole plan had been so cleverly carried out that in spite of his instinctive wisdom, Belarmino did not suspect he was the victim of a practical joke. Some twenty people in all—the most outspoken Belarminians and anti-Belarminians—filled the small room. The shutters of the windows were partially closed so the street noises wouldn't interfere with the proceedings. They sat Belarmino down very close to an antiqued-gold velvet curtain. He seemed to be in a state of complete insensitivity, as though he had been amputated from the world of living things. If someone happened to whisper in his ear, he didn't react in the slightest. The Alligator, on the other hand, was going through one of his galvanizing crises and was shaking convulsively, already predicting that the experiment was going to fail. From time to time, the sophisticated student would go up to the curtain that veiled the phonograph. Opening the curtain a little, he would stick his nose through it and then, turning around, offer a commentary. "The room is filling up." "It's packed." "The philosopher is now walking up to the podium." "Monsieur Cleonte de Merode is going to begin his lecture." Then the rasping sound of the phonograph was heard, a sign that words would soon follow. "Murmurs of approval," commented the smart-alecky student.

Belarmino took no notice of all this; he was abstracted, off in the remotest Limbo of thought.

A metallic voice, somewhat hoarse and with a nasal twang that could have belonged either to a drunk or a phonograph, began to speak. "He who eats in front of the dictionary is in *rah-rah* until *rat-tat-tat*."

Belarmino jumped up from his chair as though somebody had given him an electric shock. He turned deathly pale. His eyes instantly developed dark rings under them and his pupils, shiny and aflame, seemed to be moving in every direction.

The voice continued in an even, strident, steady, and inexorable stream. Belarmino was transfixed, his arms wide open as he sat back in his chair in a state of near unconsciousness and with his face turned toward the curtain. He looked like those replicas of saints who have received the blessing of the stigmata. He was panting weakly as he gathered up his fading strength to be able to mutter continuously, "Of course. Naturally. Who could doubt it?" and then, intermittently, like some sort of arbitrary watch, he would energetically produce rhythmic onomatopoetic sounds at the end of each sentence uttered by the invisible speaker. It sounded something like "tris-tros, tris-tros, tris-tros." Then the bodiless, nasal voice pronounced, with the cool deliberateness of a prophetic judgment, "The toad does not register belligerence, the inquisition, or the give and take of boarders. The toad sprinkles the balloons and the stumbling of the boarders with calyxes. The toad adopts the tetrahedron. The toad strips the tetrahedron." At that point, Belarmino put his hands to his temples, threw back his head and shaking it from side to side with unreasonable yet controlled enthusiasm, muttered a few words, "How right he is! How absolutely correct!"

When the lecture had ended, Belarmino went into a state of abstractedness or paralysis. The Alligator, triumphant, was winking and making all kinds of faces as his way of asking the others what they had thought of the experience. Most of them were having convulsions and trying desperately to keep from laughing out loud. Some just arched their eyebrows and pursed their lips, refusing to accept the experiment as a valid proof of anything.

When Belarmino finally straightened up, the glassy look of the dream-magic was still there in his eyes.

"And you say," he asked, "this philosopher's name is Meonte de Clerode?"

"That's right; Meonte de Clerode," answered the young student, keeping a straight face.

111

"Well, he's a huge toad. Even greater than Salmerón."

And Belarmino returned to his cubicle, head down, his whole being immersed in these thought-provoking problems.

"Now then, what do you have to say for yourselves?" asked Escobar in a frantic state quite unusual for someone as temperate as he.

"We had a ball," answered the young student.

"That's a frivolous answer and this is a serious matter," replied the Alligator severely.

A dentist by the name of Yagüe joined the conversation.

"There is no doubt that the shoemaker knows what he's saying and he always uses the same words to describe the same objects. This seems to me to have been conclusively proven. But two other things occur to me. First, is what he's saying in his own way at all important? Should anyone bother to study his demoniacal language to find out what it's all about? Secondly, perhaps what he has to say *is* important. Then why does he have to invent an unintelligible language to express it? I would like Escobar to reply to these two observations of mine, since he is the expert."

"I will be pleased to answer your questions. As for the first statement of yours, I'll just leave that up to your own judgment. You say I am an expert. What do you mean by that word?"

"Well," stuttered the dentist, slightly disturbed, "the word tells you what it means . . . an expert is one who knows something."

"Then, why don't you use the word *connoisseur,* as some people would?"

"Now, old man, you're making it difficult for me. An expert is also a person who knows more about certain things than most other people. I'm an expert in odontology."

"All right, then why don't you say specialist?"

"You're confusing me instead of clearing up my doubts. I said expert because I wanted to express several meanings in a single word."

"Exactly, that's what Belarmino is trying to do—express several things in a single word. Since the words he already knows only express one thing each, he has invented a new language in which each word indicates various things, or at least a series of things that produce the particular item he wants each word to designate."

"But you still haven't answered my first question."

"I'm coming to that. I've already put together a considerable number

of Belarminian words, and I understand some of his sentences. For example, in today's lecture, the sentence, 'He who eats in front of the dictionary is in *rah-rah* until *rat-tat-tat,*' actually means, 'Man confronts the universe as long as he lives and until he dies.' That's the literal version."

"Fine, but that sentence is a cliché, and it's not worth the trouble to learn the shoemaker's language just to end up with a discovery like that. In what way is the dictionary the same as the universe? And why do you have to change its name?"

"Exactly. That's an argument that can be used against the greatest philosophers. Stendhal, a French writer, once wrote that he had exhausted himself by assiduously trying to fathom Kant's philosophical system, only to discover afterward that there was nothing there everyone didn't already know through sheer common sense. And as for changing the usual meanings of words, I can assure you that all philosophical systems necessarily have to begin by doing this. You think you have the meanings of words like *intuition, idea, spirit, will, extension* all at your fingertips, isn't that so?"

"Of course I do; at least enough to satisfy my mental needs."

"Well, every one of these words has a different and even opposite meaning for different philosophers, and this is because these philosophers, like you, wanted to satisfy their mental needs."

"The only conclusion I can come to then is that philosophy is not good for anything except to patch up shoes and let you walk around dressed like a bum."

"At least in Belarmino's case, his philosophy has helped him to become a saint. I think we all agree on that."

"Well in order to become a saint," answered the dentist petulantly, thinking the objection that had just occurred to him was irrefutable, "it isn't necessary to invent a new and unintelligible language."

"All saints," answered the Alligator, "speak a unique language, through their words and actions, and those who are not saints do not understand that language. Every man who has a part to play speaks a special language which another man who does not play that same part cannot comprehend, for each is animated by a different spirit. The horse trader speaks his particular language, the smuggler has his own brand of speech, so does the politician, the artist, the hardware dealer, the soldier, and the dentist; they all speak their own languages. The world

is like a great market filled with deaf people trying to carry on their business. Everybody is shouting and there's a horrendous racket. But because people don't listen to each other, nothing gets done."

After the Alligator had left, that same michievous student said aloud what the rest had been thinking to themselves, "That bundle of rags is as crazy as the shoemaker."

But there was one truth, diffused and substantive, that remained floating in the air. Escobar had won—Belarmino spoke a language intelligible to himself, and even somewhat comprehensible to Escobar. It seemed evident both of them belonged to a species different from the common run of men; it was even possible they belonged to a higher order of nature.

The news of what had happened reached Apolonio's ears. Envy is the same as clear-sightedness, but it sees everything through a magnifying glass. Apolonio clearly evaluated the event as a triumph for Belarmino, but he exaggerated its dimensions. For Apolonio, the incident had been the supreme consecration of Belarmino as a philosopher, and from there universal acclaim would be only a step away. Nervous, shaky, Apolonio paced up and down the shoe store, his coxcomb standing straight up, a fierce look on his face now ravished by this exaggerated fury. The only thing he needed now was to sprout cockspurs. He couldn't resign himself to the humiliation. It was absolutely necessary and urgent for him to prove to the world that his brain towered over Belarmino's as a cedar of Lebanon over hyssop. Just then, Novillo entered.

"What's the matter with you, dear friend? You look as though you have a fever."

"Don Anselmo, I must tell you that the moment for a friend to fulfill his sacred promise has arrived."

"Well, let's have it."

"In this very place, and I swear to it by the name of my lady, you promised me you would have my play produced."

"And I still hold to my promise. But the problem is that no dramatic company has come to town."

"That is true and 'tis a pity, but time is on the wing. There's a group now in the city."

"Yes, but they can only sing," rhymed Novillo.

Apolonio replied that this made no difference to him. The important thing was for the play to be produced. As president of the Subscription

Committee, Novillo could demand it. Novillo promised he would do just that. He carried the script with him to the theater that night, tucked tightly under his arm. During the intermission, between the performance of *The Little Acolyte* and *The Bells,* he went to the dressing room of Celemín, the clown, director and lead actor in the company. He handed him the manuscript and explained, "This play must be put on. We subscribers demand it. The author is a local talent. Basically, it's a serious drama, but your company can present it anyhow."

Celemín kept the work, saying he would read it and let Novillo have his decision by the following day. Like all men who are devoted exclusively to making other people laugh, Celemín was a rather superficial spirit who realized right away that if the play were produced as a farce, it would be the comic success of the season. The next day he told Novillo that rehearsals would start immediately.

Apolonio swelled with pride to a degree incompatible with the elasticity of human skin. Seemingly disinterested, he went to all the rehearsals as though he were God attending to the supervision of the daily but muddy job of Creation. He let Celemín do whatever he pleased, just as God allows despots and tyrants to play their game, knowing that their will and authority are useless; firm in the knowledge that providence, or the providential plan of the author, resides within each one of the characters in the drama like a fatal law, an ineluctable norm of action.

Instigated by the malicious Celemín, word got around in Pilares that opening night would turn out to be a great farce. Finally, the big day arrived.

Groups of students were distributed in strategic places in the theater. They carried garlands of onions, garlic, leeks, and other violently malodorous vegetables, two owls, several bats, and an assortment of other frightening and repulsive birds. The plan was to crown the author with these garlands and send the nocturnal creatures winging their way through the hall at precisely the right moment.

The students had decided it would be funny to give the impression they were tremendously enthusiastic about the work. From the very opening verses, they began to applaud catastrophically. Apolonio, in the wings, heard the racket, calmly taking the applause to his bosom as Olympian Zeus had done with his thunderbolts. The malicious Celemín had prepared several grotesque tricks. He had dressed the actors up as buffoons, decking them out in brightly colored muslin. Every time one of them appeared on the scene, there was an outburst of laughter and applause. In the second act, there was a duel between the Lord of Oña and Estoiquiz, the one-eyed Lord of Orduña. Celemín had staged the duel so that one of the participants faced the audience and the other had his back to them. He had tampered with the knee breeches of the actor whose back was to the audience, and he had done this in such an ingenious way that at a given moment they would come apart in that area most roundly prominent. This, naturally, would expose certain parts of the actor's anatomy. That's exactly what happened. When his pants split, there was a ripping round of applause from the audience. After things had quieted down, a servant, who was supposed to be watching the duel, shouted

> Help! My Lord has need of aid!
> A mule would not be in vain.
> In spite of the masquerade,
> What is showing, is his pain.

The servant could not complete the quatrain. Before he had finished reciting the second verse, a chorus of students interrupted, shouting out the name of an animal they felt would be more appropriate. The actor tried again, but the second time he just raced through the four verses.

How well the malicious Celemín had calculated exactly what would happen and how this chivalric scene would change in tone, becoming transformed into low comedy merely by placing the participants as has already been described and opportunely weakening the rear seams of a pair of breeches! Even the most sublime scenes in Shakespeare would have come undone in such circumstances.

In the third act, one of the characters had the lines

> For the conquering of Orduña,
> Especially with his raw recruits,
> The Lord of Oña played a "tuña"
> On one of his shimmering flutes.

As a result of the insistent applause, the foregoing quatrain had to be repeated half a dozen times, and there were clamorous shouts for the author. As Apolonio at that moment moved forward toward the foot-

116

lights in a kind of bow, spine doubled over yet not losing his marvellous bearing and pontifical dignity, a voice was heard from the crowd.

"Show us your shimmering flute!" (Fierce applause.)

The voice actually belonged to a student who was studying veterinary medicine, but Apolonio, smiling to himself with infinite joy, thought, "That is undoubtedly Belarmino, the reptile! I recognize your venomous hissing. The effusive applause has asphyxiated your intempestuous commentary. That should serve as a lesson for you to mend your ways. Tonight, the pain of my triumph is destroying you. Die! Die, you miserable wretch!" To be perfectly truthful, it should be said that at this very moment Belarmino the reptile was forming arpeggios with his hissing, but in bed, where he was sleeping and snoring to his heart's content. He was stretched out next to Xuantipa, dreaming that he was having an exquisite colloquy with Meonte de Clerode, the distinguished philosopher from Königsberg, while the two of them were seated high above the clouds.

When the drama was over, the acclamation and ovation raised a cloud of dust. Apolonio, standing in front of the prompter's box, was all puffed up with pride, but he received the homage of the multitude with a look of indifference. Garlands of onions, garlic, and leeks, all decorated with colorful ribbons, began to pile up at his feet. Apolonio gathered them up, accepting them with resigned beneficence and not even deigning to look at them closely since he assumed they were wreaths made with the bulbs of sweet-smelling plants. At that moment the students unleashed the repulsive nocturnal birds. Blinded by the gas lights, these creatures careened crazily from one side of the theater to the other, flying directly into the faces of the spectators. Utter pandemonium. The ladies howled as if they were in labor; as a matter of fact, two pregnant ladies actually did abort. Exactly the same thing had happened during the tragedies of Aeschylus.

With his prodigious ineptitude for perceiving external reality, Apolonio returned home convinced that in the annals of dramatic history there had never been a triumph equal to his own. When he was in his underwear, getting ready to bury himself in bed, he placed his index finger right between his eyebrows and said to himself, "I have now charted my course. From this time forth, my true occupation will be to give poetic form to the dramas that are fermenting in here." The result of such a beautiful decision was that he began to neglect his shoemaking business, to treat his clients badly and to alienate them little by little. Because he was assaulted by the debts resulting from his losses in the cockfighting enterprise, he, in turn, assaulted his customers; either out of negligence or forgetfulness, he tried on occasion to collect twice for the same bill.

At about that time, Martínez, a former employee of Belarmino, opened a store on Ruera Street, a thoroughfare that for some reason seemed to have a particular attraction for shoemakers. This shop carried machine-made shoes, and was called "Solidity, Incorporated." Martínez stocked merchandise from Majorca, Almanza, Barcelona, and he even promised future shipments from the United States.

Apolonio considered a pair of boots a work of art in the same way the Renaissance princes used to look upon a book as a work of art. For those exacting tasters of beauty, a book had to be written by hand, bound with expensive fabrics, and fastened together with jeweled brooches, although one *might* be permitted to experiment with printing dies in certain unimportant sections of the work. In Apolonio's view, a machine could intervene in some of the accessory stitching, but the important seams of the boots naturally had to be sewn by hand. When the emissaries of Cardinal Besarion saw the first printed book at the home of Constantine Lascaris, they made fun of the stupid invention. "Only among barbarians could such a thing have occurred; naturally, it had to be in a German village. Frederick of Urbino would have blushed with shame had he owned such an ugly book as this." When Apolonio saw his first pair of Yankee shoes, he exclaimed, "Only savages could have invented this. I prefer the *alpargata,* which at least is made by hand. That new store should be called 'Stolidity, Incorporated,' not Solidity." And he offered a prophetic statement, which to date has turned out to be quite valid. "The making of luxury shoes is, and will always be, a matter of handsewing." Nonetheless, Apolonio was well aware that Solidity, Incorporated or "Stolidity, Incorporated," threatened him with serious, even ruinous competition.

Martínez filled the newspapers with attractive advertisements, something Apolonio considered unworthy of real art. Besides, this same Martínez, a true representative of the pure and applied sciences, had invented a shoe polishing cream, Zenitram, whose name was an anagram of the inventor's last name spelled backward. In one of his newspaper ads, the owner of Solidity, Incorporated announced——All shoe polishes known to date have been devised according to the following formula:

Whale Oil, white or red	45%
Linseed Oil	30%
Tallow	20%
Coloring	3% to 5%
White Wax	2%
Alcohol	2%

And he included eight more combinations. The advertisement continued, *"Solidity, Incorporated,* under the ownership and management of the well-known industrialist, Claudio Martínez, offers five hundred *pesetas*—500!— to anyone who can demonstrate that any of the polishing creams now on the market are not made in accordance with the foregoing formula. Another five hundred *pesetas,* for a total of one thousand —1000!—to anyone who can prove Zenitram is not different and superior to all other polishes. Zenitram Cream will keep your shoes new and sparkling for eternity. We invite all our competitors to win the one thousand *pesetas* by denying our claim."

One day, the Duchess of Somavia entered Apolonio's store and spoke to him calmly about the situation. "In the letter my brother Deusdedit wrote to me before he died, and that's now about nine years ago, he told me you were an ass. Don't scowl at me . . . I know you're an artist, but that doesn't stop you from being an ass. Look, Apolonio, we're now living in a period of businessmen; these are not times for art and philosophy. This is the era of the Martinezes and not the Apolonios and Belarminos. As for Belarmino, he's nothing but a mender of shoes now. I have it on good authority that things are not going too well with you either. The same thing that happened to Belarmino will happen to you if you don't sharpen your wits and shake off that stupidity of yours. I've always said exactly what's on my mind, and I'm telling you now that you had better wake up. If you don't, you can be sure you and Belarmino both will end up in the poor house."

Chapter Six

DRAMA AND PHILOSOPHY

It is an age-old tradition that once a year during the September equinox, the angelic and gentle shepherd, Saint Francis, feels out of sorts. He unties the cord from around his waist, and aims it like a slingshot in the direction of the heavens. Flocks of clouds appear, the urns where the winds are kept burst open, the floodgates holding back the celestial waters give way, the seas become angry, fishing vessels capsize, migrating birds flee, wild animals race to their lairs, men take refuge in their homes, and the heart becomes drenched with a sadness that is like the lament of all perishable things.

It had already been raining for more than a week. From the earth to the heavens dense streaming cataracts made a thick forest, the gray and livid clouds forming an impenetrable vault of branches in which the tremorous lament of the church bells sounded lost and dejected.

It was Sunday night. Apolonio was pacing the length and width of the dining room, humming the "Spirto Gentil" from *La Favorita*. Ascending with the impetus of the ecstatic music, his pupils had risen to where they were hidden behind the curtains of his upper eyelids. His eyes were as white as those found in ancient statuary and his soul was equally blank, like the virginal page that hopes to receive the most sublime concepts written in an indelible script. At that moment, Apolonio was floating above the sadness of the world and above the gloomy clouds like the melodious spirit of Jehovah high above primeval chaos.

"Sir. The beans'll be overcooked," sourly muttered the maid as she stuck her nose through the door. "It's already ten o'clock."

"What are you saying, you uncouth creature?" answered Apolonio, startled.

"I said that it's ten o'clock and if you want to have supper tonight . . ."

"There'll be no supper until Don Pedrito arrives."

"But Don Pedrito's not eating home tonight."

"Who told you that?"

"Well, I'll be! . . . why he said so himself, and what's more, he left you a note."

"A note? Where is it?"

"Right in front of your long nose, on the table—there on top of your plate."

Apolonio read the letter. "Father, forgive me," said the text. "I was not born to be a priest. I am going away with the woman I adore. We will be married and I trust that in spite of everything, you will bless our union. Pedro."

At this moment Apolonio actually did turn into a statue, not only around the eyes but in every part of his body. Even his soul became pale and hollow. Finally, when his blood had started to circulate again, he said to the maid, "There will be no dinner tonight. You can go home now. Give me my raincoat."

He headed for the house of the Duchess of Somavia, who, just the day before, had returned to Pilares fleeing from the inclement weather, melancholy, and boredom of the village. Apolonio was carrying the note in his hand, forgetting to keep it out of the rain.

"What's the matter with you, Apolonio?" asked the duchess, somewhat alarmed by this stonelike man. "The catastrophe I spoke to you about, bankruptcy, you've been wiped out? I could see it coming."

"Would to God it were only that!" murmured Apolonio, his voice hollow. He handed her the note.

"But my young friend, this piece of paper is sopping wet. The ink has run and the letters are all blurred. How do you expect me to read that?"

"Would to God I had gone blind before I had a chance to read it! But now, what am I to do? Ah-h! resign myself and forgive the hand that has wounded me. Let me drain the cup to the very dregs and read the note for the second time."

He read the letter to the duchess. Deep down inside himself, so far down that not even *he* realized it, Apolonio felt extremely proud of his behavior, and believed that at this very moment he was truly a tragic character, imagining he had awakened a powerful, pathetic interest in the duchess.

"Bah! When I saw you, I was afraid it was a question of something serious. Sit down. Even though this has to be solved quickly, it's necessary to think slowly to come to a quick solution. Sit down!"

"Sit down"; the phrase was the one Napoleon used with the Queen of Prussia on that occasion when the sovereign, in order to get from him a treaty less harsh, had tried to move the Corsican to sympathy by staging a painful, theatrical scene for his benefit.

How well Apolonio knew that tragedy requires speaking on one's feet while wearing buskins. As he sat down, he understood he was worse than ridiculous, he was humiliated, like a fallen idol. He lowered his head shamefully.

"Let's take this one step at a time. Undoubtedly you don't even know who the woman adored by the disobedient Pedrito is." Apolonio shook his head, no.

"How could you possibly know, since you don't even live on this planet? Not even an inkling?" Another shake of the head. "Well friend, I'm going to tell you—it's Belarmino's daughter."

"No. Not that! Death would be better!" roared Apolonio, leaping to his feet, this time really frantic. "I was already willing to forgive, to give my blessing. I was even thinking about my little grandchildren . . . but this, never!"

"You're really off on a tangent . . . you were thinking about grandchildren and I brought you back to earth. But, sit down! Of course you don't know or can't even guess how, when, at what time or in which direction they fled, and you have no idea how to find out." Another mute negation. "So, I'm the one who has to do everything. Let's talk calmly. There's no doubt in my mind Angustias is the lady who has been carried off. I knew that rascal Pedrito liked the girl—they saw each other very often during vacations, and he used to write to her from the seminary—but, to tell the truth, I didn't think he would go this far. The things children do! Who could have helped them to elope? Only one person comes to mind—Felicita, the Consumptive."

"The loathsome bawd!"

"Don't use those foul-sounding words. That whole business of procuring is a very relative matter. When women reach a certain age and still feel amorous, and if they're no longer ripe enough to be loved for themselves yet still have to live in love's ambience, all of them would do anything to protect and encourage the loves of others. This is a forgivable weakness and even more so in the case of Felicita, who in spite of being a bit dried out, loves and is loved, although she can't manage to have her desires satisfied. Angustias always used to go and visit the old maid, and if she didn't appear, Felicita would send someone to fetch her. Everyone on the street knows about it. Your son also used to visit the old maid. You didn't know that either?" Mute negation. "Well, help me tie up the loose ends. The idea of this flight was inspired, encouraged, and resolutely approved by the old maid. She knows everything. How can we get it out of her? Before you answer, it's necessary for you to tell me what your plans and wishes are in this matter. Do you approve of what's happened and will you consent to the marriage?"

"Never! Never, never!" screamed Apolonio, again leaping to his feet.

"Sit down old man, sit down! I agree with you. That foolish Pedrito has a lovely future ahead of him. It would be stupid for him to throw it away just like that. What would he do without a profession or a pension after he had married that little thing, the daughter of a shoemender who doesn't even have a place of his own to drop dead in? I couldn't approve of such nonsense. There is still the question of conscience, of morality. Personally I can't take other people's ideas of morality seriously. It must have something to do with heredity, just like scrofula and the shingles, for no matter how I inquire into the matter, I can't find any traces of having inherited in my ancestors' blood any of that moralizing nonsense others seem to think is so important. I can recognize that the girl is going to have a rather hard time of it for a while because of the way people see things. But people do forget and they forget rather quickly. Time erases the creases of memory even faster than it does the scars of the flesh. If we were to weigh the matter carefully, we'd have to admit that your son stands to lose more in the way of reputation than Belarmino's daughter. But we must consider one particular issue that has to be seriously taken into account. If we prevent the marriage, are we dooming Angustias to a life of misery? No, I don't think so, for this kind of thing happens every day. Anyway, if she is miserable, it'll be her own fault for not accepting this as a natural occurrence. But even so, I'm convinced she'd be much more unhappy if she were to get married under these circumstances. Later she would probably ask herself infinitely more often, 'Oh why did I ever get married?' instead of 'Why did they stop me from getting married?' Bearing that in mind, my conscience is clear and I can see no objection to breaking up this ill-conceived informal wedding. Now let's go and get all the necessary information out of Felicita. We have discussed this slowly and now it's time to get a move on."

The duchess pulled a bell cord and mobilized the servants. She ordered one to get the carriage ready immediately for at least a day's journey, and perhaps even for a day and a night; she sent another servant to Novillo's boardinghouse to tell him to pack a suitcase and come right over so he could set out on the road without delay (the duchess knew Novillo would be useless if he didn't carry his cosmetic kit with him), she told Patón to get dressed, and ordered another servant to bring her writing paper. She dashed off a succinct note.

"From reliable and confidential sources, I have learned you are not uninvolved in the elopement of Pedrito Caramanzana and Belarmino's daughter. Anselmo Novillo is leaving at this moment to capture the fugitives. We have no doubt you will supply us with the necessary details. If, due to other preoccupations, you cannot remember those particulars we require, we would be most pleased to take you to court so your memory might be refreshed without delay. Sincerely yours, Beatriz, Duchess of Somavia."

She dispatched the servant to Felicita's house with the missive. He returned with a reply before any of the others. It was written in a shaky hand and stated, "Illustrious Madam, Pedrito and Angustias left by coach for Inhiesta at five o'clock this afternoon. They adore each other. They want to get married. I thought I was performing a charitable action by helping them. They have two hundred and fifty *pesetas,* which I loaned to them; and I do not mention this so the money can be returned to me. Forgive me and forgive them. If we have erred, it was from an excess of love. Your servant, Felicita Quemada."

"That crazy dame!" exclaimed the duchess. "What fools cupid makes of us. How I wish I could do to him what people do to cats and oxen," and here she burst out with a lively oath.

Novillo arrived when the duchess was in that antiamorous, antitaurine mood; the servant appeared with the information that the carriage was ready; Patón showed up dressed for the journey, complete with high boots and a cape.

124

"What does my lady wish?" asked Novillo, bowing ceremoniously. In his hand he held a little bag that contained dark secrets of cosmetic alchemy.

"What are my wishes? I was saying if it were up to me, I would fix it so there wouldn't be any more young bulls, or 'novillos', around because I would have them all turned into oxen; they are more useful in agriculture. Stop twitching your nose; I wasn't referring to the fact that your name also means 'young bull', Novillo. This is not a question of personalities, but of an understanding of the general order of things. You're an inoffensive and sweet little bull. And now, off to Inhiesta. Apolonio, you'll go as the father and you, Novillo, as representing my authority. Since Pedrito is an energetic fellow and stronger than both of you put together, and since he's probably also become too stubborn and spoiled by this time to let himself be taken from the manger right after having gotten close to it, I'm sending Patón with you. He's as crude as a mule and he'll take care of Pedrito if it becomes necessary. Now, straight to Inhiesta and bring the fugitive back here to me. I'll have him kept in custody for the few days left before courses start again in the seminary. And Apolonio, be careful; no threats or reprimands. That part's up to me. Now let's get to it, before the love birds take the train from Inhiesta tomorrow."

The scouting party left in accordance with the duchess's wishes. It rained and rained. The coachman and Patón rode up front in the box. Inside, Novillo and Apolonio sat rigidly, without exchanging a word, like two idols being carried to virgin territories to spread the power of a new cult. An hour passed, a long drawn out, threadlike, lazy and interminable hour, as though it had been spun in slow motion by the tips of numb and rigid fingers—the little bells on the horses. Ding, ding, ding, the bells slowly sounded as they swallowed the bulky and dirty skein of the nocturnal hours that had to be spun and wound.

After what for Apolonio was an eternity of silence, he dared to speak.

"I don't know the topography of the province because I am not indigenous to it. I don't even know how far Inhiesta is."

Novillo took out his watch and struck a match.

"It's twelve o'clock. We'll reach Inhiesta at seven in the morning."

"It's that far? . . . well, I think it would be a good idea for us to get comfortable and have a snooze."

"I am disturbed, my friend. The cold damp air doesn't agree with

125

me at all. I forgot to bring a lap blanket. But, what's to be done now? Let's try to sleep."

Feeling his way, Novillo opened his suitcase and took out a jar that had once held olives but was now filled with clear water. Secretively, he removed his false teeth and placed them inside the jar. He wasn't able to get to sleep with those foreign teeth in his mouth because no matter how he tried to stop them, they used to bite his tongue, as if the former owner were taking advantage of the mist of sleep to come back and avenge himself for this macabre usufruct. That is to say, Novillo imagined that just as the hair of his wig belonged undoubtedly to a dead man, the same thing was true of his teeth. Sometimes, under the influence of a particularly unpleasant experience, or when he was troubled by his amorous timidity, he was convinced of all this, for he had the sensation that the hair of his wig was standing straight up. What could this mean except that the spirit of the dead man was rising in anger against the profaner of his mortal remains? But Novillo bravely and firmly withstood these chilling skirmishes with the supernatural and supersensory, for they were preferable to appearing bald and toothless before Felicita.

Novillo also shed his wig, spread a Pompeian ointment on his face to keep his skin from developing additional wrinkles, and settled down for a nap. Apolonio and Novillo both dozed off to the sound of creaking and jingling. They were awakened by a sudden silence, as if somebody had suddenly grabbed the pillow out from under them.

"What's the matter? Why has the carriage stopped?" they both asked at the same time, straining to hear.

"Who are you, boy?" shouted the coachman.

"I am Celesto, the shepherd from Cachan," replied a voice. This Celesto had been Belarmino's apprentice many years ago.

"Where are you coming from, pal?"

"From Inhiesta."

"Who'd you take?"

"Two friends of mine."

"Can I know who they were?"

"No, you can't. So good-bye and we're off."

A flutter of bells was heard, dividing into two separate coveys as each flew in the opposite direction. Recovering their pillow of noises and movements, Novillo and Apolonio dozed off again. Novillo was the first to awaken. The morning light was already being diluted in the grayish rain. Before Apolonio awakened, Novillo placed his apocryphal capillary and osseous excrescences in their respective places. He felt a chill from his scalp down; "That's bad," he thought. "I've caught a cold. And colds are really bad for me." He sneezed, and at the sound of the sneeze, Apolonio opened his eyes.

They reached Inhiesta at eight o'clock in the morning, pulling up to the town's only inn.

"Those love birds are probably deep in sleep," said Novillo. "It breaks my heart to think I have to nip this idyll in the bud. But I am not the will, only the arm that carries it out. We've got to get this over with as soon as possible and return to Pilares immediately. I've just caught a cold and I don't want it to get worse."

A servant girl from the inn accompanied by Patón went up to the lovers' room. She rapped on the door.

"Who's there?" asked the seminarian.

"Sir, someone is waiting for you downstairs."

"Let him wait; I'm not going down."

The girl insisted. After a while, the seminarian, only half dressed, came to the door with the intention of angrily sending the girl on her way. Patón tied him up, put a gag in his mouth, carried him down the stairs on his shoulders, and put him in the carriage. Novillo paid the innkeeper, and that was that. Upstairs, Angustias continued to wait. Apolonio didn't even want to think about her. Novillo, with his cold, couldn't think about her.

At five o'clock in the afternoon, the hunting party with its captive was back at the Somavia palace. Novillo went directly to his boarding-house, suffering from a severe pain in his ribs. The duchess had the seminarian locked up after first saying to him in an arch and ironic tone, "You'll be very safe here until the school year begins. Meditate, my son, meditate in tranquility and in the shadows on the asinine thing you were about to do—abandon the service of God and His bountiful wages in order to serve a mortal creature, the daughter of a shoemender, neither one of you having enough for a crust of bread."

Overwhelmed with bitterness, Don Pedrito managed to murmur, "But they won't let me in at the seminary." "Well, the little priest has a head on his shoulders after all," thought the duchess.

"I hadn't even considered that possibility. So, they won't let you in, eh? They'll let you in all right, or my name isn't Beatriz Valdedulla."

She gave orders for them not to unhitch the carriage and had herself driven to the episcopal palace. When the duchess arrived at the entrance, Father Aleson was just coming out. "Those idiots have gotten here before me."

As a matter of fact, the Dominican fathers had gotten there first, because the bishop belonged to the same order.

"But that's no skin off my umbilical," murmured the duchess in an audible voice as she went up the stairway side by side with a green and sickly priest, a relative of His Holiness. Upon hearing what for him was a totally strange and inexplicable expression from the duchess, the young priest had such an intense attack of confusion that he tripped on one of the steps and almost fell flat on his face.

"What's going on here, I wonder. In what kind of a mood will I find Facundo, narrow-minded fool that he is?"

When Angustias ran off, not daring out of fear to let Xuantipa know, nor wishing out of love to tell Belarmino, she had used a subterfuge, a flanking maneuver in which she had been drilled by Felicita. The day of her flight, Angustias told Belarmino and Xuantipa she would be having dinner with the old maid and planned to spend the night there as she had done on other occasions. The next morning, Father Aleson, without knowing why or wherefore, received an anonymous note written to look like print. The anonymous message was a literary creation composed by Felicita; with cloying sentimentality she described the unhappy loves of Don Pedrito and Angustias up to the very moment when enslaving passion had swept them up in a veritable whirlpool and forced them to elope; she told how some heartless persecutors were planning to pursue the runaway lovers with the intention of destroying their happiness; with heavy charcoal she sketched the future portraits of a young girl without honor, despised by all, and of an unworthy priest; she hinted at what would become of them both if they were not permitted to marry. As an epilogue, she begged the Dominican fathers, as well as the Marquis and Marchioness of San Madrigal, to intercede with the bishop, with whom it was well known they were heavily involved, so that the wayward seminarian would be obliged to behave like an honorable man in his actions toward the girl. A dizzying and deep shudder of almost earthquake proportions spread through the huge humanity of Father Aleson. Angustias was a part of their establishment;

she lived under the protection of the robust Dominican order as the rose lives under the shelter of the cypresses in the conventual cloisters. The religious orders maintained this sanctum, this law of internal ego-centric peace, this defensive wall, this impregnable fort. At one time these orders enjoyed the holy right of asylum, which had been uni-versally respected like the outside moat of the cloister; they were not yet resigned to the fact that they had lost this privilege and those who came to them for protection and help were no longer inviolate. As far as Father Aleson was concerned, it wasn't Angustias who had been carried off, but the order of Saint Dominic. More important, the mem-bers of the Pilares chapter had been violated and threatened. A just sanction, adequate reparation had to be imposed, and this could only mean that Don Pedrito would have to give up his career and marry Angustias. Carrying this anonymous letter as though it were a mani-festo, the voluminous Dominican went to see Don Restituto and Doña Basilisa, who in his opinion had also suffered a small rape. The Neiras had made substantial gifts to the diocese and the bishop was very much in their debt. Together with Father Aleson, they came to a mutual agreement that they would humbly but energetically ask the bishop to force the seminarian to carry out the law of God and the law of man.

Until mealtime, Belarmino and Xuantipa didn't know anything at all of the elopement. Xuantipa, who had become converted into a rabid devotee of religious functions, had just come from spending three hours in the church of San Tirso. Father Aleson told them what had hap-pened, infusing them with faith in a happy ending. Belarmino put his hand to his heart, lowered his head and sobbed. Xuantipa, a diabolical joy showing in her face, gave free reign to the bitter gall she had been storing up. "The daughter of sin returns to sin, her natural element. I couldn't care less whether she marries or doesn't marry. What's more, I think God doesn't want her to marry."

"Silence, you scorpion-tongued creature," said the friar, irritated. "How does frequenting the temple benefit you?"

"It helps me to know God's justice," answered Xuantipa boldly.

"We would be in fine shape," replied the friar, "if divine justice were based on your sense of jurisprudence." The word *jurisprudence* was like a leaden slab falling on Xuantipa's tongue.

In the afternoon Father Aleson visited His Eminence. The bishop showed himself completely in agreement with his religious brother's opinion. The priest left the interview absolutely radiant. When he left, the duchess entered.

"And to what do I owe the honor of seeing my lady the duchess in this humble house?" asked the bishop gallantly, bowing profoundly as if he were dancing the pavane and looking quite silly.

"For the time being, ask this melancholy young man to get out, because I don't want any eyewitnesses around," said the duchess nervously pointing her finger at the timid and suffering relative.

"Manolín, leave us. And now, to what do I owe the honor which in this humble house . . . ?"

"Cut out those priestly habits and commonplace greetings. What are you talking about, humble houses? This is one of the best homes in the city."

"Well, but humility dwells within."

"We'll see about that in a minute."

"To what do I owe the honor . . . ?"

"You're asking me? Can't you guess? Well you should know, since that whale just floated out of here."

"Don't be cruel madam; calling poor Manolín a whale . . ."

"Don't pretend to be stupider than you are. I'm talking about Father Aleson."

"Ah-h-h-h!"

"Ah-h-h! Don't just stand there dumbfounded with your mouth wide open. I'm here for the same reason he was. What did you talk about?"

"Madam, I have not forgotten my past, my childhood. In any way I may be able to serve you as a man, I will do so willingly. As a pastor, as a prelate, however, I will do my duty with complete independence. If you ask me things about my life, I will reply; if you ask about matters concerning my office, I will be obliged to offend you, and mine is not the blame."

"Why don't you just take your bishop's crook and hit me with it a few times? That's the only thing left for you to do now. You were born a shepherd and you are a shepherd, thanks to whom?"

"To the duke, your husband; I don't deny it."

"You behave like a sheepherder and it seems that as far as you're concerned all of us are just so many sheep. You don't want to tell me what you talked to the friar about? I'll tell *you*, Facundo, because I'm not afraid to speak my mind. You spoke about Pedrito and Angustias. You want to marry them off. What a monstrosity, what an aberration, what a . . . !" And she broke out into a lyrical and resounding obscenity.

"You cannot refuse to give me your reasons."

"My dear duchess; the reasons are very clear. On the one hand, that young man is no longer in a position to be a good priest. On the other hand, an honest girl has been seduced and dishonored; she has lost her virginity. He who has wrenched this from her must return her honor."

"I'm going to answer only the last part, because that's what I find most amusing. What a joke! You speak about virginity the way children speak of fairies or the way older people talk about hidden treasures. You, who are supposed to be an erudite naturalist, what do you have to say about virginity among insects? What can you tell me about the virginity of the *Draco furibundus*? Isn't that the name of it?"

"We are not talking about insects but about Christians."

"Come on, Facundo! Since you live in another world, you haven't found out yet that virginity has the same value among Christians as among insects."

"Holy Mary, Mother of God! Don't get delirious, madam."

"You affirm that the girl's virginity has been wrenched from her. Would you swear to it? Did you examine her before the elopement? Were you there to see the spoliation?"

"Quiet. Quiet, madam, I beg of you."

"Why should I be quiet? . . . I like things out in the open. Does the truth frighten you?"

The duchess just waited. The bishop didn't know what to answer. The lady had begun to get the upper hand. Her tactics were the ones she always used; to baffle him and then leave him totally perplexed. Friar Facundo looked at her with distress and rancor in his eyes; he was resolved not to be won over.

"Who was the first one to use that word, was it you or me? You said that the girl's virginity had been wrenched from her, and you said it with as much aplomb and conviction as if you were speaking of a pickpocket you had seen stealing somebody's wallet. And if it should turn out there is neither pickpocket nor any such theft there, but rather two friends, and one of them, freely and willingly, gave his wallet to the other? Didn't that ever occur to you?"

"What occurred to me, madam, is what would have occurred to any pure and religious individual, that a man and a woman have run off alone and, consequently, the gentleman dishonored the lady."

"Those who dishonor her are you, all of you pure religious types. In this way your purity grows according to the facility with which you can invent impure acts; your religiousness multiplies with your malicious skill in imagining sin. What disgusting materialism! What lustful and tortured brains you pure and religious people must have! Your heads must be like those secret booths in carnival stalls with their wax figures and their 'for men only' signs. As a result, in your brain there is no room for the idea that a man and a woman can travel together very properly and purely. I'll make sure you never accompany *me* on a trip. How hideous! . . . I'm beginning to see you as a type of satyr . . ."

"Madam Duchess . . ." begged the prelate, almost with tears in his eyes.

"Don't be intimidated, Facundo. I've gone a bit too far, but I was joking. I know you could be left alone with impunity in the harem of the Great Turk and even with the choir of the eleven thousand virgins. Let's get to the point. I'll agree with you the young girl has suffered a certain . . . modification, and that after the trip she is not the same as she was before the trip. But, for God's sake! . . . that's just an insignificant modification. If they had cut her hair, it would be more noticeable. Nevertheless, and *this* I can't swallow, you called that slight modification a dishonor. What an absurd exaggeration! My ancestors had seigneurial rights to any bride's bed, and those maidens on whom this right was exercised thought it all a great honor. And your ancestors, by this I mean the bishops in those days, sanctioned that right without being scandalized or acting prudish about it."

Friar Facundo put his hands over his ears and shouted out in a burst of courage, "With all due respect, Madam Duchess . . . I cannot listen to such things."

The lady waited for the bishop to uncover his ears and then said, "Facundo, don't come to me with the scruples of a nun. If you don't want to listen to me, rebuff me with intelligent reasons, and I'll be quiet. Otherwise, I'll be forced to think that you're either stupid or obsessed."

"My lady, I recognize that you are much more clever than I and have a way of putting things so that I cannot respond correctly. But since I

132

respect and admire you, I am sure that in your conscience you recognize I am right and you are, however ably, defending a lost cause."

"That's enough hypocrisy! So you've turned out to be a mind reader, Facundo. Listen friend, I haven't come here for you to deal out the cards and guess my thoughts. I've come here, and you listen carefully to this, to stop the marriage. I'll use all the means I have to do it; if I can't achieve it with decent methods, I'll resort to indecent ones."

"Indecent, madam? What could a servant of God possibly fear?"

"If you were only a servant of God, perhaps you'd have nothing to fear. But since you also serve your vanity and ambition, you also must serve other people, particularly me and my husband."

The duchess had expected to see Friar Facundo become flustered at this point but the bishop, on the contrary, answered calmly, "That is true; a servant, a slave, as long as I am not ordered to do something that goes against my conscience."

"You want your nephew to get to be a deputy. That doesn't go against your conscience. Well, he won't make it. And as for you, hold on tight to your miter, because it could fall right off your head. On the other hand, if the idea seems more appealing to you, we'll send you somewhere where you can hide it—to the Republic of Andorra or to a diocese *in partibus*, where you'll be just like Quevedo or like the soul of Garibay.*"

The duchess was on the way to losing her case, already having lost her serenity.

"I cannot conceive how my lady the duchess is capable of such petty vengeance, particularly when, by refusing to oblige you, I am not allowing my lady the duchess to be responsible for an unworthy action."

"Well, I don't even recognize you any more. Now you've attacked me where I'm most vulnerable. You're right. I would be incapable of taking petty revenge; petty as it refers to me, but it wouldn't be so petty for you. I also think if you ever had the chance to take revenge,

---

**In partibus (infidelium)* literally means "in the lands occupied by the infidels" and refers to a bishop whose title is purely honorary and without power or jurisdiction. Francisco Quevedo y Villegas (1580–1645) was an important poet, novelist, and essayist whose turbulent life at Court made it necessary for him to flee to Sicily. The soul of Garibay was not wanted by God or claimed by the Devil.

you'd do it. Not me. That's the difference between those of noble birth and those who aren't. But you're not right in calling my attempt to stop this marriage an unworthy action. I've thought about it carefully. Both for him and for her, the best thing is not to have the wedding take place. It's best in every sense, including the religious one. At the beginning you said the young man was no longer in a position to be a good priest. That's where you're wrong. He is most certainly in a perfect position to become just that now that he has tasted both the sweetness and the pain of life. God prefers repentant sinners. Remember Saint Paul and Saint Augustine. Who is to say that by cooperating in this foolish marriage you're not nipping a future father of the Church in the bud? A great idea just came to me. Couldn't we put the girl in a convent? What a blessed solution to this conflict that would be! . . . In your hands, Facundo, you hold the power to perform a great service or do great harm. Make up your mind."

"What pleasure it gives me, madam duchess, to hear you offer arguments I can understand. You make me hesitate."

The prelate looked pensive. The duchess thought to herself, "It's in the bag now. He really did give me a hard time. My threat really hit the bull's-eye." The prelate was meditating, eyes cast down, the fingers of one hand twisting the topaz-encrusted cross hanging on his crimson chest. When he looked up, he pronounced the following words:

"This marriage must be consummated. If it is not wise, God will forbid it."

"Is that your final word?"

"That is my final word."

"I am really disappointed in you . . . Well, now I've got to make tracks."

"There will be many other occasions when I may be able to oblige you."

"Fat chance! Beatriz Valdedulla will never ever ask a favor of you again. Don't bother to see me out."

In the midst of her disappointment, the duchess had a pleasant and happy sensation. "This visit," she was thinking as she went down the steps of the episcopal palace, "has made me appreciate Facundo a bit more. He's a man of will and he does have a conscience after all. What a shame he doesn't have more brains in his skull. Before this, I used to pity him; now, I almost admire him." At any rate, the duchess was resolved not to agree to the marriage, convinced that it would turn out to be a very unhappy one. In the meanwhile, she kept Don Pedrito prisoner and let time run its course.

Angustias, on finding herself alone and abandoned in Inhiesta, wrote to her father, "I didn't leave you because I didn't love you, Father. We ran off only because we were sure we were going to be married, Father. We wanted you to come later and live with us, Father. Pedro loves you as much as I love you. Father, I have been abducted. I don't know what's happening to me, Father. I want to come back to you, Father." This letter crossed with another that Xuantipa had written right after dinner in the first flush of anger when she heard the news of Angustias's flight. "Do not come back to stain this house. Hide your shame where no one can find you, where no one knows you, where you don't know us." When Belarmino received Angustias's letter, he laughed and cried at the same time. He enthusiastically kissed the paper itself and sobbed, "Oh, daughter of my entrails, daughter of my entrails," as a mother might say. He went upstairs to see Father Aleson and ask him if Angustias was on her way.

"Well, of course she's coming. She's going to get married. Tomorrow's the day. Early in the morning we'll go to get her. I'm going with another member of the order."

"She is coming, she is coming," sobbed Belarmino, his eyes filling with tears, a smile on his lips.

When the priests reached Inhiesta, Angustias had disappeared. The innkeeper's wife handed them a piece of paper the girl had left behind in the room. It was Xuantipa's letter.

"If that woman were here," said Father Aleson after reading the letter, "I swear to you, Father Cosmén, I would strangle her with my own hands; that's how enraged I am by her infamous action. Poor child, poor infant; now lost forever! And this is going to kill Belarmino, our inoffensive, crazy, and angelic Belarmino. We'll have to invent a kindly deceit. God won't hold it against us since He will realize our good intentions." And over the face of that huge mass of a man there spread a lachrymose, human tenderness as if the sun were melting the snow on the peaks of the highest mountains.

The kindly deceit of Father Aleson was to tell Belarmino that Angustias, for the sake of appearances, had taken up residence in a convent, there to await her wedding day. So that, for the time being, and in order to avoid problems, the best and most prudent thing would be for father and daughter not to see each other.

Father Aleson had Xuantipa come to see him alone; he asked her to sit down and then leaning over in order to intimidate her with that massiveness of his which threatened to annihilate her, he said, "You infernal woman, you are damned without remission. It wasn't enough you mercilessly made a martyr of your husband. Now you have dashed an innocent creature into the abyss. Revel in your satanic joy! You are damned without remission."

In order to have been as imposing as he would have liked, Father Aleson needed a much more thunderous voice. But since Xuantipa was so afraid of Hell, the flutelike voice of the friar sounded to her as if it were a trumpet being played on Judgment Day.

"Father, forgive . . ." she stuttered, completely shaken.

"Shut your sulfurous mouth. In order for your terrible crime to be forgiven, you will have to manifest an inflexible desire to mend your ways and promise me that never, never, for any reason whatsoever, will you say an unpleasant word to Belarmino, nor will you mention his daughter, that child who is more than just a daughter to him although not of his flesh, that creature whom he has now lost, thanks to you."

In effect, Xuantipa left this interview completely annihilated, frightened to the marrow of her bones for the rest of her life.

And it continued to rain in the old city of granite; and there was heavy affliction, tears, and mourning even in the most hardened of hearts. Imagine, then, how it must have been in the tender and sensitive ones.

Felicita had not seen her adored Novillo for three days, the only three consecutive days of absence in many a year. No matter how much it rained, Novillo had never stopped coming to Ruera Street, well protected by his galoshes, leather breeches, a hooded raincoat, and an umbrella. He would take shelter in a doorway and there keep watch over the sovereign queen of his heart. What could have happened now? Wrapped in a cotton robe and wearing cloth slippers, Felicita spent hours and hours, day and night, immobile, dried up, calcified, waxen, in the glass enclosed balcony; among those withered flowers that seemed to be made of rags, and behind the little birds stiff with cold, looking as if they had been stuffed, she looked like a museum mummy in a glass case. From time to time, an old woman in wooden shoes would pass by with her underskirts of yellow flannel lifted up over her head like a kerchief. The sound of the shoes against the paving stones resounded with a funereal echo, as though she were walking on empty tombs. What could possibly have happened to Anselmo? Could he be angry? Could he have been opposed to the marriage between Don Pedro and Angustias? Had he found out that the anonymous letter written to Father Aleson was Felicita's doing? My God, my God, what gnawing uncertainty! Felicita sobbed silently, wishing for death. She couldn't sleep; she couldn't eat.

"Eat something, even if it's only a hard-boiled egg," said her servant Telva. "Look, you're already too thin and if you don't eat, your bones are going to poke right through your skin."

"Oh, I wish they would make holes in it like a screen to let my soul push through like wheat through a sieve. Why do I want a soul in my body? What good has it done me? Who has offered to buy it, to use it as a fertile seed?"

These rhetorical plaints left Telva completely cold. "The mistress is as crazy as a loon," she thought to herself.

After four days, Felicita couldn't stand it any more and sent Telva to the Commerce Hotel to inquire discreetly what had happened to Don Anselmo. When she came back, Telva didn't beat around the bush and just blurted out what she had learned.

"Well, Don Anselmo is very sick with pneumonia."

Felicita swooned. When she came to, and in spite of the fact that she didn't have the strength to stand up, she asked for her overcoat, her kerchief, her boots.

"What do you intend to do, miss?"

"Fly to his side."

"Don't forget he's a bachelor and you're a maiden lady; idle tongues are bound to talk about whether you did or you didn't."

"He is my fiancé. I don't care what they say. The heart has its reasons above and beyond mere human habit. I cannot leave the man I love to die alone, abandoned in a lonely hotel room."

"If that's the reason you're going, don't bother. Don Anselmo is well taken care of. He's got a nun there, and, besides, the duchess and Apolonio won't leave his side for a minute. Anyhow, as far as I could make out there's not much chance of his dying. Sit down; calm down; have something to drink—a cup of tea."

Completely unraveled, Felicita stretched out on the sofa; her eyes, open wide, fixed on the ceiling.

"Telva."

"Miss."

"Go see how he is."

"Miss, I just came from there."

"Do as I say. Go and see how he is. Come back with all the details."

Telva went, mumbling unhappily to herself.

"What's that noise?" murmured Felicita, trembling as she tried to raise herself up. "It sounds as if someone's nailing a coffin shut . . . Now they're digging a ditch."

But it was just a pair of wooden shoes striking against the pavement. Felicita stretched out again on the sofa.

"What's that noise?" she murmured, standing up completely terror-stricken. "It sounds like a swarm of spirits buzzing around. Can I be hearing voices from the other world?"

But it was just the wind blowing through the cracks. Felicita lay down again on the sofa.

"What's that noise?" murmured Felicita, falling to her knees, delirious. "I hear the droning of prayers and the sound of sputtering candles. They're offering up the prayer for the dead. It's Anselmo. Anselmo is dead!"

But it was the sound of rain against the windows.

When Telva came back, Felicita was on her knees, praying.

"Don Anselmo is a little better."

Felicita began to touch the servant. "Am I dreaming? Is it really you? Am I still made of flesh? Are we both ghosts?"

Telva thought to herself, "You, flesh? Pure bone, and already gone brittle. Goats? You're a vain goat all right."

Felicita continued, "Did you speak? I thought I heard a voice. What did you say?"

"I said that Don Anselmo is a little better."

"Bring some oil, all the oil we have in the kitchen."

"Well it's about time you decided to eat something."

"Get me a large bowl and bring the box of prayer candles. Find all the candles we have in the house."

On top of the bureau was an image of the Virgin of Covadonga. Felicita lit a virtual bonfire in front of it. Kneeling, she pleaded, "Oh, dear lady, save his life! You were an unblemished virgin, but you were married. Save his life, dear lady! Dear lady! You were married and you had a son! Save him for me, dear lady, so that we too may get married even if I remain a virgin and have no son at all!"

Felicita felt her breast to be overflowing with faith. She returned to the sofa and rested her head, deep in thought. "The Virgin will preserve him for me and we will be married. It's foolish for us to go on like this." A mental pause . . . "I went a bit too far when I told the Virgin that I didn't care about having children. I would very much like to have children. Well, the truth is I didn't really promise her that I wouldn't have children. I'm sure she understood."

"Telva, go and see how Don Anselmo is."

"Señorita, I just came back from there."

"Do as I tell you. Go see how he is."

Telva started off again, mumbling as before.

"Telva, don't go; don't leave me alone. I am frightened." A brief pause. "Go, yes, Telva—go. I will overcome my weakness . . . No, don't go! I'm frightened, so frightened . . ."

"Well, what am I supposed to do, split myself in two?"

Felicita began to cry.

"How should I know . . . how should I know? Split *me* in two; leave the dead part here and take the living part with you. Carry me off in your arms, hidden away, like an infant child."

"Miss, you're losing your marbles. Come now, calm down—go ahead and cry if you want to; tears will do you good."

Night had already fallen. With her tears Felicita had become more sweetly and unconsciously disconsolate and resigned; stretched out on the sofa, she went off to sleep like a child. Telva didn't want to disturb her sleep and left her alone, but only after mumbling, "When she wakes up, she'll go to bed. Christ, what arrogance . . . and what lusting after anything in pants!"

Felicita awakened at dawn. A livid and inanimate clarity poured in through the balcony window; it was like dawn beyond the grave. The

139

candles on the bureau had burned out. The small prayer candles that were still glowing, had begun to sputter with an incorporeal shudder like a vague, golden memory. Felicita felt that an invisible hand was pressing against her heart. She couldn't breathe. A rooster crowed. An incredibly strange voice echoed inside Felicita's head, "This is the hour in which Lucifer falls into Avernus, and the souls of the just fly up to God." Felicita began to shriek wildly. Telva came running, half dressed.

"Hurry, hurry!" gasped Felicita, "come with me."

The servant wondered whether she should use force to control her mistress, but the light in Felicita's eyes was so phosphorescent, that Telva could do nothing but obey. They went out into the street. There was a driving rain. They huddled under their huge, violet-colored umbrella.

"But where are we going at this hour? It's too early for mass."

Felicita heard nothing. Telva insisted. Felicita then said, as if talking to herself, "Anselmo is in the throes of death."

They reached the Commerce Hotel. It was open and there was a waiter standing watch.

"Don Anselmo is dying," said Felicita.

"Yes, madam, he's croaking for sure," answered the waiter.

"I'm going up to his room. Show me the way," ordered Felicita.

"But no one's allowed in. The oven isn't hot enough yet for the biscuits."

"I'm going in because I have every right to go in. No one has more right than I. Show me the way. Don't even bother, I don't need a guide. I will go straight to his side. I have never been here before, but the eyes of my soul will lead me there."

"Wait, madam. I'll go with you to let them know you're here. Who shall I say is calling?"

"Felicita, just Felicita."

Novillo was close to the end. At the head of the bed stood Apolonio and Chapaprieta, the chaplain of the Somavia household, who held in his hand the book from which he had just read the prayer commending Anselmo's soul to God. On the other side of the bed was a nun who was wiping away the sweat that ran in streams down Novillo's forehead and bald spot. The wig could be seen hanging from one of the bed-posts. His false teeth were submerged in a glass of water on the night

140

table. Without his teeth and his toupee, his skin having turned a greenish black and sagging in spots like an animal hide, his eyes deep in his head, his beard and moustache completely white, Novillo was not even a shadow of his former self. The only thing that still remained of his former splendor was the bulging stomach that formed an arch under the sheets. That beautiful heart of his, so overworked by its constrained love, no longer wished to be in charge of things. Novillo was choking to death. The first-aid attendant who was standing next to the nun had given him an oxygen balloon to help him breathe; the truth of the matter was, there was no sure way of knowing if the balloon was inflating Novillo, or if Novillo was blowing up the balloon. He hadn't lost consciousness. Every so often he raised his arms and then let them fall heavily to the bed. From time to time he struggled to pry open his fleshy eyelids, and his deepset, sad eyes looked gratefully at those who surrounded the bed.

When the waiter knocked at the door, the duchess was looking for a bottle of medicine among the jars in the cabinet. She held a flask in her hand that was labeled, "Essence of the River Lethe. Indelible Hair Dye." "I'm going to try this stuff," she thought to herself. "It was undoubtedly a present from that crazy husband of mine." When she heard the knocking at the door, she made a gesture to the others not to move as she went to open it.

"Who is it?"

"Felicita," answered the waiter.

The voice and the name reached Novillo's ears. He was overcome by an attack of intense trembling. With awkward and useless movements, he reached out toward the toupee and his false teeth. The duchess, who had slammed the door shut, was looking at Novillo.

"Don't let her see me like this . . ." stammered Novillo in a thin voice that was hardly audible.

At that, the duchess went outside, grabbed Felicita by the arm and dragged her away to an empty room where she pushed her into a chair. "You just be quiet in here."

"My place is at his side, at the head of the bed, so I can breathe in his last sigh. Let them marry us in *articulo mortis*. He is dying."

"Unfortunately, that's true. And if you love him, the least you can do is let him die in peace."

"He will not die in peace if I am not there beside him."

"You're all wrong on that score. Anselmo doesn't want you to see him in this condition."

"That is a lie! Calumny! Did he himself say that?"

"Yes, he said that."

"This is impossible, impossible!" shouted Felicita, frenetically. *"Articulo mortis, articulo mortis!"*

"My dear lady, don't create such a scene . . . all the other guests are sleeping; and don't make me waste any more time. I'll explain it all to you later."

And the duchess left the room, locking Felicita inside.

Novillo died an hour later. Before he passed away, he motioned to the duchess and mumbled his last words to her. "Felicita . . . forgive . . . not to marry . . . loved, I loved . . . I am dying . . . I love . . . she . . ."

They closed Novillo's eyes, tied up his jaw with a handkerchief, intertwined the fingers of his hands, and then all of them knelt down sadly, deeply touched with pity and sympathy. They prayed briefly. The duchess, in the low and unctious voice customarily used in prayers for the dead, slowly pronounced a few words, as though she were thinking out loud. "The duke will not again find a political servant who was so humble and at the same time so daring. It doesn't seem possible that this man, a terror at the polls, a man who was better than anyone at thinking up illegal rackets and carrying them off by sheer nerve, was basically a simple, frank, sentimental, and frightened creature. That's life," and, after a pause, she added, "And that's death! Rest in peace, brave Novillo; good Novillo; faithful Novillo; lover Novillo."

The duchess went to communicate the sad news to Felicita. During the duchess's absence, a singularly brilliant and sharp idea had made itself felt vividly and with penetrating pain in Felicita's soul. "Anselmo caught this case of pneumonia, or rather this case of pneumonia caught Anselmo . . ." and here Felicita's imagination actually saw this pneumonia as a nocturnal vampire, flying in the dark of night through wind and rain. She continued with her thoughts, "This pneumonia trapped Anselmo when he went to Inhiesta in pursuit of Don Pedrito and Angustias. If those two had not run off, Anselmo would not have been caught by pneumonia. I was the one who organized their elopement. Therefore, I am the one who is guilty of Anselmo's death. I am the assassin; I have treacherously killed him; yes, I murdered him."

The duchess went up to her, but before she could open her mouth,

Felicita spoke. "I know what you're going to tell me, my lady. I know, and I'd rather not hear the accusation from someone else's lips. I am guilty and I confess. Take me off to prison, lead me to the vile garrote. I have killed him."

"Don't get delirious, dear woman. Take courage and listen to what I have to say. I am bringing you a very bitter pill to swallow, but with a small grain of sweetness as consolation."

"There is no consolation for me. I have killed him and he has accused me of the crime; that is the reason he didn't want to receive me before he died."

"If Anselmo refused to see you, it was because of his love for you. He wanted you always to remember him as a pleasant and attractive man, and not in that deplorably sad state to which he had been reduced by his sickness. That was the reason. Before he died, he entrusted me with a message for you. He wanted you to forgive him for never having married you. He always loved you and he died loving you. Those were his last words."

A few moments of stupor. Felicita remained motionless, as if congealed. She lost her will and her self-control. Her flesh, so thin and dried up, finally split, and out through the openings, in clamorous torrents, spilled the most secret particles of her soul, those feelings that only rarely escape from the mystery of consciousness—the very marrow of the spirit that fears the light and is terrified of words.

"He desired me and I desired him!" shouted Felicita, pulling at her hair, the only young and beautiful thing she owned, and letting its black abundance fall loose about her shoulders. "Why didn't he speak? What do I mean, speak? A gesture, one single gesture, a look in his eyes, the lifting of a finger, the slightest of signals, and I would have thrown myself into his arms; I would have given myself to him . . . he would have embraced me and annihilated me with love. I would have been consumed with passionate kisses . . ."

"Felicita, don't forget there are guests in the rooms next door who can hear everything you say."

"I will shout it to the whole world. Let the heavens and the earth, God and Satan both hear me. I will even send word to the newspapers. Everything, everything, everything; my life, the small fortune I inherited from my parents, my well-being, my honor, all of this I would have given just for one second, only one second of love. Why do I want to go on living? Why should I want wealth? What well-being can I now have? What good is honor and virginity to me now?"

The duchess thought to herself, "Felicita's ideas about virginity are different from the bishop's. I wish poor old Facundo could hear this."

"Get hold of yourself, Felicita," advised the duchess. "You're right, but nothing can be changed by these belated lamentations."

Felicita fell into a kind of torpor, but it didn't last long.

"I want to see Anselmo," she said, standing up.

"I don't approve of this whim," commented the duchess. "The shock will be too unpleasant for you."

Felicita obstinately insisted, and the duchess finally gave in. On the way to Anselmo's room, Felicita spoke. "The ground is fleeing beneath the soles of my feet, the walls are undulating, the world is being carved into bits and pieces, and the pieces are circling in the air." These strange phenomena or hallucinations in which Felicita felt herself involved and which were probably caused by her weakened state, became exaggerated when she entered the chamber where Anselmo's body was lying. It semed to her that the decomposition and quartering to which the world had fallen victim were more furiously and absurdly verified, as if by some diabolical scheme, in Anselmo Novillo's cadaver. His hair had come loose from his scalp and it was swinging on one of the bedposts. His teeth, even and sparkling white, had leapt, gums and all, right from his mouth into a glass of water. His terrifyingly huge stomach seemed to be expanding, and it was almost at the point of breaking the ties that connected it to the rest of his body.

Felicita couldn't hold back a heart-rending cry as she covered her eyes with her hands. Just as the Duke of Gandía had reacted when he stood before the cadaver of the empress, Felicita also decided then and there never to fall in love again with changeable and perishable images, but, instead, to consecrate her virginity to God.

The human soul possesses greatness because, like all great things, it is comprised of an infinite number of small things. For that reason, during those painful crises when the soul necessarily revolves around itself, it can happen that the rotary axis is some ridiculous and petty object. Felicita, a few days after she became a widowed virgin, went to visit Father Aleson in order to inquire about the monastic regime of the various available feminine religious orders, and also to find out about a ridiculously petty item that, for her, was of extreme importance

—the habits worn by the nuns in each one of these orders. Felicita knew that some of the habits were lovely and even quite elegant, if one could be permitted such a profane expression to describe these things. On those two points, the regime and the habit, would depend Felicita's choice. When she entered the Neiras' house, she was surprised not to see Belarmino in his cubicle. Where was he?

Father Aleson had told Belarmino that until the day of her wedding, Angustias would live in the Carmelite convent located on the outskirts of Pilares. Belarmino asked for permission to walk around the convent grounds every afternoon.

"As long as you promise not to try to see your daughter, I grant you permission."

Belarmino promised and he kept his word. It was still raining those first few days. Sloshing through puddles, Belarmino would reach the convent all covered with mud. He sought shelter under the portico of the convent, and there, squatting like a philosopher, he let the hours pass by. The tremolo of a harmonium could be heard coming down to him from above and then, moving along the silent pavement, the sound would reach him in short, buoyant skips and jumps, like birds hopping along the ground. He also heard the monastic chants. Belarmino was fond of religious chanting—*ne impedias musicam* is what the Bible says. "Perhaps Angustias is also singing in the choir; they have undoubtedly taught her how," thought Belarmino. And he made an effort to unravel the blue, celestial voice of Angustias from the polychromatic skein of the chorus. No, Angustias was not singing. If she were, the unique ray of light of her voice would have penetrated the penumbra of Belarmino's soul, just as only one beam of the sun's rays penetrates the vault of a church.

Then the weather cleared up. It was the autumnal season, honey-colored, a silvery velvet mist covering the earth and making it look like a fuzzy ripe peach. Above the walls of the convent garden arose the rigid, black cypress trees like the prologue to a mystical trance, the perfect model of the vertical will and aspiration toward this moment of rapture; and, too, there were the anemic, long-suffering willows—called "swoons" by the local populace—which were like the fatigue and exhaustion that constitute the sweet epilogue to the mystic spasm; and the veined, muscular apple trees, with branches like gnarled fingers displaying small red apples that didn't at all suggest the image of sin but only peccadilloes. To the eye, all was peaceful in the convent garden; for the ear, there was the querulous racket of the evening sparrows.

Belarmino sat down at the foot of the walls and contemplated the fields with their yellowish fuzz, and he saw how they exhaled an opalescent and tenuous vapor. His soul too was like a soft, level field shaded in mist. No longer using words, or even representative signs, he thought and felt within this internal mist. He felt that his daughter had not been in the convent before and that the others had wanted to deceive him out of kindness. That is to say, they hadn't really deceived him, he had deceived himself and the rest of them had also been duped. But now his daughter *was* in the convent. How could that be? Outside of one's self, thought Belarmino, nothing existed. The world was a sensual illusion, a mirage of the imagination. The outside world was an apparent and deceitful creation of the inner world. Therefore, Belarmino resolved to put his inner world in peaceful and harmonious order and, in that way, the exterior world—nothing but an echo or a sensual image of the other—would also be ordered. He would chase away, or pay no attention to, the hidden specters that occasionally forced their way in and disturbed the harmony of the soul's dominion, beclouding the heart's warm light. They were phantoms that illogically emanated from the imagination and projected themselves against the outside world in the form of hateful and aggressive figures, as if they really existed in flesh and bone and were not merely hallucinations. Belarmino resolved that Xuantipa no longer existed; that Bellido, the usurer, did not exist; that neither Apolonio nor his son, Angustias's seducer, existed; and that the elopement had never taken place—how hard it was for him to suppress in his soul this budding hallucination, this illusory reality! . . . Angustias, yes, she existed—as if he himself had conceived and created her; she was the daughter of his soul and of his entrails—how could she not exist? She existed, and of her own very free and unanimous will (hers and her father's), she was now under the protection of the Carmelites where the scorn of the outside and apparent world and her desire for absolute and perfect peace had led her. She had no faith in the exterior world either. It was not just by coincidence that Angustias was Belarmino's daughter. And every day, Belarmino took his afternoon walk around the Carmelite convent that he might communicate by mysterious and wondrous means with this imaginary daughter of his who had been entirely engendered by him in his paternally tender and creative soul.

It was then that Belarmino abandoned the philosophic profession and gave up shoe repairing. Formerly, when you saw Belarmino, you couldn't help but think, Saint Francis of Assisi must have been like that; at least he must have had the same kind of face. Now, Belarmino was the living image of another Saint Francis, the one sculpted by Luca della Robbia, with his pure, childlike features, his glassy eyes and his broad temples. Plato also had broad temples. The friars and the Neiras left Belarmino in peace so that he could live as he wished, as an innocent child of God who could do no harm to anyone. One of his last lessons consisted of a kind of very brief epilogue which he confided to Escobar, the Alligator, and which the latter was fortunate enough to be able to translate into everyday language. It went like this:

Once upon a time there was a man who, because he felt and thought so much, used to speak very little and very softly. He didn't speak much because he could see so many things in each individual thing that he could never find an adequate way to express himself. Everyone called him a fool. This same man, when he learned to express all the things he discovered in one single word, spoke more than anyone else. Everyone called him a charlatan. But when the man, instead of seeing so many things in one thing, reached the point of seeing one and the same thing in all different things— because he had penetrated the sense and true meaning of everything—he never spoke a word again. And everyone called him mad.

Chapter Seven

PEDRO AND ANGUSTIAS

After preaching the long Good Friday sermon, Don Guillén's voice was used up, cracked, and even a bit coarse. Standing for two hours before an audience of kings, heirs to the throne, and other members of the courtly retinue, he had enacted the drama of dramas, the Passion of the Son of God. His face had not yet cast off the expression of the actor, of the tragic mask. I don't mean to give the impression that Don Guillén was merely a histrionic player and that, returning to the wings after a great hypocritical performance on stage, he only pretended to be still dominated by terror, rigid with pathos, and unable to recover the elasticity and mobility of his facial muscles. The story has it that when the Greek actor Polus used to perform in Sophocles' play *Electra* he would bring the urn that held the ashes of his own son on stage so the expression of his pain would be sincere and touch the audience. That afternoon, while portraying the drama of Calvary, Don Guillén had undoubtedly brought forth the urn hidden in his heart which contained the ashes of his own life, ashes smoldering still. Here it was, hours later, and his eyes, his cheeks, his mouth, the position of his head, his torso and his arms were like graphic signs that could be easily interpreted—where one could read a transcription of the divine words, *Tristis est anima mea usque ad mortem;* my soul is sad even unto death.

I feared that if Don Guillén remained in this frame of mind he would not continue to tell me the story of his inner life. I remembered what he had told me the night before, that his father, Apolonio, believed in the Buddhist principle that each man's destiny is written on his forehead in invisible letters. Perhaps, I thought, the letters inscribed on

148

Don Guillén's forehead are not completely invisible and the diversity of his baptismal names indicates a corresponding diversity of personalities. And so, I hoped that, after an adequate period of time, the personality of the peaceful and expansive man would overcome the passionate, sad, and taciturn one and then Don Guillén would continue his account. In order to make this transition easier, I spoke about things not related to what was troubling him but not so irrelevant as to be frivolous or silly. I noticed that the storm clouds of the tragic mask were passing away and that the weather showed signs of improving. A hint of a smile insinuated itself across his lips. It was the advent of the effusive man.

"Last night," Don Guillén said finally, "I began to tell you innumerable trivial things of only slight interest. But even the merest flicker of interest would fade away if we left the story unfinished. Last night I said good-bye to you from the doors of the conciliar seminary in Pilares. Now, I invite you to enter with me. Twelve long years of residence; but don't get frightened. We can compress these years so that they will be reduced to a mere quarter of an hour. To consider time to come is frightening; and yet time doesn't take up any space; we do not realize that it doesn't exist until it has passed. We are proud of ourselves if we can very quickly conquer, piece by piece, this great block of future time. But then we are in the same position as the miser who did nothing else but put away pieces of gold in a coffer while each ounce disappeared without ever reaching the bottom of the chest. Just consider the inadequacy of language as regards time and a man's age. In Spanish one says, 'this child has only a few years,' or 'this old man has many years.' How foolish! The child is the one who has many years and the old man is the one who has a few, very few years, perhaps months, perhaps days, perhaps only hours—because past time no longer exists."

Those ideas, although subtle and original, did not seem at all pertinent to me. What I wanted to know were not Don Guillén's ideas, but his life and feelings. I cut him short with what I thought was clever irony.

"You are quite right. I never imagined that in the seminaries students were taught to converse in paradoxes in such a synthetic, expressive way."

"Of course they aren't!" exclaimed Don Guillén, laughing happily.

"I understand, I see what you're after . . . you want me to realize I have put you in the seminary for just fifteen minutes and you don't want to stay in this place for a second longer than is absolutely necessary. Well the door has been closed behind us. In your nostrils, your eyes, your ears, on your tongue, in your sense of touch, and in your soul, you receive an impression of mildew—Pilares mildew—that spongy and viscous mold found, together with earthworms, in humid, dark, and quiet corners. We will remain in one of those corners for only fifteen minutes; then we might live for another hundred years, and yet our senses could never shake the sensation of mildew, of that mossy verdigris, that clamminess in the marrow of the bone and the proximity of so many bloodless worms, of those ductile and undulating yellow wax candles. The candles referred to are, of course, my fellow seminarians. Most of them came from very humble backgrounds, from the brambles and bowels of the soil; they belonged to poor peasant families who had saved just enough to cover the modest room and board expenses of the seminary for one son—at that time, little more than a *peseta* per day.

"They belonged to a species somewhere between pure animality and a rudimentary branch of the human race. Good Lord! What loves and what hates! . . . Some had heads perfectly flat and obtuse in the back— where there couldn't possibly be room for a cerebellum. Others among them had heads that were pyramidal and came to an exaggerated point on top. I remember wondering, where are they going to find space on those heads for the tonsure? Some of the owners of these craniums sit beside me today on the cathedral council; all of them have been invested with great authority and hold sway to some extent over the private realm of the family as well as over the more public realm of society. The strange thing is that those wild and muscular creatures with their narrow foreheads and closely knit brows, their animal eyes and bronze-colored skin, had hardly entered the seminary before they acquired the colorless, bloodless pallor of worms and wax. Nonetheless, it was certain that although they ate quite badly in their new residence (wormy chickpeas, lentils mixed with pebbles, sebaceous strips of meat, ratty cheese, fruitless hazelnuts and walnuts), they still ate better than they had in their own homes. An inexplicable phenomenon! There were about two hundred of us. Among so many, it was only natural there would be sons from families that were well-off financially, some whose fathers were prosperous artisans, or shopkeepers, and even a couple who belonged to the middle class. In this last category there was the son of an attorney, one Stanislao Correa; a very timid, delicate young man, virginal and lily-white, whom the others jeeringly called by the nickname of Saint Stanislao of the Powder Puff, thus in their gross way making his life miserable. How barbaric they were! I also had some pretty bad moments. What really bothered them was the fact that I didn't lose my healthy complexion. I've always been as rosy-cheeked as I am now. The most boorish and poverty-stricken among them would fall all over those of us who had some money, demanding that we share it with them whether we liked it or not. They would bribe the servants and have them buy bits of food and drink, particularly white wine. They were inordinately fond of white wine. Because wine was prohibited in the seminary and no one was allowed to have bottles around, they hit upon a rather repugnant scheme to keep it hidden; they poured it into chamberpots and drank from them as if they were earthen jugs. We used to sleep in large communal dormitories that were practically never swept. The floor was covered with nutshells, orange peels, and the skins of other fruits in season. Some of the older ones and even the senior members of the group would escape at night to 'chase girls,' as they put it. The rest of us used to witness the escapades, that is, the act of flight. On the side of the bedrooms, the seminary gave onto a very high cliff situated on the outskirts of the city. The fugitive had to be in good physical condition and able to stand heights without getting dizzy. The escape apparatus was made up of no less than twenty bed sheets, which some of the seminarians, those coming from the coastal villages, would tie together with sailors' knots. Many times, as a joke played on these revelers, the others removed the sheet ladder and didn't throw it down to them until early in the morning, just in time for these gadabouts to appear at early morning inspection; as a result, many of those who went out at night had to spend several anxious hours down below among the brambles and the filth of the ditch, sometimes even in the rain. Well, that was the atmosphere in which the future ministers of God were hatched. How many of them really had a vocation for it? How many of them had headed for the seminary following the dictates of a persuasive inner voice, of an unavoidable star?

"I used to hear them tell spicy tales about the village priests, their drinking habits, the comfortable life they lived, the love affairs they had for amusement and the respect and obedience they enjoyed from the faithful. They would be panting in anticipation of how they would spend such a delightful and lazy life in a rural parish, side by side with a housekeeper and a niece, for almost all of them believed theoretically and cynically in polygamy. Did I have a vocation? I'm not sure if by reacting in anger against my companions, I had reached the point where I was convinced that I felt a great vocation. At times I'm very sentimental. In those days I was even more so. Canonical duties, Church ceremonies, the sound of the organ, the glowing of the lights, the mysterious coyness of the religious images; all this touched me deeply, stirred me to the very depths of my soul and this grew to be even more the case as I began to understand Latin.

"It is true that the liturgy of the Catholic church is very beautiful, very beautiful and very sensual—just right for temperaments that are delicately voluptuous. Upon reading the lives of the saints, especially the female saints, you can observe that their wild seizures and mystical agitations coincide with the two critical ages: puberty and menopause. A materialist would give a low and vulgar significance to this phenomenon; he would say that religious sentiment is just a disguised sexual emotion. For a spiritualist, the phenomenon has a more natural and deeper explanation. Since in these critical ages it is the body, which with indefatigable tenacity tries to impose its control over the soul, it is only natural that in the case of those individuals with fine spiritual textures, the spirit should desperately attempt to divorce itself from matter and, in opposition to the precarious and fugitive desires of the flesh, offer up an absolute and incorruptible object in which the most exalted yearnings can be found, extracting the purest and most lasting delights from it. Someone is bound to say to me that this only happens in the case of sickly or abnormal individuals. I concede that. But extraordinary intelligence, noble and uncommon sentiments, the rare ability to produce beauty . . . aren't they also abnormalities, sicknesses . . . just as the pearl is a sickness in the oyster? Inert matter in a state of equilibrium is only partial reality. Substance in transformation, in its decompositional stage, is integral reality because in it life and new energies are being created. And energy is the spiritual element of the universe. I don't mean to sound boastful . . . What would be the sense of boasting about this? . . . I am a rather normal and stable individual. But my boorish classmates were even much more so. I would attend the Church services with deep feelings of emotional involvement, even though I never reached the point of ecstasy or rapture; *they* were like a pack of dogs at mass. During the first four years in the seminary when it is customary to devote most of your time to the study of Latin, I applied myself to perfecting my knowledge of that language; they finished their four academic years knowing less Latin than a Miura bull. I liked languages. The duchess had begun to teach me French and later, on my own, I worked at it some more until I knew it well. I also began studying English. My only distractions came from studying and reading, and this was something my fellow seminarians couldn't understand. My favorite book was the breviary.

"Now I ask you to bear with me if I speak at some length about the breviary."

Don Guillén's Disquisition on the Poetry of the Breviary

"How lucky I am that its hymns have influenced my life! . . . I know many of them by heart and have even translated some of them into Spanish. What a pity I'm not a good poet. Spaniards don't know Christian poetry. The great French poets, Corneille, Racine, and others have transposed these hymns into delightful French verse. People spontaneously show their true nature and bare their souls by the way they love, through their preferences. Passionate Corneille always translates the equally passionate Saint Ambrose; the more cerebral and refined Racine translates Prudentius, that meticulous artisan of liturgical poetry. In the second stanza of the hymn to *Laudes,* to be sung on the sixth day of the week, Prudentius says, *Volvamus obscurum nihil,* and in the third stanza, *Ne noxa corpus inquinet.* In these two lines of poetry, Racine thought he had come upon a remote harbinger of Boileau's *Aesthetics,* and he therefore translated them as *Et que la vérité brille en tous nos discours,* and *qu'un frein legitime—Aux lois de la raison asservisse les sens.* I know of no Spanish poet who has had the idea of anointing himself with the dense and amorous oil of Christian poetry. The most primitive and archaic hymns were the ones that touched me with the sweetest violence. So, ever since those very first years in the seminary I have been rash enough to think that the Christian church has changed in temper over the course of centuries; at first a spiritual power and apostle of social charity, it was later transformed into a political force. With this change, what it gained in wealth and influence it lost in effectiveness, in stability, for all political powers are hateful and therefore perishable. These early and infantile hymns suited the simple and inflammable souls that used to chant them together in the humble temples of worship. Those innocent and pious creatures considered it proper and wise for the clergy to live with women, and the Church permitted ecclesiastical concubinage. I used to ask myself then why the Church nowadays does not allow its priests to marry. It would alleviate so much pain . . . and I used to think about it not because I felt particularly inclined, nor because I had fallen in love with any particular woman, but because I used to observe and feel compassion for my companions. My falling in love came later; and the go-between was the breviary.

"The first Christian bard was Saint Ambrose of Milan whose heart was like a grain of incense among the burning coals. One author has said of Saint Ambrose that he taught Latin how to pray. In the hymn *Aeterna Christi Munera,* which is sung during matins on the day of the Apostles, Saint Ambrose expresses himself thus:

> *Devota sanctorum Fides,*
> *Invicta spes credentium,*
> *Perfecta Christi charitas*
> *Mundi triumphat principem.*

'In you, the religious faith of the saints, the triumphant hope of all believers, the perfect charity of Christ, triumph over the princes of the world.' Isn't that admirable simplicity and clarity? Nothing here of authority or political power. Faith, hope, and charity, that's it; love willingly offered and not out of a sense of duty. These three theological virtues suffice to allow the Christian to triumph over decaying earthly principalities. That was the social and spiritual mission of the early Church, of the Apostolic church. To celebrate the day of the Apostles Saint Peter and Saint Paul, the breviary has a hymn composed by Elpis of Sicily, the wife of Boethius, the philosopher. This hymn is sung in the Vatican, to the music of Palestrina, by a very large chorus situated above

154

Saint Peter's tomb and under Michelangelo's dome. The last stanza proclaims

> *O felix Roma, quae tantorum Principum*
> *Es purpurata pretioso sanguine:*
> *Non laude tua, sed ipsorum meritis*
> *Excedis omnem mundi pulchritudinem.*

'Oh fortunate Rome, you are red with the precious blood of those martyrs (Christian princes). Not because of your splendors, but for their merits, you outshine the beauty of all the world.' Doesn't this clearly show the opposition of the early Church as a spiritual power to the ostentatious pomp of unstable temporal powers? There can be no doubt that the setting, the surroundings in which this hymn is presently sung in Rome are magnificent and imposing; but what would Boethius and his wife say if they were to raise their heads now? Please don't become impatient with me, for I will return to my story immediately, but this preamble is essential."

The Narrative Continues

"I will not even mention to you the recisions, reworkings and revisions that the breviary suffered at the hands of successive popes, because this undoubtedly wouldn't interest you and even if it did, it would be out of place here. I only want to tell you that the second edition of the breviary was published under Clement VIII, with the assistance and direction of Cardinal Belarmino. You will recall that last night I mentioned another Belarmino to you, Belarmino the shoemaker and philosopher, father of Angustias, my little girlfriend. Well, I couldn't help but see in Cardinal Belarmino someone who was the reputed or adoptive father of the breviary. The name Belarmino appears frequently and no matter how I tried, I couldn't shake myself free from this fanciful idea. On the other hand, I had discovered that Belarmino, the shoemaker, was not Angustias's real father, but rather her putative parent. He claimed to teach philosophy, but I say there was much of the poet in him; just as my father, Apolonio, who claimed to be a dramatist, was quite the philosopher. A strange and mysterious association of ideas and sentiments was slowly beginning to have a deep effect on me. The poetry of the breviary, the inexpressible, penetrating, dizzying essence that springs from its melodies and clings to the heart forever, bursting inside of it, was the same poetry and essence that sprang from the soul of Angustias, that young girl whose purity and freshness made her seem like a beloved rose of the Supreme Being. The breviary conveyed to me not only the spiritual presence of Angustias, but her sensual presence as well. The breviary abounds in extremely vivid and expressive phrases and images and my adolescent imagination freely supplied what might have been wanting in its evocative and plastic power. Besides, the liturgical psalmists, afflicted lovers of chastity, often make great gestures of exorcism to expel evil visions. These severe adjurations are undoubtedly extremely useful in purifying and tranquilizing souls that harbor memories of their own impure experiences, where the lewd images are either actual memories or fragments of memories that have been retouched and embellished by the imagination. But in pure souls, those virginal in experience and memories, the effect is different, and far from expelling nonexistent disturbing visions, those adjurations provoke them.

"As I mentioned before, the hymns in the breviary were born at different periods in the life of the Church; some during the infantile or adolescent period—they belong to the primitive Church—others appeared during the adult or mature period, and others, very few, were composed during the age of senility, a very sterile age. Since the substance of poetry is, by necessity, love, so too the liturgical hymns are emanations of love, of a love especially abundant and ambitious because it aspires to an absolute and incorruptible object. It is said that the hymns of the primitive and adolescent Church are inspired by a love conceived in the heart, while those of the mature Church spring from a love conceived in the mind. In spite of what superficial intellectuals think and say, it is more natural for adolescents to be inclined toward pessimism and desperation than mature men; most of the people who commit suicide are young. Chamfort* tells of a young man who was not old enough to know anything of the world but who in spite of this was as sad as if he knew everything in it. This is a superficial observation, since it was probably his youth that made him so sad. For an intelligent and sensitive young man, the world is pure chaos engulfed in gloomy dark-

*Chamfort (1741–1794) was a French moralist and author of a collection of maxims.

ness. The young person has vast desires, he wants to order and illuminate all things with the order and light that emanates from his own heart. This light, light and fire, clarity and passion, is love. If someone from the outside, the evil spirit, extinguishes this light, then the world has collapsed irredeemably. This was the psychology of the early Church; that was my psychology during the first five years I spent in the seminary. I was afraid of the darkness, of cold chaos, of a gust of breath from the evil spirit; I was possessed by a desperate desire for light, for warmth, for love. All the hymns in the first part of the breviary are a continuous and anguished cry for light. Every time I read, my heart almost suspended, *claritas, lux lucis, lux refulgens sensibus, lucis aurora rutilans,* 'clarity, light of lights, light that illuminates the senses, sparkling light of dawn,' I actually saw the image of Angustias and I would exclaim in the words of Saint Ambrose, *os, lingua mens, sensus, vigor—confessionem personent,* 'may my confession of love resound in my mouth, on my tongue, in my mind, through my senses, with all my strength.' Every time I read, *Virgo super omnes speciosa, flos, dulcedo,* 'gentlest of all maidens, flower, sweetness,' or as that aesthete of the primitive church, Prudentius used to say, *Thesaurus et fragans odor—Thuris Sabaei ac myrrheus;* 'treasure, fragrant perfume of Arabic incense and myrrh,' it was then that I would actually see the image of Angustias. Other times, when I came across the adjuration of Saint Gregory the Great against lust, *Absint faces libidinis—Ne foeda sit vel lubrica—Compago nostri corporis,* 'far from me the torches of libidinous conduct; may filthy lewdness find no place in the joints of my body,' the image of Angustias would appear to me prettier, fresher and more adorable than ever, and my arms, of their own accord, would reach out to hold her tightly against my breast. And when I read in Saint Fortunatus, *Membra pannis involuta—Virgo mater alligat—Et manus pedesque et crura Stricta— cingit facia,* 'of how the Virgin Mother wraps the awkward limbs of the newborn Son in swaddling clothes and binds his hands, his feet and his legs with strips of cloth,' I also saw Angustias with child and my heart would melt with tenderness. Alone with my conscience, I would ask myself if these were examples of Satan's cunning evil which were leading me into impure fantasies or, rather, if they were divine clues meant to convince me I could best serve the Lord as a good husband instead of as a melancholic priest. I discussed this with my confessor and he answered my first question in the affirmative; these were Satan's evil ways and I could conquer them without effort. Without effort . . . A saintly man, an albino and adipose, my confessor had not the slightest inkling of what the word effort meant. Nevertheless, I followed his advice and opinion, for I knew God's voice seeks out, as instruments to express itself, those hollow and limpid souls who are like solid wooden flutes— not dried out, split, or obstructed. I made a great effort . . . how eagerly I tried! . . . to expel those soft, amorous images from my mind and heart. But the harder I tried, the more insidiously they pursued me, encircling and penetrating my defenses. This emotional state reached its painful climax when I was finishing my fifth year of ministerial duties and had already begun my first year of philosophy. My discomfort increased as vacation time approached. During the previous vacations at the end of my first two years, and even at the end of the third, Angustias had still been just a little girl, and in spite of my black priestly robes, which aged me prematurely, I too was only a child. There was nothing strange in our renewing our old friendship every summer although things were not as lively as they used to be now that Celesto, Belarmino's former apprentice, was no longer around, for when Belarmino became a mender of shoes, Celesto had gotten a job as an assistant coachman in a coach-rental firm. Despite the separation, the new assistant coachman was still very fond of Belarmino, Angustias, and me. But my relationship with Angustias was totally innocent. My passion didn't reveal itself until my fourth year. Leaving the seminary at the end of that year, I found that Angustias had become a woman. The first time we ran into each other in the street I felt so confused that I couldn't move or even speak to her. I realized I had turned deathly pale. During that whole summer we never talked to each other once. Every time we saw each other I turned pale and she blushed. And thus the fifth year in the seminary started, nine months of martyrdom before I once again had my vacation. I was horrified by the idea of having to see Angustias again. I was even tempted to beg the duchess to let me spend my vacation in her country house even if it meant I would be her servant, but I didn't follow through with that idea. And it happened one day that an old maid by the name of Felicita Quemada, who lived two doors down the street from my father and who used to invite me to her house for tea when I was a child, stopped me when we met in the street and said to me, 'My dear Pedrito, you *have* turned out to be a handsome lad, a real man! But you won't mind if I continue to address you in the familiar form. For me, you will always be a little boy, even if they make you the Bishop of Barataria Island.* But, really, you *are* a handsome fellow. What a shame you're on your way to becoming a priest. Otherwise, the girls would be chasing after you all a-flutter. And in spite of everything . . . who knows? I mean . . . I have an idea . . . but let's do change the subject. There is no reason why you cannot come to visit me as you used to years ago, as you always did. It is true I am a single woman, you are most certainly a handsome youth, and people *do* have venomous tongues; but that ought not to concern us because I know that the most important person in my life will see no harm in it. And besides, you are already half a priest and priests can go anywhere they please. So, tomorrow I will expect you for tea.'

"The following day I appeared at her house. That woman was the victim of an impossible love and, unable to find a happy ending for it, she tried everything in her power to bring others in the world together in an intimate and indissoluble lovers' embrace. Her chatter was enough to make anyone dizzy, but that afternoon what really almost drove me to the edge of unconsciousness was not the form, but the content and subject matter of her babbling. Through veiled hints and allusions sprinkled through her long, empty sentences, she somehow managed to convey to me that Angustias was madly in love and couldn't live without me. I was not unaware that Angustias used to visit the old maid's house frequently and at times even slept there. I began to make frequent visits. With each successive tea she served me, the old maid's intentions became more and more transparent. One day she proposed a meeting between me and Angustias right there in her house; she would make all the necessary preparations and nobody would be the wiser. I absolutely refused. Only God knows the agony and effort the refusal cost me. And my confessor had tried to pursuade me that whittling down one's amorous inclinations was an effortless task! The old maid answered, 'Don't worry about a thing, Pedrito—I am convinced you have a real vocation for the priesthood.' It was plain she was well aware of my love and my anguish. She continued, 'There's nothing wrong in what I propose to you nor is there any real danger, because you are so staunch in your religious vocation. We will just be performing an act of charity for the benefit of poor Angustias. Just by seeing you up close for the last time,

*Barataria was Sancho Panza's land-locked "island" in Cervantes' *Don Quixote*.

she will be happy for the rest of her life. You might even be able to instill a religious calling in her and convince her to become a nun.' I continued to reject her plan. The old maid said, 'So be it. Each one of us is sovereign over his actions.' Me, sovereign of my actions? . . . 'But just the same, what we have talked about here should not stop you from coming to see me from time to time. I will do everything possible to avoid a chance meeting here between the two of you. When will you come again? Next Thursday?'

"Having left my house the following Thursday in order to visit Felicita, I noticed that a woman was going into the old maid's house. I didn't really get a good look at her, but only managed to see the flare of a skirt and a foot moving up from the sidewalk to the front step. That was all I needed. It was Angustias. I fled, leaving the city behind, heading for the countryside, walking, walking for several hours until I ended up at the duchess's house. When I arrived there I was still in shock. I told the duchess I didn't feel well and I was going to the village to convalesce. The lady asked me if I had had an argument with my father. By the tone of my reply, the duchess, who was a very shrewd article, guessed the hidden cause of my emotional state. 'Poor little Pippin, my poor little child,' she said as she patted the top of my head. 'Now the thing to do is take long walks, go fishing, hunting . . . amuse yourself, lose yourself in your animal instincts. Don't exaggerate the importance of inconsequential things. You'll get over this slight ailment.' But I didn't get over it. A month passed. Summer was running out. The sky had already become colorless and sad. In less than three weeks I would have to be back in the seminary. I could hold out no longer. I returned to Pilares and to Felicita's house. Before she had a chance to speak, I just blurted out, 'I want to see Angustias.' 'I was expecting this,' replied the old maid. 'You have a heart of gold. Come back tomorrow for tea at the usual hour.' When I arrived the next day, Felicita led me to her sitting room and, once I had stepped inside, closed the door behind me. Angustias was standing there. I was a mere three steps from her. We looked at each other without saying anything. Her eyes filled with tears; mine also began to blur. We continued to look at each other without a word being said. How long did this last? I have no idea. Nor do I have any idea how I found her in my arms, our lips joined. How long did we stay like that? I don't know. There was a chest of drawers in the sitting room and on it an image of the Virgin of Covadonga with a small candle

160

burning beneath it. I took Angustias by the hand, we knelt down before the Virgin and I said, 'Here before the Heavenly Queen, I promise to marry you.' Felicita came in. 'Children, sillies, it *is* getting very late. Every owl to his olive tree and every chickadee to its perch.' I couldn't bear to be separated from Angustias. 'How rash Pedrito is,' said Felicita; 'That's only natural, for he has been hungry for so long. You little ninny, it's your own fault. But we'll take care of everything, lickety-split, so you won't be eaten up by your impatience.'

"Just the same, I didn't want to leave Angustias without at least having a photograph of her that I could look at during those hours of separation. Fortunately, Angustias had a small picture at home. We agreed Angustias would bring it to Felicita's house and the latter would send it to me immediately. Within a few days (and not one went by without our seeing each other), Felicita had incubated, hatched, and prepared the plan we were to follow. Angustias and I did nothing at all but let ourselves be carried along by Felicita and, to tell the truth, our happiness was no greater than the joy experienced by the poor old maid. Only rarely did she take time out to complain softly, 'How envious I am of you little love birds! . . . but don't fall into the sin of pride or egotism, for you are not alone in the world. My time will also come and I will soon be married. When Anselmo and I wed, all four of us will be good friends, even though you two belong to the lower classes. But I don't take such things very seriously, and if *I* don't, neither will Anselmo.'

"Felicita was of the opinion that if we handled this matter without deceit and in the usual and customary manner, we would never get married. Therefore, it was necessary to devise a rapid and energetic plan. We would elope and then by letter ask our parents for their forgiveness and consent. In order to avoid any scandal, these two requests would be granted and everything would turn out perfectly. Angustias did not want to hurt Belarmino and the idea of elopement repelled her. 'Why do we have to run off? People who sneak away like that have done something evil, and we haven't. What will my father think?' said Angustias with angelical timidity. As for me, my love had made me violent and this violence was reflected in my speech. 'We will elope because that is the only way open to us, and if you won't go along with me it's simply because you don't love me.' 'Don't say that,' sighed Angustias and the tears began to appear in her eyes. As I tried to stop them with my lips, the old maid began to squeal in a comical way, 'Children, for the love of Christ, don't be sinful. You are whetting my appetite and making me blush.' Poor woman, poor generous and fruitful soul, like a grapevine with its sinuous and mummified stem! There was no problem or obstacle to our planned elopement that she didn't sweep away with a suitable solution. She advanced us the money, which I later turned over to Angustias, she suggested to us that we contact our faithful friend Celesto so he could furnish us with a carriage and also serve as our steward, she handled all the details and when it finally came time for us to leave, like a selfless priestess of love, an aged vestal virgin, she gave us her tender blessings. How it rained on the day of our happy exodus! How the water resounded like crystal, like the bells of Heaven! It was a new deluge drowning all humanity; our carriage was like the ark and only *we* would survive the universal disaster; we were destined to be the creators of a new race of mankind. Soon, like a rainbow, wedding rings would sparkle on our fingers.

"Early the next morning there was a knocking at our door. I got up. Angustias, pale and fresh, with her head tucked under her arm continued to sleep like a dove. The chamber maid shouted through the closed door that some gentlemen were waiting for me downstairs. Undoubtedly they had come after us, to destroy our happiness. I was resolved to be killed rather than give myself up. I had nothing to defend myself with. I looked around. There was no object there I could use as an effective weapon. Outside the room the maid kept insisting. What I was afraid of most was that Angustias would awaken. I threw on some clothes and went to the door with the intention of bribing the chambermaid. A pair of hands with an iron grip (they belonged to that barbarian Patón, the duchess's servant), grasped my limbs, gagged me, lifted me up and carried me down the hall where my father and Novillo, Felicita's suitor, shoved me into a waiting carriage. In the meantime, Angustias slept like a dove and was perhaps even dreaming she was happy. Those iron hands did not reduce their savage pressure until we reached Pilares. I was like an invalid, like a useless and paralytic thing. Patón, the barbarian, just hauled me off as if I were a bundle of rags. And I was carrying my own life, my poor soul, like another bundle, untenable and oppressive. As we raced along in the carriage I thought that if I could only secretly bite an artery with my teeth and slowly bleed to death . . . It was all useless. My heart was numb, unfeeling. I cried, I wept then like a frail woman, crying for the treasure I had not been able to defend like a man; I wept during the whole trip. My father and Novillo didn't open their mouths once on the way back. The duchess locked me in a dark room and kept me there for the week that was left before I was supposed to return to the seminary. I couldn't imagine how they would let me back in after the scandal. While I was locked up no one told me anything. On the first day of the academic year, the duchess herself took me in her own coach to the seminary. What had happened? As time went on, I found out. The bishop, under the influence of the Dominicans and the Marquis and Marchioness of San Madrigal, wanted me to get married. The Duchess of Somavia strongly opposed this plan and insisted I be allowed to continue my studies for the priesthood. Since Angustias had disappeared without leaving a trace of her whereabouts, the duchess finally won out and I returned to the seminary; seven more years . . . " Don Guillén rested his elbows on his thighs, holding his head in his hands. There was a long silence. He finally sat up and once again took up the interrupted thread of his long discourse.

"Seven years . . . The almond of the Church tree, the Holy Bible, dogmatic theology, moral theology. Seven years of a triple martyrdom, no longer only of the heart as in previous years, but also of the flesh and conscience. The images of temptation that had existed in the past were no longer tentative images of the imagination springing from my heart; now it was the experience of the flesh, the memory of what had happened. Even though it was in the past it stayed with me—on my skin— like a scar. My contact with Angustias had impregnated my whole nervous system and would be there forever—the sensation was always with me, on my flesh, like an almost pleasant chill. Angustias continued to form a part of me and I ached as if they had amputated an arm or a leg. Martyrdom of the heart, martyrdom of the flesh, and, perhaps the most miserable of all, martyrdom of the conscience."

Don Guillén's Drama of Conscience

"In contrast to my fellow students, I continued to read and study. No one seemed to care that I was reading nor did they worry about the books I read. And what I read were French and English books as well as German works of biblical criticism translated into French and English. I began to meditate on the problem of the first three Gospels of the

New Testament. It was evident, oh how evident! that the Gospels had no historical value. They were not personal testimonies of the life and teachings of Jesus Christ but had been fabricated many years later, almost a century after the facts. The cornerstones on which the Church rested were fraudulent. The name of our Scripture teacher was Solomon Caicoyas. Solomon, the son of David, had only briefly visited the intellect of his namesake. What an ignorant, arrogant, self-centered individual! . . . He wore his cloak slung to one side, his headpiece cocked, and looked in every way like a nineteenth-century Spanish dandy. In the seminary it was said he was quite a lover and would always show up in crowds or crowded places so he could rub up against the women. His voice was like the grating of a knife against a plate. I couldn't even listen to him without gritting my teeth and feeling sick to my stomach. In addition, and I can't imagine why, he openly bore me a grudge and never lost the chance to remind me in public of the serious offense I had committed. Well, this was the man who was supposed to dissipate the black clouds that darkened my conscience. Imagine! . . . I would have to find my own salvation; I, myself, with the help of God and Saint Paul, the Apostle to the Gentiles, the one who did not know Christ. Saint Paul's Epistles are the oldest and most trustworthy documents of Christianity; they are really the work of faith, of the will to believe. Saint Paul didn't demand heroic virtues, only moderate ones. The Paulist doctrine speaks of the relevance of virtue. To Saint Paul, true religiousness is based on something more important than proved acts and rigid conduct. In the second Epistle to the Corinthians, Saint Paul says, *O Khirios to pneuma estin,* 'the Lord is the Spirit.' Although they were spiritualists, the Greeks were unable to sublimate the idea of the human soul except by concretizing it, and they therefore gave it the name *psyche,* the word for butterfly, which in their minds was the image of maximum weightlessness. What a miraculous advance in the spiritualization of the soul from the word, *psyche,* matter still, to the word *pneuma,* immaterial matter, ethereal substance, divine breath! . . . The Lord is the Spirit—God resides in our soul. Everything else, testimonials and dogma, all of that is secondary. We have only to strengthen and exalt the spiritual element of our being. That is our primordial and only religious duty. Christianity enriched the history of the human consciousness by an act of creation—the creation of the spirit. The spirit is something finer and more elevated than the soul. The Egyptians, too, be-

164

lieved in the soul; but the spirit is the soul that has been freed. On earth the spirit exists conscious of itself—before it had only existed blindly—and thus it has existed for nineteen centuries, from the days of Saint Paul. Perhaps an experimental psychologist would sarcastically say to me, 'But the spirit still has no existence . . . I have never come across the spirit in my experiments.' I would merely answer, 'So much the worse for you, because that's a sure sign you have no spirit and cannot be a Christian.' The spirit is far superior to the *psyche,* and you can't reach it through psychology. Saint Paul was also the bitter apostle of chastity. It is better to marry than to burn, but chastity is still the mother of fortitude."

Don Guillén Takes the Vow of Chastity

"One sleepless night while I was meditating and speculating on what might have happened to Angustias, I thought I heard a voice from within, a voice that reasoned with mysterious conviction, 'That woman is a lost soul. You have caused her perdition. She is incapable of sin, for she is innocent of her fall. Her sins weigh on your conscience. Whenever she may sin it will be you who are sinning; she will remain pure because the sin is not hers. Everything will be forgiven her because she loved you so. It is you who must make amends for all the guilt, nullifying with stringent chastity that chain of sins you yourself have forged and which now shackles your wrists and ankles.' And with a firmness that arose from the very marrow of my bones, I exclaimed, 'I will comply.' And so I did. I believe that basically I am continent; the rest is secondary. Once my soul was stronger and healthier, I went back to immersing myself in the warm and invigorating currents of the breviary. Now there were three hymns lodged in my breast, and they burned there inextinguishably like an oil lamp with three identical flames. These were the three hymns to Mary Magdalene; one actually composed by Cardinal Belarmino, the other by Saint Gregory, but touched up by Belarmino, and the third by Saint Odon of Cluny in another arrangement by Belarmino. Saint Odon says:

> *In thesauro reposita*
> *Regis est drachma perdita;*
> *Gemmaque lucet inclita*
> *De luto luci reddita;*

'The lost drachma is replaced in the king's treasury and the pearl, recently snatched from darkness, shines again in all its brightness.'

"And Saint Gregory says:

> *Nardo María pistico*
> *Unxit beatos domini*
> *Pedes, rigando lacrymis*
> *Et detergendo crinibus;*

'With a crushed spikenard, Mary anoints the holy feet of the Lord, sprinkling them with tears and drying them with strands of her hair.'

"And Belarmino writes:

> *Amore currit saucia*
> *Pedes beatos ungere,*
> *Lavare fletu, tergere*
> *Comis, et ore lambere;*

'Wounded by love, she races to anoint the holy feet, to wash them with her lament, to dry them with her hair, to caress them with her mouth.'

"Thus, one day the woman whose perdition I caused will come to me and innocently ask me for forgiveness. I will then tell her, 'Stand up, woman. You are the one who must forgive me. I kneel here at your feet.' That was what I thought then . . . and later . . . for many years afterward. And I have always carried the image of that girl with me, a picture of the way she was before her misfortune and mine; and since I couldn't make her my mistress, I made her my sister."

After a brief pause, Don Guillén continued, "I performed my first mass in the country home of the Duke and Duchess of Somavia. The duchess was my patroness and she made me the gift of an exquisite cassock, embroidered in gold. Hidden in the delicate embroidery was the figure of a heart squeezed by a hand; from this heart trickled a delicate stream of blood that, in its convolutions, formed a somewhat blurry letter *A*. A large white banner was hanging from the top of the chapel. At the request of the duchess, the bishop officiated with me, but His Eminence had never forgiven me my Easter escapade and I had barely been ordained when he sent me to an inhospitable rural parish— San Madrigal of Breñosa. The Neiras had a beautiful estate there and it was from this place that their original title of nobility derived; but they never went there because the region was so craggy and isolated. It happened that during my two years' stay in that lonely place, Don Restituto died. Doña Basilisa, the widow, went into mourning in the lonely reaches of San Madrigal, and since she was very devout and heard mass every day before breakfast, she designated me as her private chaplain. She was a plump little lady, not at all ugly, still young, very white skinned and as naïve as they come. Her ideas on religion were capricious and even downright comical. She believed that the paradise of the blessed was a theater, with a stage and seats for the public. According to her, Don Restituto, her husband, had gotten to the theater before her to find a good seat and reserve it for his little woman. The fact is she soon forgot her husband was waiting for her with a reserved seat and fell in love with me. She didn't make a secret of it either. She was like one of the Ephesian women. There was nothing strange about this, since you must realize I was the only person around there who looked the least bit like a man. Besides, her husband had been much older than she, and she also had a very tender, generous heart. Last, but by no means least, was the fact that I dressed in long black skirts just as she did and this, in spite of her natural timidity, made her bolder and more confident in revealing her sentiments. She knew about my flight with Angustias and must have calculated that I would be an easy prey to love. I used all the tricks I knew to dissuade her. With what I must confess was rhetorical fervor and emotion, I managed to convince her we ought to establish our mutual relationship on a purely spiritual level. I didn't forbid her to love me since God does not demand the impossible of his weak creatures and it is impossible to uproot deep emotions merely through the exercise of the will, but I did forbid her to declare her emotions publicly, since God does demand we overcome our weaknesses or passions, and this can be accomplished through our own volition.

"I myself spoke to her about the great sin I had committed as a rash adolescent and how repentant I was. I made it clear to her that my desire to make amends was unshakable. In order to soften the blow and make it easier for her to bear the burden of her eagerness, I falsely led her to believe I was equally fond of her but that my priestly state forced me to blindfold myself against temptations of the flesh. I would be her spiritual father and she, my daughter. In confession, as a penitent speaking to her confessor, she could confide to me all her lovelorn afflictions; but as woman to man, never. She was amazed by what she considered to be my strength and fortitude, which was really only a wish for peace and a desire to be left alone. 'You are a saint, a real saint—the only saint I have ever known,' she used to say to me from time to time as she looked at me adoringly, her hands clasped in prayer. I always had my meals with her. Sometimes she would interrupt her swallowing to contemplate me with sheeplike, tear-filled eyes. Other times, after the dishes had been cleared and the servant had left, she would disgorge some heart-rending sighs, but it went no further than that. I also slept in the main house. But to avoid gossip I chose a comfortable room at the far end, beyond the servants' quarters. It was sparsely furnished, like a cell, but it had a northern exposure and a permanent silver light streaming in through the window. I was master of my time and I spent hour after hour studying books as well as the country people around me. There, in contact with the slaves of the soil, the great tragedy of human society was revealed to me. I then became interested in the social sciences, which have continued to preoccupy me."

Don Guillén Feels a Vocation to Become a Social Reformer: Disquisition on Happiness

"I was born to be a social reformer. It is evident that society is badly organized and must change. Men have a right to happiness, all men, and they have the right to it here on earth. The most vehement and constant stimulant, the most powerful and active incentive that God created in uniting the human body and soul is the pursuit of happiness. Therefore, since it is by divine plan that the pursuit of happiness is the foremost human desire, man's right to happiness is clear. All important conscious activities (and there is no need even to mention the unconscious and automatic ones) spring from that fatal and inevitable incentive, the wish for happiness—thus, religion, morality, law, art, science . . . From their beginnings, all these activities have conspired to perfect society for the ultimate purpose of providing the greatest happiness for the greatest number. But because of human failings, to date all these experiments in social organization have been founded on a narrow concept of happiness which emphasizes only one of man's conscious activities to the detriment and omission of all the others. The Church was born as an attempt to organize society for happiness' sake. Saint Paul's Epistles unequivocally state that the apostle believed himself immortal and was convinced that all who professed faith in Christ would also become immortal. According to him, the Saviour would return to establish the kingdom of happiness on earth for the faithful, what he called *Parousia*. All Saint Paul's followers believed what he preached; but when some of his converts in Thessalonica died, the Thessalonian Christians rose in revolt and branded him a deceiver. The same thing happened with the Ephesians. Finally, the apostle realized that he and all Christians had to die; but since he could not renounce happiness completely, he decided that only the body died, and the spirit, which was immortal, entered into the kingdom of Christ, into paradise. Thus, the early Church was a gentle and uncultured anarchy, an effort to organize society in order to secure happiness after death. In this attempt at social organization for happiness' sake, all kinds of conscious actions besides religious ones—scientific, artistic, political and even ethical acts— were dismissed and looked upon with contempt. Our current social organization, what people call capitalist society, is another attempt at organizing in order to achieve happiness by emphasizing two types of activity, the political and scientific, to the exclusion of all other pursuits. It is a state of cruel and productive anarchy just as the primitive Church constituted a state of gentle and uncultured anarchy. Socialism, the heir apparent to capitalism, is a social experiment that bases itself solely on scientific activity. Up to now all experiments to institute happiness have been failures. Although they are all different, they all have as a common trait this underlying anarchy which is disguised, shamefaced, and inhibited. Although it may seem paradoxical, couldn't it perhaps be that anarchy is the only possible social organization leading to happiness? On the day when all kinds of conscious activity, including politics and the administration of justice (by which I don't mean the art of governing but the art of communal living without bothering or harming one's fellow man), attain complete maturity and total autonomy, existing in harmony among themselves without denigrating or causing harm to each other, won't the result be a spontaneous organization of perfect anarchy, of absolute liberty, and of unsurpassable happiness?"

The Narrative Continues

"Well . . . this isn't the time for me to expound all my ideas about society. It's just that in San Madrigal I often used to think, 'If I had the means, the wherewithal, I would found an experimental community that would make men happy. It would be an experiment similar to previous ones except I would have the advantage of knowing the mistakes others had made.'

"One day, out of the clear blue sky, the widow told me point blank she planned to make me the sole heir to her fortune, which came to some ten million *pesetas*. Of course I didn't know what to say, but after a short while God granted me enough tranquility and peace of mind to be able to answer her, 'Madam, I am grateful to you. I could never hope to express my emotions to you in words. But I do not accept your generosity, nor will I ever accept it; not so much because of me, but because of you and your good name. People would think the nature of our relationship had given rise to this posthumous proof of your love for me.' And Doña Basilisa, usually so silly, spoke exceptionally well on that occasion, even with a certain amount of eloquence and good sense. 'What such rash judges may say is their business and a question of their own conscience. My conscience is clear and I commend it to God who knows my secret intentions. This is not a gift of love, no, nor is it a prize for your saintliness and virtue, but it's merely an unworthy token of my gratitude to you for having persuaded me to preserve my virtue and for serving as my guide on the rough road to righteousness. When I join my Restituto in the celestial coliseum, I am sure the first thing he'll say to me will be, 'Don't think what I am now applauding are the mellifluous tones of the heavenly choir; what I am doing is applauding your performance.' Nevertheless, I insisted I would only accept the inheritance on one condition—that it be stated in her will that she was leaving me her fortune in trust for me to use as I saw fit, in useful and charitable undertakings for the benefit of my fellow men. This was the agreement we reached.

"I had been in San Madrigal for seven years when the Duchess of

Somavia died. I attended her in her last moments. Up to the very end, she never lost her good humor or her spicy use of language. In the midst of the anguish and grief we all felt on seeing her die, she still made us laugh with her outbursts. I had always thought her hair was naturally very curly but, in fact, she curled it strand by strand every night, twisting each one of them around paper rollers that stuck out on both sides of her head like white butterflies. Even on her deathbed she had her maid brush her hair every night, placing those strange butterflies in it; and there they stayed throughout the next day. The total effect was rather funny. Well that is how she died, her head covered with paper butterflies. And since I must have looked rather surprised the first time I saw her in that get-up, she gave full play to her sharp tongue and said, 'What are you looking at, you silly ass? Haven't you ever seen a woman in bed without her street clothes on? Or do you think it's evil for us old women to try to hold on to and even nurture the paltry bits of beauty we still have left? And don't start imagining things like the typical malicious priest that you've probably become, since all of you are like vicious mules and have picked up the vice of thinking the worst of people from your experiences in the confessional. You don't learn anything there but what's ugly and evil although there is a lot you're not told . . . don't start imagining I've put on these things out of vanity . . . it's a little late for that! I'm doing it out of a sense of propriety as well as for another good reason. The primary duty of all decent and well-born human beings is to respect the decorum of their own person. And besides, I have done this all my life just to have at least one unpleasant obligation, the only annoying one I've ever had, an act of patience and discipline—a mortification of the flesh as you of the cloth would say. I want to die with these *papillons* on my head and when my soul escapes through my lips, may all these butterflies whisk it away, fluttering straight to the lap of God, He who created me Beatriz Valdedulla, who sustained me all my life as Beatriz Valdedulla, and who will accept me in his eternal mercy as Beatriz Valdedulla. After all, is it my fault I'm Beatriz Valdedulla?' Just remembering those words moves me to tears. One morning in the duke's presence, the day before she commended her soul to God, she said to me, 'Pedrito, my son—I love you almost as if you were my own flesh and blood. But since words are like so many flies that can't be caught by the tail, I have wanted to leave you something more substantial than the verbal ex-

171

pression of my affection. Through the intercession of the duke, my husband and master, who also happens to have good connections in the government, I have obtained a canonical position for you in Castro-fuerte. No matter what they say, it is not a great benefice. If I were to live longer, I would see you a bishop. You with your cleverness and charm will achieve by yourself what I have not been able to achieve for you. As I leave you all, I have misgivings and feel uneasy only about one thing, and that is your father. His name should have been Bolonio and not Apolonio. There is no hope for him. My suggestion to both you and the duke is that when your father is finally penniless and without a roof over his head—and that day is not far off—you find a rest home for him, where you'll send him those little things he needs to feed his vanity and without which he couldn't live.' Before she died, she expressed herself further, 'My dear duke, you have not fulfilled your duties to me properly as a husband, but I forgive you. I also ask for your forgiveness if I have failed you in any way, because it was without my realizing it. And you, my beloved son, I have nothing to forgive you for since I feel that children owe nothing to their parents, that, on the contrary, it's the other way around. If some day life weighs heavily on you, then forgive me. I only wanted to give you a life filled with happiness and good fortune. As for you, Facundo (the bishop was also present), how many times I've called you an ass for no reason at all except that you really are one! . . . But you know I have always held you in high esteem, I never intentionally harmed you, and, in fact, I even helped you as much as I could. On one occasion I actually admired you, but you have probably already forgotten that. I ask you to forgive me for calling you an ass. Pippin, I will tell you more or less what I have told my son; if some day you feel life is a burden because of me, forgive me. That was not my intention. If I have offended or caused pain to anyone, forgive me all of you. And you, my Lord Jesus Christ (here she kissed the Crucifix), I already know you have forgiven me as you forgive all in your infinite goodness; otherwise, fire would rain down on earth at least every ten minutes. I will see all of you soon— life is short. I'll be right there, my Lord Jesus Christ.' She died like a saint. In her own way, she was a saint, for there are many different ways to be one. I have noticed that there are many more saints in the world than one usually imagines. As a matter of fact, I think the world is in such a bad way because there are too many saints; because people in general are too good and too resigned to their fate . . . but let's not have any more footnotes. The duchess died.

"I became a Canon in Castrofuerte and vegetated there for some years. Doña Basilisa continued to write me those long and affectionate letters of hers. She informs me that lately she hasn't been in very good health, though she says nothing to me of the inheritance. I have no idea if I am still heir apparent or if some monk has been paying her visits in San Madrigal and has managed to trick her out of my inheritance for his own religious order. My father and Belarmino, now a widower, are both in a rest home just as the duchess predicted. I wanted my father to live with me. I even took him to my house in Castrofuerte where he stayed for a short period of time. But it was totally impossible. In the first place, he made love to all the servants in the neighborhood. On one occasion he had a local paper publish a declaration of love, in verse, to the mayor's wife. Besides, he began to owe people so much money that my modest canonical stipend wasn't enough for us to live on and so, in spite of my feelings of regret, I had to put him back in the shelter. In accordance with the duchess's wishes I did send him whatever little gifts I could afford. The one who now has a large department store of ready-made shoes in Pilares as well as barrels of money, is that Martínez, Belarmino's former apprentice. Paradoxically enough, living in the same charity ward with my father and Belarmino is a loanshark called Bellido, who caused Belarmino's ruin and was himself ruined at the time of the famous bankruptcy of Hurtado and Company.* Quirks of fate."

And Don Guillén sat there with vacant eyes, as the English so expressively put it; eyes that were blind to things around him but perhaps penetrating some inner and remote perspective of motionless memories. While he had been talking and I listening, the nocturnal, black-caped hours had harmoniously wandered off; the early morning hours were now dancing on the threshold of a new day and a ripple of their violet-colored tunics flickered into the room through the balcony window The pink knuckles of dawn rapped silently on the crystals of our eyes. As if reacting to this gentle appeal from the radiant sky, Don Guillén exclaimed, "It is Saturday and it is Easter. The almond trees are covered

---

*This incident appears in another novel by Pérez de Ayala, *La Pata de la Raposa* [The fox's paw].

with a pink veil and the apple trees are all in white. Soon the joyous bells of all Christendom will resound. Christ is resurrected.

Sat funeri, sat lacrymis.
Sat est datum doloribus,

intones the Easter hymn, 'an end to mourning, no more tears, no more deep anguish.' And the inaudible voice of the angelic choir adds, 'peace on earth to men of good will.' All is peace and contentment in this vale of tears. The children of God embrace, kiss each other on the cheek, and softly whisper, 'Greetings, brother; greetings, sister; may the Lord be with us.'

"And you, my sister," continued Don Guillén, taking the miniature in his hand and looking at it with an expression filled with pity and bitterness, "Where are you, in what dark dungeon did I blindly imprison you so that I cannot find the entrance, even though my hands and feet are bloody from so much groping and walking? I looked for you and did not find you; I waited for you and you have not come. My soul will be sad unto death; my ears will be deaf to the bells of Resurrection; my eyes will be blind to the colors of Spring."

I naturally judged the small rhetorical outburst of Don Guillén to be spontaneous, sincere, and, therefore, legitimate, given the circumstances. Barely had he finished and lowered his head dejectedly, than I immediately spoke up.

"I have already told you I know that woman and I am going to bring her here right away."

I suppose when I left him he was about to explode and couldn't even utter a word or, for that matter, any articulate sound at all. I left without turning to look at him, without hearing him gasp. The city was wrapped in the cold, ashen light of dawn. I headed rapidly for the small cafe. There, in her usual corner and with her usual watered-down coffee in front of her, Angustias was waiting for Tirabeque.

"Come with me, girl," I said to her in an emotional and threatening way. Angustias got up. "Follow me."

"Has something happened to Tirabeque? Has he had a fight? A brawl? I don't want to see anything. I'm not interested. I'm no prisoner," she said out of breath from trying to keep up with my impatient gallop as we hurried along.

174

She hesitated for a minute when we reached the door of the house.

"What is it you want of me? You're not trying to deceive me are you? I always thought you were a good man . . . Oh, how miserable I am."

"Just come with me," I insisted as I took her by the hand.

"But where are you taking me?"

I didn't know what to say and what I ended up saying was stupid.

"To the Resurrection. Don't you know it's Easter?"

She stopped, trembling.

"Are you mad? Oh, Lord, take pity on me!"

I dragged her up the steps with me.

"Just come with me."

"Holy Virgin of Covadonga! I'll scream. I don't care if there's a scandal and they carry me off to the police station." She wouldn't budge.

"Angustias, don't be a child," I began speaking without realizing I had called her by her real name. "How can you even think I am trying to do you any harm? On the contrary, I am leading you to happiness, to a meeting with someone you have been hoping to see again for many years." The match I had used to light our way burned my fingers. I let out a suitable expletive as I threw its stub to the ground. We were in total darkness. Angustias was frightened and moved toward me. I could feel her trembling, with fear in her heart.

"Let me escape," she begged. "How can I dare to appear in front of him. He probably knows everything by now. You yourself must have told him. He will spit on me. Wouldn't he be right to push me away? And then, Tirabeque will come after us; he will kill me and leave a gash on his face."

"No, Angustias, let's not worry about Tirabeque. Pedrito is waiting for you. Don't you want to see him? Don't you want to be saved?" I uttered impatiently as I lit another match.

What an expression Angustias had on her face! It was a childish, contrite look as though she were being tormented by some obscure, barely perceptible pain!

"I want to be saved! I want to be saved!" she sobbed, desperately seizing my arm as if it were a life raft.

We reached Don Guillén's flat. She didn't want to go first and I had to enter before her. My plan had been to leave her inside and discreetly withdraw to my rooms. Against my wishes I was forced to witness the beginning of the scene because it all happened so quickly, and then I saw its continuation because I had become too involved and too caught up in its suspense to be able to make a move.

Angustias threw herself at Don Guillén's feet, she clasped them to her, bathed them in tears and dried them with her long, copper-colored hair. And there it was, the same touching picture that had been so innocently and transparently sketched by the holy psalmists of the breviary.

"Forgive me! Forgive me!" implored Angustias with all the purity of her innocent soul. "I am evil, but I have loved only you. Love has been my downfall, the hopelessness of love. I will tell you all about it and you will forgive me."

Don Guillén was livid and stiff. Stammering, he pleaded, "Arise, sister!"

Angustias obeyed like a passive creature. Then Don Guillén kneeled down before her.

"You are pure. All your sins revert to me. You and God are the ones who must forgive me, and you will forgive me because I have loved and suffered so much. Say you forgive me, say yes with your lips, nod with your head, even if it isn't from your heart."

"A thousand yesses," said Angustias in a suffocated cry, shaking her hair from side to side.

Don Guillén got up from the floor and Angustias flung herself into his arms, her head falling back lifeless against her shoulders, her parched lips lifting toward him. Don Guillén gently touched her face and kissed her on the forehead.

I understood it was the right moment to sneak away and as I turned on my heels to make my escape, I heard Don Guillén addressing me in a surprised, even severe tone.

"What are you planning to do? Wait a minute, I have a great favor to ask of you. You've got to help me improvise a place where my sister can rest for a few hours. If there's a sofa or even an easy chair in your room I can sleep there, if you don't mind, and Angustias can stay in this room."

We arranged the accommodations as Don Guillén wished. He insisted on stretching out on my sofa. This piece of furniture was flush against the wall that separated his room and mine. On the other side of the partition was the bed where Angustias was resting.

Once we were both lying down, Don Guillén spoke to me from the sofa, "I've already thought about the most immediate and urgent matter. Within a few hours Angustias will take the first train to Castrofuerte; she'll be carrying a letter addressed to Abel Parras, an old, fat, peaceful, and good natured priest who happens to be my best friend. Angustias will live with him; that will keep people from spreading malicious gossip. Later on we'll see what's to be done . . . *In thesauro reposita* . . . the lost drachma has been returned to the king's treasure, and the pearl, brought out of the darkness into the light, glows once again. Now if the unhappy Doña Basilisa doesn't decide to change her will! . . . Oh what beautiful possibilities there are for worshipping God while serving mankind!"

He rapped gently against the wall and there was a cautious answering rap from the other side. He began to laugh as he turned to look at me.

"Did you realize what we said to each other?"

I answered in the negative, dully; I was exhausted and sleepy.

"Well, I said 'sleep in peace, my sister, you are resurrected with the Lord.' She answered, 'May God reward you; protect me always.' "

What a revelation! They have been given the gift of language as if it were Pentecost instead of Easter. These were my vague thoughts as I began to sink into dark sleep.

The last words of Don Guillén that I heard were, *Sat funeri, sat lacrymis, sat est datum doloribus . . . O Khirios to pneuma estin.* And then from the very depths of my waking consciousness, which was just about to fade, I thought I commented aloud, "The gift of language! Pentecost!"

I woke up at two in the afternoon. Don Guillén had disappeared from the sofa and from Madrid. On the table there was a note that said, "Good-bye, my dear friend. I gave you a farewell embrace filled with gratitude but you were too deep in sleep even to realize it. You will be hearing from me. Your friend eternally, Pedro Guillén Caramanzana."

And, as a matter of fact, many years later, I learned great things about him, some of which I even witnessed. I intend to write about them on another occasion if the opportunity should ever arise and I have nothing better to do.

Chapter Eight

SUB SPECIE AETERNITATIS

Easter Sunday. Time: a little before noon. Place: the outskirts of Pilares. A typical northern spring day. Earth and heaven, two feminine graces. The earth, dressed in thickly woven perennial green, is gorgeously embellished, though winter snow and rain have been its sole cosmetic and repair. Bright-green folds and pleats of baize adorn the eternally virginal Mother Earth; here and there are scattered fresh apple blossoms, innocent ornaments. The graceful sky, pure and bright, is like a nubile schoolgirl dressed in her springtime Sunday best—snowy-white translucent hoopskirts on a background of blue silk.

Seen from the village, the city is a dark mantle covering a distant hill, a scaled breastplate resting on a sleeping body; a dented piece of armor hewn from copper and steel; dusty gold, reddish grey in spots, green and rusty in places from the corrosion of the years. The cathedral tower rises from one end of the town like a splintered spear still firmly tucked under the warrior's arm. Birds warble, bells sound.

A fat, dark man, whose silvery goatee shines like aluminum in the early morning sun, proceeds along the main road from the city. He is sweating profusely. Behind him another man and a young boy, both wearing white jackets and carrying baskets on their heads.

"Sacrebleu, sacrebleu," mutters the dark, fat man as he wipes the sweat from his forehead. "Walk alongside me, Nolo. I have to talk to someone and much better to find a faithful soul to confide in than mumble to oneself. Oh God, I'm tired! . . . I'm tired of my wife, my dearly beloved wife. Women are thrifty in my country, and I love thrifty women, good managers. But my wife is too much thrifty; too, too much.

178

I put my head in my business and work like a mule after morning until night to make good money. I love good money to enjoy life and eat to my pleasure. That's what remains to me. *Voilà*"—patting his stomach— "This friend is very demanding. But my wife, she doesn't eat at all, or she eats like a little bird, and she thinks the rest of us have no need to eat as it is necessary. So, to eat in my own home, I have to invent certain mystifications. Is it not surprising and very unpleasant? Now, even that does not work. How I am tired! . . . I will tell you what happened the other day, a lean day, or, how do you say it? . . . a fast day. I adore salmon but my wife does not buy salmon because it is too expensive. Then I myself went to the market and I bought a *magnifique* salmon for sixty *pesetas*. I sent the beautiful fish home as if it were a gift from the part of a friend; otherwise, if she knows that I bought it, my wife makes a terrible scene. So I go home happy thinking to myself, salmon today, all I can eat. My wife receives me with amorous kisses and says we have good luck; someone has made a gift to us of a very large salmon. 'Since it was too big for us to eat,' she tells me, 'I have sold him for forty *pesetas*.' *Sacrebleu!* No salmon, and twenty *pesetas* less. What do you say to that?"

"I'd have given her such a wallop she'd never sell fish again."

"*Voilà*. In this country, you men are not cultured. One should never hit a woman, not even because of food, and less for more unimportant reasons—infidelity, for example."

"Whoa!" commented Nolo. "I'll let the one about food pass—but the other! That's another matter! As for me, death is the answer."

"Ah! You would kill yourself? That is different. It's barbaric, but I understand."

"What do you mean, kill myself? Kill her!"

"*Mon Dieu,* you *are* a savage!"

"There's no other way, señor. Either you give the orders or the woman will; and if she gets out of line, take a stick to her. Either you hit her or she'll hit you. Remember poor Belarmino."

"What are you telling me? Was Xuantipa unfaithful to poor Belarmino? I did not know that."

"The itch she didn't lack. What I'm talkin' about is that since Belarmino didn't know how to cure his wife, when he had her, with a stick— the best medicine for bossy women—well, she was always after him and her remedy was to cover his back with blisters."

"Yes, yes, I knew all about that. The poor man. My dear, dear friend

179

. . . I miss him now that he is put away in the rest home, which you people call the insanitary, a name I find most amusing."

"It isn't insanitary. The insanitory."

"Isn't that the same thing?"

"No, sir."

"Then what do you mean by insanitory?"

"I'll be damned if I know."

"Oh well, it doesn't make any difference. But let us return to the subject of dear Belarmino. I cannot get along without him. I come to visit him every week, or every two weeks, for the past ten years—in spite of this abominable hill I have to climb to get there. He never says anything, he never speaks. He is the sweetest of souls and I maintain he has a great intelligence."

"A muttonhead, a nut; just like the other one, that Apolonio."

"Be quiet, Nolo. You don't understand. Belarmino is a great man and Apolonio, he too is another great man. I want to show them how much I love and admire them. That is why I am bringing them these fat, juicy Easter pies, these big bowls of whipped cream and dozens and dozens of delicious pastries, so many of them! Just as I do every year on this very same day."

"Those gluttonous little nuns and the other inmates will eat them all, just as they do every year on this very same day."

"Ah, *naturellement!* But the pastry belongs to Belarmino and Apolonio, and they enjoy themselves more inviting than being invited. They have always given them away without keeping anything for themselves. I never even used to talk to Apolonio in other times; I only started after he was put into this home. Very interesting, very interesting. It is a strange thing; Apolonio did not want me to have anything to do with Belarmino. He hates him, that is to say he thinks he hates him. Very amusing. But Belarmino pays no intention if I talk to Apolonio. He has contempt for him, that is to say he thinks he feels contempt for him. Very piquant situation. I have to be very tactful. But it is all so extra-ordinary, so extraordinary . . . of course I love Belarmino more, that goes without saying—it is an old friendship. But I also love Apolonio. Well, here we are. Now remember, the wife mustn't know we brought these gifts. She would make a great fuss."

By some mysterious pull of gravity, Colignon heads straight for Belarmino.

It is a common error to think that the force of gravity causes bodies to fall. The concept of falling presupposes the existence of higher and lower, and yet out in infinite space there is no high or low. Sometimes bodies and souls rise down and other times they fall up. The second phenomenon was taking place in the case of the epicurean Colignon who, panting and wheezing, periodically climbed up the hill to the rest home, attracted there by the ascetic Belarmino; that is to say he involuntarily fell while climbing toward him.

Now a much older Colignon penetrates the entrance to the home. It is a long room with bare walls and four broken-down wicker chairs. Opposite the main door there is a wooden bracket hanging on the wall with a sad-looking plasterboard figure of Saint Joseph. At his feet are half-a-dozen stringbeans, another half-a-dozen chick-peas and a little jar containing a thick olive-colored liquid, marked "kooking oil." These offerings to the saint apparently indicate what is most needed by the institution, reminding the charitable souls who occasionally pass that way in order to perform an act of mercy, that their gifts ought to be the things most lacking in that humble establishment.

The clink of a small bell with an old, cracked voice can be heard receding. A painted black door opens and out comes a little old nun whose flowing skirts cannot disguise her wasted, skeletal body; she has the face of a mummy. Her big, tired eyes light up as soon as she sees Colignon who runs to greet her with open arms.

"Ah! Felicita; dear, kindly Felicita."

"Sister Dolores, if you please, my dear Colignon," corrects the nun.

"But I cannot forget."

"How true, how true. But we must forget, and if we cannot forget we must appear to have forgotten," says the sister with nunnish unction as well as a trace of nostalgia in her voice, making it clear that in spite of everything she has not forgotten. How could poor old Felicita have forgotten! And especially when Colignon refreshes her memory and causes Sister Dolores to feel a tug at her heart. These effects are produced unintentionally and unwittingly by the Frenchman . . . it's all because of his girth. Since all the old men living in the asylum as well as the religious hypocrites who come to visit are, without exception, emaciated types, every time Sister Dolores sees a fat man she thinks she's in the presence of her beloved, dear-departed Novillo. At those moments she feels like the Felicita of yore. She is standing now with her eyes obstinately lowered so as not to receive the image of that round, devilishly evocative stomach of Monsieur Colignon.

"But, *mon Dieu!*" exclaims the visitor, laughing, "it must be difficult for you to forget and hide your feelings . . . This is just a branch of Ruera Street as it was in other times. Belarmino is here; Apolonio is here; the pawnbroker is here; you are here. I am the only one who is missing and I am here right now. And the rest who have not come to this *rendez-vous* are not here because they are dead and living in the land of eternal nothingness."

"Aye!" sighs the sister without raising her eyes, and thus going against all the rules governing sighs. "Those of us who are here are also dead and we gaze out at the world with eyes fixed on eternity."

"What an idea! We still eat pastry. As long as we can eat pastry, God be blessed." And here Colignon laughs as he always did, clucking like a turkey while his stomach vibrates. He continues, "I notice that string-beans, chickpeas, and olive oil are needed here. So much the better for eating pastry."

"May God bless you, Señor Colignon. You and your Easter gifts are even more dependable than the sunrise. For eight days now the poor old folks have been licking their chops in anticipation, and talking only about Señor Colignon's delicious delicacies. How little is needed to make some people happy!"

"Very little—six pounds of flour, a pound and a half of sugar, three dozen eggs, three sticks of cinnamon, and two of vanilla. But you must realize it is not I who invites the little old people for pastry, but Belarmino and Apolonio."

"How little is needed for happiness and yet it almost never comes!" mutters Sister Dolores to herself without, naturally, referring to the flour, sugar, or even the eggs, since she hasn't paid any attention to the Frenchman, but is lost in her own thoughts. She comes out of it, however, and adds, "Leave the baskets here, they'll come to pick them up later. Now go along, Señor Colignon, to see your friends until dinner time. You already know the way. They are undoubtedly in the garden waiting impatiently for you."

Colignon walks down passageways that have a strong smell of rotten meat and comes out into the garden, so called because it is an open space spotted with grass and with sandy pathways cutting across it, where the only flowers are a few scattered day lilies. A couple of wooden benches are set along the paths; the leaves of the acacia trees like canopies spread over them. The smell of wet earth is in the air. The tenuous, yellow sunlight dissolves the outline of things, insinuating the fleeting and immaterial qualities of dawn or twilight into them; and yet it is noon. A golden vapor melts everything into one flowing and indecisive mass that could be either memory or hope. Elysian light. Every time solid, fleshy Colignon peers out at that garden, he imagines he is treading along the fringes of the Elysian Fields inhabited by the spiritual images of those who were and are no more—those who have left their solid flesh behind on earth, that seat of carnal pleasures. They now only preserve an appearance of life, but still experience their former passions, because passions are of the soul and the soul is indestructible. Colignon shudders, feeling the dampness of the earth deep in the marrow of his bones.

But that is exactly what he likes—to penetrate momentarily into a kind of great beyond, a world of illusion or memory, to seek pleasant companionship among its strange inhabitants and to be convinced that even there people eat pastry, and, while in this simulacrum of the world beyond the grave, to know full well that he can leave whenever he feels like it and return to the delights of the physiological and active life.

As soon as Colignon pokes his head into the garden, all the old men who up until that moment have been scattered here and there, shuffle toward him, moving slowly and jerkily like characters in a dream whose movements are obstructed by heavy and invisible obstacles. One of them quite flagrantly lags behind. He moves majestically, with an expression of indifference on his face, determined not to display common haste—it's Apolonio. There is someone else who has already greeted Colignon with a slight wave of the hand and, detached from the rest of the pack, remains seated on a bench—it's Belarmino. Belarmino and Apolonio are quite a bit younger than the other residents.

The nun who watches over that flock of decrepit men is walking along one of the footpaths and comes face to face with the slow-moving Apolonio. She is Sister Lucidia. Not old, but not particularly young . . . on the right side of her face, from the temple to the corner of her mouth, cutting right across her cheek, she has a livid birthmark that seems to be sprouting tentacles. It looks like the flaming imprint of a slap on the face—a slap fate had given her before she was born. Sister Lucidia always holds her head slightly tilted to the right as if ashamed of that mark, as if she were trying to hide it or turn the other pale and unblemished cheek to this misfortune perpetrated by an aggressive Providence. The stain, which seems to have been rubbed on with the skin of a black grape, by a lewd satyr during the bucolic delirium of the grape harvest, suggests an intimate, tragic, and secret tale of love. To a passionate and dramatically inclined spirit like Apolonio, the nun must seem pretty in spite of her humiliating stigma and even something more than pretty because of it. Apolonio approaches the nun, and with contained passion, which he wouldn't want anyone to notice, he murmurs, "Oh, comforting angel on my right! I adore you; I adore you day and night. You are both a fiction and delight, pale and bright, like Heaven's light. Day and night both leave a trace in your very beautiful face. On this side calm as a lagoon, deathly pale; Diana, the moon. The other side is red with strife, like Apollo, flaming father of life. Oh terrible battle! Joy or pain; I look first at the calm side and then at the flame; looking at your face night and day, the hours of my life pass away."

"Señor Apolonio, that's enough of your rhymed couplets. When you speak to me that way, it's because you want something. I know from experience. Speak to me as a creature of God and tell me what's bothering you."

"Do I want something of you? Yes, what I always want; let us run away together. We are not so far apart in age, if one takes the time to look. I am over sixty, but so what? I am as agile and playful as a newborn calf. As for earning a living, I have just finished writing a drama that will make us millionaires. That's right. We will live in Madrid and have our own carriage. What kind of horses do you like most? I think I prefer sorrel-colored ones or maybe a pinto. Come, make up your mind; we could be so happy. One day, when we come to understand each other, you'll tell me your drama, the horrible drama I can imagine but which I do not wish to know about quite yet. I would not want to force my way into the hidden vault of your consciousness. Make up your mind, my precious Lucidia."

"I will think about it, Señor Apolonio. But aside from the elopement, which is in the future, you have a more immediate request. Don't hesitate to tell me what it is."

"You, divine creature, have a clairvoyant soul; a sibyl's soul. You read what is written on my heart. Why should I speak? Save me the trouble of having to tell you myself."

"Oh, for goodness sake, Señor Apolonio, out with it. I really don't go in for guessing games."

"So be it. Your wishes are my *ukase,* as if dictated by the Russian emperor himself." Apolonio continues speaking but now feels somewhat intimidated and stumbles a bit over his words. "It is not conceit, nor is it Satanic pride; it is the truth. What can I do? I am a man infinitely superior to all those living on charity in this holy sanctuary. I mean everyone, and I am not leaving anyone out. I am superior in family background, superior economically, and superior in intelligence. I have had an academic education. I even wear goatskin slippers whereas they, the rest of them, wear just ordinary cloth. A drama of mine has been performed on the stage with inexpressible success. I have a very delicate stomach."

"Your superiority in this last respect is well known to all of us."

"I'm coming to that. I must drink Vichy water with my meals. I realize that I am the only one with a bottle of Vichy water under my arm when we stand in line in the dining room and all the others envy me for it— or, yes, I will dare say it, even hate me. They would give anything to have a weak stomach and a priest for a son who sends money for Vichy water and other luxuries. I could live with my son if I wanted to, but he prefers me to be here, as a distinguished guest who has everything he needs and is cared for by you charming virgins. Well, I do need something now. I drank the last bottle of Vichy water yesterday. The mother superior tells me that my son's money has not arrived and she cannot buy any more. I understand his forgetfulness because in one of his last letters my son told me he was going to Madrid to preach in the royal chapel; imagine, the royal chapel no less! He can probably think of nothing else these days. But how am I going to enter the dining room today, today of all days, a holy day, without my bottle of Vichy water? What will the others say, particularly one whose name I will not even deign to mention? What humiliation, what mockery, what jeering will they subject me to! No, no, a thousand times no; I would rather die first."

"And what can I do, Señor Apolonio?"

"I was coming to that, celestial Sister Lucidia." Apolonio's voice trembles. "I wanted to ask your permission to allow me to get one of the empty Vichy bottles and fill it from the faucet out there among the laurel trees. No one will see me and no one would be the wiser."

"I see no reason not to. You have my permission," answers the nun, smiling placidly.

They separate. Apolonio feels wondrously relieved. A great burden that had been weighing on his heart has now evaporated. Since he assumes that for the others this bottle of mineral water is a hierarchical emblem, for him too it has become a symbol of superiority. A symbol, perhaps, of economic superiority? Of course, but for Apolonio this is secondary. The essential thing is for the bottle, with its therapeutic and hydraulic contents, to be seen by everyone as a tangible proof of Apolonio's intrinsic and physical superiority. As he himself has just boastfully stated, this irrefutable superiority consists in the fact that he supposedly suffers from a stomach ailment, although the truth of the matter is he has the belly of an ostrich and could even digest volcanic stone. Apolonio is a dramatic author *a nativitate* and this has its effect on his mind— he assumes that the affection or preference the gods show for certain mortal creatures is expressed through some stigma or unusual trait. As a result, the true heroes of human tragedy suffer from and display one sickness or another, some ill that flesh is heir to, as a sacred sign that distinguishes the protagonist from the plebeian chorus. For himself, Apolonio had chosen indigestion. He would have preferred having a blood-stained birthmark on his face like Sister Lucidia, and for that reason he loves and reveres the nun. But for his purposes, indigestion is quite sufficient. And what are his purposes? To offer some tangible proof that he is different from Belarmino. Belarmino can lock himself up in philosophical and hermetic silence, with that smile on his thick, colorless lips as he tries to give the impression that he is beyond and removed from all earthly things. But who would believe him? There was nothing wrong with Belarmino's digestion. How could anyone be convinced that he had seriously pursued intellectual goals, if he had never had stomach trouble?

And Apolonio, with the tragic and wretched expression of one who is favored by the dismal gods, walks toward the group made up of Colignon and the bony old men who surround him. All those old inmates dressed the same way; dark brown burlap . . . homespun woven by hand on the looms of the provincial orphan asylum; hand-woven by those born anonymously for those who will die anonymously. Their garments hang loosely on them; all look as if they are wearing shrouds. They lean on canes of stripped beech which are like so many old bones scraped clean. All of them speak with shaky voices that sound like the last dying re-verberations of an echo.

OLALLA [*an old man who used to be a drunkard*]. Listen, Señor Frenchy, sweets'll do for the kiddies and mushy ladies, but let's have some cider —good old cider with bubbles in it. It's been a long spell since I tasted any!

MONASTERIO [*an old man who used to be a dandy*]. How about a tie, sir, just a little tie you have hanging in your closet—one you don't wear any more. And if it could be turquoise, which is a fashionable color these days . . . only servants don't wear ties. They keep us here without ties and that's worse than not eating.

CILLERO [*an old glutton*]. Oh, shut up, you hissing snake. What are you talking about? Sir, the lentils and the stringbeans and the chickpeas are all wormy. The rats have gotten into the cheese. Someone's got to tell His Excellency, the president of the provincial delegation. And the meat? There's not even enough to smell. It's so stringy and shredded, if you tied the strips together, all they give us wouldn't be any bigger than my fist.

MONSIEUR COLIGNON [*touching himself, satisfied as he confirms the fact that he is so alive and so fat in comparison with the plaintive shadows of these former men who surround him*]. Come, come, my dear little old people; some day it will rain cider, cigarettes, ties, and an *épatant filet mignon* . . .

BELLIDO [*the pawnbroker*]. What do you mean, cider, cigarettes, ties, *filet mignon*? I'm not interested in drinking, smoking, walking around half nude, or eating lentils mixed with pebbles. I'm not a drunkard; I'm not a chimney; I'm not a fop, and I am not a pig. An honest man is what I am, hard working and fair. Justice! I demand justice. I want what belongs to me. I will not die in peace, Señor Colignon, until I know that Hurtado the crook, the one who robbed me of the fruit of my deprivations, has been hanged. You, yourself, Señor Colignon, know that Belarmino owes me money. You were his partner. It's up to you to pay me what's still due on that loan.

SEVERAL VOICES. You're the crook. Thief! Pig! Shame on you, you foul man. Even here you're trying to take things away from us. We have no money left!

BELLIDO [*irritated and convulsed*]. Shut up, you conniving beggars. These are legitimate transactions, lawful business dealings. Whose fault is it if you're a pack of dogs and loafers?

SEVERAL VOICES. Lies! He has a shirt that belongs to me. He walked off with a pair of my shoes. And what about my handkerchiefs? And he has plenty of cash stashed away, Señor Frenchy. He's got a cat hidden in the woodpile and I know just where it is. One night, some smart fox is going to haul it way.

BELLIDO [*livid, enraged, and intimidated*]. You thieving unicorns! I have no cat, not even a mouse. You're all mistaken. I am an honest, God-fearing man. Everyone steals from me, including all of you lazy beggars who come to me to pawn things but then don't want me to get paid for my trouble.

At this moment, Apolonio, like some inflated, round-masted, fantastic sailing ship, enters the scene. The old men's storm dies down and they all move away.

The French pastry maker and Apolonio are left alone. Apolonio speaks with his usual rhetorical flair. The Frenchman listens with his usual mirth. After a short chat with Apolonio, Señor Colignon walks toward the place from which Belarmino has not budged all this time. The bench where Belarmino is resting is set against a stand of laurel trees that form a kind of semicircular wall behind it. From beyond this green enclosure, the sound of rushing water can be heard. Colignon sits down next to Belarmino and affectionately takes hold of both his hands. Without once letting go of his friend's hands, the Frenchman speaks with his usual profusion. Belarmino listens with his usual smiling muteness.

"What's going on over there?" asks Colignon, as his attention is caught by the unusual activity and racket taking place near the main house where the old men had gathered. Belarmino doesn't even turn his head to look. Nothing seems to awaken his curiosity any more. Time passes.

Sister Lucidia approaches Belarmino's corner and gives him a little bluish green piece of paper tightly folded. It's a telegram. In a gesture of indifferent resignation, Belarmino opens it. Scarcely has he begun to read, when he turns white. A tear trembles on the edge of his eye lashes. He rubs his forehead with his free hand.

"Is this a dream? Am I dreaming? Me, am I really me? The belligerencies, the inquisition, the give and take of the boarders do not register as far as I am concerned. *Resurrexit.* Hallelujah."

Sister Lucidia, who has never heard the taciturn Belarmino speak in quite this way before, or for that matter in any other way, thinks he has suddenly gone mad. Colignon lifts his arms skyward in a gesture of triumph and thanksgiving.

"Finally, *a la fin,*" he exclaims. "That sweet and delicious tongue of yesteryear has become untied. Speak, speak, my dear, beloved friend."

But Belarmino, teary-eyed, holds out his arm and says in a dark voice, "Not now; not now. We will speak some other day; we will speak, my very dear Colignon; we will speak until our hearts melt and become pure saliva, and the saliva, words, and the words like the wind."

Belarmino gets up and goes behind the laurel trees to hide his emotion.

Sister Lucidia and Señor Colignon withdraw. Before he leaves, the Frenchman looks for Apolonio but can't find him anywhere and decides to leave without saying good-bye. Apolonio has also received a telegram. After reading it, he speaks to his fellow inmates.

"Gentlemen, I am a satrap. I am richer than Prester John, Croesus, and Montezuma all put together. I promise all of you that I will build a palace where you shall live and where each one may lead the life that most appeals to him." And this was the cause of the activity and clatter mentioned earlier. The old men dance around Apolonio, all trying to tug at his jacket and, naturally, formulating their future requests. Drunk with happiness and pride, Apolonio receives the supplications of those poor unfortunate men like a false idol. At this moment he remembers he doesn't have any more Vichy water and has got to improvise without wasting any more time, for it is already one o'clock in the afternoon. He escapes from his companions and makes his way down a hallway, looking for an empty bottle; he takes a circuitous path through the garden to avoid arousing suspicion as to the real purpose of his maneuver. In his wanderings, he comes across Sister Lucidia and shouts to her on the run, "I've just had great news! We will be joined in nuptials, consoling angel. Our wedding bed will be carved in sandalwood. Oh! What am I saying? What impropriety! It will be made of more precious woods and adorned with oriental gems."

Apolonio has now reached the spring beyond the laurel trees and fills his Vichy bottle with the apocryphal water. Since he finds the squatting position rather uncomfortable, he turns half way round and . . . there, opposite, looking straight at him and with a compassionate smile on his face (at least Apolonio sees it as a compassionate smile), stands Belarmino, in person. In person? Apolonio's legs give way under him. He falls to his knees. Belarmino is standing quietly motionless.

"Are you Belarmino, or are you an illusory phantom?" stutters Apolonio.

Belarmino doesn't utter a peep nor does he make a move.

"Whether you are Belarmino or some astral body," continues Apolonio, uncontrollably swelling from his wounded pride, "I assure you I do suffer from a stomach ailment; the Vichy water I have been drinking up to now was authentic, and I didn't come here to fill up the bottle, but merely to wash it out because I have to put some cologne in it for a long trip I am planning to take. And if you doubt my word, which is better than the King's own word—oh, how His Majesty would like to be as truthful as I—I challenge you to single combat."

And, standing up, he grabs the bottle by its neck. A dark thought passes through Apolonio's brain. There stands Belarmino, emaciated and inert, completely at his mercy. A bop on the head with the bottle and everything would be settled. They might bring him to trial later, but so what? With money, even judges can be bribed. But before doing away with Belarmino and thus satisfying his ancient desire for revenge (although no matter how hard he looked, Apolonio couldn't find in his heart any reasons for feeling this way), he decides instead to humiliate and debase him, making Belarmino envy *him* for the first and last time.

"Look at this and read," says Apolonio frowning and contemptuously shoving the telegram that he has just received in Belarmino's face as if it were a death sentence.

After reading Apolonio's telegram, Belarmino takes one out of his own jacket and hands it to Apolonio. Then he opens his arms wide, looks toward the heavens and sighs, "Look and read. Blessed be God!"

Apolonio's telegram said, "When I returned to Castrofuerte I was informed that I had inherited a fabulous fortune. I am coming for you immediately. Together we will live a life of prosperity.—Pedro."

Belarmino's telegram said, "I am saved. Pedro has saved me. Pedro himself will take you out of that place and he will bring you to me immediately. We will all be so happy.—Angustias."

Belarmino's arms are still spread like a cross, but he is not now looking toward the heavens. He is looking directly at Apolonio.

Apolonio hestitates for a second, but only a second. An ineluctable force, fate itself, pushes him, his arms also open, his hand holding the bottle over his head, and he moves aggressively toward Belarmino. Belarmino comes toward him. Apolonio and Belarmino . . . embrace silently, tightly, profusely, and fraternally.

"I have never really hated you, I swear it," says Apolonio finally. "I have never hated you, even though you despise me."

"I never despised you," murmurs Belarmino softly.

This is the first time they have ever uttered a word to each other and yet they spontaneously use the familiar form of address, because deep in the mysterious workings of their hearts they have both been intimate friends for many, many years.

"I admired you and envied you," confesses Apolonio, blushing.

"I was also jealous of you," declares Belarmino with sincerity.

"You're like my other half."

"Yes, and you, you're my other figurehead [figurehead = hemisphere]."

"Now we are finally united. What dramas I will now be able to write! You will be my inspiration, just as Socrates was for Sophocles; at least that's what Valeiro told me."

From a distance the dinner bell can be heard.

"Finish filling your bottle," suggests Belarmino.

"Oh, of course. But I swear to you it is the first time I have done anything like this."

"I know that."

Arm in arm, wrapped in a golden, sunny mist that creates the fuzzy illusion of weightlessness in all material things, they walk through the garden of day lilies.

"But, aren't we dreaming?" asks Apolonio with some anxiety in his voice. "I don't seem to be touching the ground."

"It seems like a dream. The tetrahedron is a dream. Only love, goodness, and friendship constitute reality."

Inside the house, the residents are standing in line waiting for Apolonio and Belarmino to arrive so they can all go into the dining room and eat their pastry.

"Where could those nuts be?" asks Sister Dolores. She goes out to find them.

On seeing them approach, arm in arm, from the other side of the garden, the nun crosses herself.

"Jesus, Mary, and Joseph! Can I be dreaming? What miracle is this? No, it isn't a dream. It's actually happening!" When they finally reach her, she adds, "Thank God you two have become reconciled. The Lord has touched your hearts. There's nothing more delicious than forgiveness that comes after resentment. Because today is the day of Glory, I also dare to ask you to forgive me. Many years ago, quite unintentionally, I made you both suffer. And what is worse, with my senseless blundering I contributed to Angustias's unhappiness as well as to Don Pedrito's. I have paid for it! God will forgive me. Now I ask for your forgiveness."

"What are you saying, Felicita? Don't be foolish. Without realizing it, you, with your meddling many years ago have been the *deus ex machina* for what has happened today, the happiest day of our lives— Pedrito's, Angustias's, Belarmino's and mine."

"Quite true," commented Belarmino. And suddenly becoming pensive, he adds, "How long will it last?"

"The rest of our lives," affirms Apolonio making broad, circular, theatrical gestures.

Both show Felicita their telegrams. Sister Dolores has an attack of anxiety and, on the verge of fainting, she brings her hands to her heart.

"Everyone's moment of happiness has arrived," she mumbles as if talking to herself, "except mine. God will have to make it all up to me in the next world!"

Belarmino and Apolonio are now standing in the double line of refugees. The lines are moving sluggishly, to the accompaniment of asthmatic gruntings, the scraping of canes, and the shuffling of feet. Belarmino moves as he always did—his head down, a smile on his face, withdrawn into his inner world. Apolonio, as always since the days of his youth, moves in his bristling way, his head erect and with a gait that is pontifical in pace and rhythm. He holds the bottle of apocryphal Vichy water very conspicuously under his arm, assuming that everyone is gazing with envy at this sign of distinction, this testimony to his wealth, this proof of his bellyache.

Epilogue

THE GRIND

Froilán Escobar, alias the Grind and the Alligator, died of hunger; a fact that falls well within the immanent logic of things. He himself must have had an inkling of the disastrous end in store for him, because among the notes and jottings he left behind after his death, I came across these statements, "He who dedicates his days to the search for and the exercise of truth, goodness, and beauty, will be at odds with life, at least with life as we have it in today's society. Modern life is a negation of truth, goodness, and beauty; conversely, truth, goodness, and beauty are a negation of modern life. Consequently, any one who professes, believes in, and practices these three categories, either renounces life or is considered by others to be a revolutionary anarchist." To tell the truth, whoever took a good look at Escobar, so poorly endowed structurally, so unkempt and filthy, would never have guessed that the renowned Alligator was a professor of beauty. Of course, it's true the poor fellow was concerned with supersensory and spiritual beauty and not the perishable, physical kind. And so, he was fated literally to starve to death. But the odd and paradoxical thing was that he died in the home of a butcher by the name of Serapio, a kindly soul who had charitably taken him in. This butcher gave the student free lodgings in an attic room with a cot, and he offered him scraps, leftovers, bits and pieces of the intestines of slaughtered animals to eat. Unfortunately, Escobar was a vegetarian who was so repelled by meat that he preferred to die of starvation rather than eat such a thing. What a tremendous contrast there was between Escobar and Serapio! The butcher was so plump and rosy that he himself looked like a side of

194

beef, and he was a typical embodiment of the human form in its most materialistic shape. Escobar, bilious and bluish in complexion, vibratile and almost ethereal, was a totally spiritualized projection of the human spirit in its transitory passage through the human shell.

At his death, Escobar left a great treasure of writings behind, mostly notes and outlines. I was lucky enough to see and examine them before Serapio had a chance to throw them in the garbage. Some of his thoughts, simply expressed, surprised and perplexed me. For example:

"The two historical events that have turned out to be the most harmful for the advancement of pure science and the eventual sovereignty of culture are the invention of paper and the invention of the printing press."

"If instead of filling up reams of paper, a person were forced to write on a small sheet of parchment, then the results might be worth reading, because no one would write anything that didn't deserve to be written."

"All public libraries should be closed."

"The stupidest thing I have ever read is Carlyle's statement, 'The true university of our time is a library.' I reply, the best university would be an army barracks. By that I mean a socialized culture imposed on people like military discipline. Military discipline is abominable because it is uncouth. Modern culture is abominable because it is undisciplined. No one has the right to any more culture than the exact amount that corresponds to his capabilities and to the social function in which he is to employ it. In the present state of culture there are five-star generals who are nothing more than simple mess sergeants and, on the other hand, there are lowly sergeants who are endowed with the spark of genius, frustrated and unappreciated men who would have been generals in their own right if the appropriate military-cultural organization had existed."

I imagine that when Escobar wrote the above lines, he had Belarmino and Apolonio in mind.

As I continued reading the Alligator's rough drafts, I could not help but remember the excellent Don Amaranth de Fraile. How much alike and yet how different were these two! They were like the two opposite poles of an axis. One was self-educated, the other dogmatic. Both of them suffered from *libido sciendi,* "concupiscence of knowledge, scientific lust."

But if I make mention here of the posthumous papers of Escobar, it isn't because they reminded me of Don Amaranth, but because Belarmino and Apolonio are mentioned in them; these manuscripts also furnished me with a very strange and useful document which the reader himself might find helpful.

To copy down everything Escobar had to say about the two shoemakers would be boring. I'll just note some random opinions. "Belarmino had to invent his own language because he had never been taught how to read. If Belarmino had read the classics in his childhood, would he ever have learned to speak and write? Max Müller* has said and proved innumerable times that thought and language are identical. You can come to know an author's intelligence through his style—metaphorical style, bombastic style, archaic style, colorful style, abstract style, etc., etc.; all of these styles taken separately denote a limited intelligence and a paucity of ideas. When all of them are fused together, but with the predominance of one type according to the kind of thoughts being expressed, what do you get? Cervantes; the first Spanish thinker."

And later he writes:

"The primary quality of the playwright [read, Apolonio] is an aptitude for effective imitation. Such imitation or simulation is not merely external and superficial. The playwright, from the depths of his own soul, begins to deceive himself; but the most recondite and personal *ego* always remains absent and is inhibited by emotion. For that reason, the dramatist is incapable of real love. There is a paradox in the playwright's situation; it's the same as what Diderot calls the paradox of the comedian. Emotion is not communicated but provoked. In order to provoke an emotion, one has to remain calm. The actors who can make other people cry are the ones who know how to feign tears. Those who really cry, just make the audience laugh. That's what happens to the dramatist. Drama created the man who provokes love in all women but doesn't really love any of them—*Don Juan*. The playwright goes through life inventing dramas, discovering them. One might think this gift for invention [to invent means to discover] comes from the fact that

*Max Müller (1823–1900), German philologist and orientalist, did more than any other scholar to popularize philology and mythology, particularly in his lectures *Science of Language*. Son of the poet Wilhelm Müller, he studied in Germany and taught philology and comparative religion at Oxford.

the dramatist lives his dramas. But actually, the opposite is true. Anyone who lives a drama, doesn't see it; he sees only *his* individual drama. And if by some chance the playwright happens to become the victim of a drama in real life, he stays calm and collected. He always pretends to be an actor and yet he is always the spectator—the spectator observing himself. This is the dramatist's paradox. The person who goes through life with exaggerated pathetic gestures is a counterfeiter; that is, a potential playwright. Such men are needed in the world because without their frustrated passionate drive that is naturally contagious, humanity would shrivel up and die of apathy and wisdom. But, oh, how sad it would be if such men were in the majority, for their very essence consists of a lack, an empty hole, a bubble like the one you see in a carpenter's level, a bubble almost impossible to center. If this species of man were to predominate, humanity would become more and more inflated and hollow, and would finally burst like the frog that wanted to be as big as an ox. Luckily, at the other end of the pole from the dramatist stands the philosopher [read, Belarmino]. The philosopher is just the reverse of the dramatist. On the outside he is serene and impassive; but in the most secret chambers of his being, there burns an inextinguishable flame. The philosopher is a madman preserved in ice. Ice is the great preserver of passions as well as of edible things, for when these are exposed to air and light they turn rancid or rotten. The philosopher lives every drama; he is never a spectator. He feels the pain of others as if it were his own; his own pain is multiplied by the anguish of his fellow men. Thus, through his own pain and through that of others, he is in intimate contact with those burning coals that make up the huge bonfire of universal pain—the drama of life. The playwright, disturbed and embarrassed by his inner vacuum, races toward the surface, expressing himself with emphatic largesse and, like a miracle worker, conjures up frenetic passions. Through this feigned emotion, he is searching for the corrective to his inner apathy. Besides, because he can't cry on the inside, he never manages to laugh on the outside either. As for the philosopher, in his search for serenity and wisdom, he makes use of apathy as a corrective for his overwhelming secret passions. That is his *sofrosine*. The philosopher cries on the inside and laughs on the outside. When the philosopher has his moment of drama, it is so intense that he feels the destruction not only of his own heart, but of the entire universe. Then, nothing exists for him anymore. This is the maximum apathy and indifference; *ataraxia*. But the philosopher needs the dramatist in order not to become sterile and perish. And, conversely, the dramatist needs the philosopher to keep from becoming vain and disappearing all together. Sophocles needs Socrates, and Socrates needs Sophocles. The Socratic dialogues have a dramatic structure and the Sophoclean dialogues have a philosophical basis."

Apolonio said something similar about Socrates and Sophocles to Belarmino while they were both in the rest home, experiencing a rather dramatic moment. All this makes me think that Escobar and Apolonio came to be friends and that the shoemaker was inspired by the student's theories. It will be noted that these theories are exactly opposite to those held by Don Amaranth. As far as Don Amaranth was concerned, the dramatist is the one who penetrates the individual drama, and the philosopher is the one who removes himself from it. According to Escobar, the one who penetrates the drama is the philosopher, and it is the dramatist who keeps his distance. How disconcerting it is that human beings can hold such different and opposite views! Don Amaranth's doctrine is refutable as well as sensible; and the same can be said for Escobar's beliefs. As a matter of fact, so it goes with all human opinions. The ones who are all wrong are those who claim that any human opinion expresses absolute truth. It's enough for it to be partially true, to contain a speck or a seed of the truth. When a gold digger says he has discovered gold, he doesn't mean he is now in control of all the gold hidden in the bowels of the earth; he merely means he has found some gold, a small quantity of gold. Don Amaranth and Escobar have equal claim to the truth; and between Escobar's truth and Don Amaranth's truth there are an infinite number of intermediate truths—this is what the mathematicians call the *ultracontinuum*. There are as many irreducible truths as there are points of view. Concerning Belarmino and Apolonio, I wanted to present here the points of view of Don Amaranth and Escobar because all other points of view can fit somewhere between them. Since they are the most antithetical, they are naturally the most comprehensive. And, oddly enough, I have called upon the science and doctrine of these two people in order to disguise the fact that in the case of Belarmino and Apolonio I never did have, nor do I now have any particular point of view. Belarmino and Apolonio existed and I have loved them. I don't mean they have actually existed in mortal flesh on the face of the earth; they have existed through me and for me. There is nothing left to say. To exist is to multiply oneself and to love.

I have already referred to a strange and useful document that Escobar left behind among his posthumous papers. It is a complete lexicon of all the words and phrases Belarmino used, listed together with the interpretations he gave them. I have chosen a few expressions from this list which the reader has heard Belarmino use on occasions, and they are included in an appendix to the present volume.

The vocabulary compiled by Escobar also contains a preliminary statement.

Max Müller says that by placing the twenty-three or twenty-four letters of the alphabet in all their possible combinations, one can obtain all the words that have ever been used in every language of the world and all those that may be used in the future. Taking twenty-three letters as a base, the number of words would be 25,-852,016,738,884,976,640,000; and using twenty-four as a base, 620,-448,401,733,239,439,360,000. Belarmino never reached the point of employing such lexical wealth, nor did he even come close to Dante, Shakespeare, or Cervantes, all of whom made use of thousands of words. Belarmino's figure is around five hundred. I remember having read somewhere that in his writings, Racine never used more than a few hundred words, and yet his language was so supple, elegant and suggestive.

Selected Glossary of
The Belarminian Lexicon

Abscess, *n*: system, theory; inactive tumor that is formed inside a living body.

Adopt, *vb*: to love for love's sake and not because of blood ties.

Balloon, *n*: vanity.

Belligerence, *n*: opposition, resistance, adversity, misfortune.

Belligerent, *n*: opponent, resister.

Boarder, *n*: man as a living creature, for in order to live, he must eat; refers to the base material necessities that inhibit the full life of the spirit.

Calyx, *n*: smile.

Caress, *vb*: to respect and distrust; to fawn, as when propitiating and flattering certain pets.

Class, *n*: deportment; men are classified according to their deportment.

Clothing, *n*: that which is external and superficial.

Convulsion, *n*: pleasure, contentment.

Crack, crack, *adj*: good; what is good is brief and as effective as a sharp blade.

Ecumenical, *adj*: conciliation, synthesis.

Eliminate, *vb*: to execute, to perform, to evaluate with clear and lucid judgment; to illuminate.

Flashy, *adj*: ardent, flammiferous.

Give and take, *n*: disdain.

Greece, *n*: wisdom.

Hump, *n*: responsibility, because it is bulky, heavy, and annoying.

Illiterate, *adj*: disinterested, impartial, without intellectual prejudices.

Imprison, *vb*: to understand, to take possession of an idea.

Inquisition, *n*: inquiry, pain.

Instrumental, *n*: that which is useful and efficacious.

Intention, *n*: reason; our reasons are our secret intentions.

Intuition, *n*: mastery of and familiarity with a subject, such as using the familiar (*tú*) form of address; the antonym is salute, to acknowledge, at a distance, by means of a wave of the hand.

200

Irrigate, *vb*: to have a vision of unity, to encompass at a glance; when one looks at objects, they are refreshed and unfold.

Kiss, *vb*: to envy; derived from the kiss of Judas.

Knave, *n*: *quid*; uncovering the essence of things; one realizes that it is something uncomplicated, simple, light, slippery; a knave.

Maremagnum, *n*: ideal, compendium of all things; from Latin, ocean.

Matron, *n*: a virgin mother who conceives through the good offices of the Holy Spirit.

Metempsychosis, *n*: unfathomable enigma, the essence of things; from Latin, transmigration of souls.

Paradox, *n*: orthodoxy.

Paraphrase, *vb*: to understand.

Projectile, *n*: nonsense, because it is fired and traces a calculated trajectory.

Puerperal, *n*: pregnant with pain.

Rah-rah, *n*: life; constant restlessness; the palpitation of the passions.

Rat-tat-tat, *n*: death; the last heartbeats; the blows of a hammer on the nails of a coffin.

Recreated, *adj*: uncreated and producing great joy or recreation; it applies to light or sunny places.

Register, *vb*: to endow with an arbitrary importance, to appraise capriciously something that is price-less and unimportant.

Ridiculous, *adj*: eccentric, outside its true self.

Salutary, *adj*: referring to perfunctory knowledge, as opposed to intuition; derived from salute; indicates that acknowledgment, although superficial, is always appropriate.

Scholastic, *n*: a person who irrationally follows a school, like a tail appended to the body of an animal.

Scholasticism, *n*: a borrowed and fluctuating opinion.

Scorbutic, *n*: pessimist; derived from Latin *corvinus,* crow.

Solar, *adj*: most perfect light, as in solarium; fountain of light; derived from Latin *sol,* sun.

Spectacle, *n*: receptacle; everything depends on the color of the glass through which one looks.

Sprinkle, *vb*: to perform the first stages of irrigation; attenuated expression (*see* Irrigate).

Strip, *vb*: to discover the profound truth, the cause.

Stripped, *adj*: the final cause, explanation; Belarmino was in the habit of saying that God is the devil stripped.

Stumble, *n*: foolishness; only fools fall.

System, *n*: stubbornness, obstinacy; refers to those who go around proclaiming *one* idea, if it could be called that.

Ta-ta-rum, ta-ta-rum, *adv*: evil; all evil is clothed in circumlocution.

Tetrahedron, *n*: totality.

Theist, *n*: zealot; one who brandishes his zeal.

Timetable, *n*: sphere.

Toad, *n*: sage; wisdom is acquired through ecstasy; the toad is the symbol of ecstasy.

Wan, *adj*: violent and contentious, like someone who strikes with a wand.

Weight, *n*: deep feeling.

About the Author

Ramón Pérez de Ayala (1880–1962) was born in Oviedo, in the region of Asturias, to a well-to-do family. He was educated in Jesuit schools; a high-spirited, rebellious pupil, he was known as "the anarchist." He studied science and took a degree in law at the University of Oviedo. He travelled extensively through Europe, England, and the United States, married an American, and served as ambassador to the Court of St. James for the Spanish Republic from 1931–1936.

For Pérez de Ayala, literature and politics were differing aspects of the humanist intellectual endeavor. Before turning to literature, as a young man he sketched, painted, and sculpted. He first became known as a poet, then wrote many essays and novels, among which *Belarmino and Apolonio* (1921) has been widely acclaimed. In 1928, he was elected to the Spanish Academy.